Fare
by
the Sea

with
A Pinch
of History

The purpose of the Junior League is exclusively educational and charitable and is to promote voluntarism; to develop the potential of its members for voluntary participation in community affairs and to demonstrate the effectiveness of trained volunteers.

Cover design and sketches by:
Luis Fernandez

A PINCH OF HISTORY

© 1983 Janet Snyder Matthews

Additional copies may be obtained by addressing:

FARE BY THE SEA

Junior League of Sarasota, Inc.
P.O. Box 25074
Southgate Station
Sarasota, Florida 34277

For your convenience, order blanks are included in back of the book.

Library of Congress Catalog Card Number: 82-063055
International Standard Book Number: 0-9611186-0-1

Money raised from sale of FARE BY THE SEA will support the Junior League's programs and projects.

Printed in the United States of America by:
Moran Printing Company
Orlando, Florida

TABLE OF CONTENTS

Seashell by title denotes quick and easy recipes

A PINCH OF HISTORY
© 1983 Janet Snyder Matthews

"FARE BY THE SEA"
Committee

Chairman .... Sandra Stewart

Sustainer Advisor .... Betsy Chapman

Appetizers .... Suzanne Webb

Beverages .... Diane Otis

Salads .... Patti Giorgetti

Soups and Condiments .... Linda Roe

Egg/Cheese/Rice/Pasta .... Diane Otis

Vegetables .... Jan Jung

Meats .... Vivian Clack

Seafood .... Carol Sears

Poultry .... Janice Hutchison

Breads .... Pam Steves

Desserts .... Charlotte McPheeters

Proofreading .... Linda Boring
Grace Duffey
Vivian Clack
Ellen Wells

Brochures .... Ellen Wells

ABOUT THE HISTORIAN

Janet Snyder Matthews is a Junior League member whose historical works have appeared in scholarly as well as popular publications. Mrs. Matthews is a historian active statewide as well as locally. She coordinates Governor Bob Graham's Oral History Dinner, an annual event held at the Governor's Mansion, and is a gubernatorial appointee to the Historic Tallahassee Preservation Board. Her scholarly research in regional history has extended over a period of years and has resulted in a number of works, including a settlement history of Sarasota Bay and the Manatee River.

Mrs. Matthews is a preservationist whose local efforts have included research of "The Oaks" and its successful nomination to the **National Register of Historic Places**, the first Sarasota County site to be so distinguished. The settlement history of The Oaks constitutes a chapter of her book. Her memberships include American Association for State and Local History, National Trust for Historic Preservation, and the Manatee County Historical Society. She has been elected a Director of the Florida Historical Society, appointed to the Sarasota County Historical Commission, and has served Gulf Coast Heritage Inc. as President and Site Historian.

Mrs. Matthews is a graduate of Kent State University and Ohio State University. She began her Florida residency in 1961 as a counselor at the University of Florida where she met her husband, Lamar Matthews, Jr., a Sarasota native and now a practicing attorney. Mrs. Matthews has been a faculty member of Manatee Junior College and is currently completing additional postgraduate degree work at Florida State University. She and her husband reside with their children in Sarasota.

ABOUT THE ARTIST

Luis Fernandez, a native of Santander, Spain, came to Sarasota, Florida in 1979 to study graphic design and illustration at the Ringling School of Art and Design. He graduated three years later with a major in illustration. Before coming to the United States, his only background in the visual arts was from a five-year industrial design program in his home town. During his years as a Ringling student, he was commissioned to create the art work included in this book. Luis hopes to continue to learn and improve his already highly professional artistic talent. Currently, he is working as an illustrator in Atlanta, Georgia.

INTRODUCTION

"A Pinch of History" is intended to present our Sarasota history in a light, yet comprehensive, manner. The presentation is a narrowly-couched narrative lightly flavoured with broader historical implications.

Based upon the Junior League Cookbook Committee's selection of ten historic and even some not-so-historic sites, certain themes emerge. Those themes begin with John Ringling's very visible influence and eventually lead backward — all the way to homesteaders and Indian mounds.

Our regional history, like that of most other places, is thickly layered in eras ranging from the stone age to what we think of as modern time. The entrepreneurs of Sarasota's early twentieth century permanently impressed their stamps upon the area's character. But it was the very nature of some of those influences which ultimately distinguished Sarasota from her coastal counterparts. A select few — John and Mable Ringling, Bertha Honoré Palmer, Bill and Marie Selby — are represented, but there were many others.

Interestingly, they were often from someplace else and were drawn to Sarasota for one or more of the usual purposes of their day: they came to visit friends, to invest, or to tour. Some came, at least initially, as typical "snowbirds" escaping winter. And they stayed. In their time, they bridged the bay, dredged the channels, laid out subdivisions, set up trusts and left legacies that after their lifetimes were to keep their names alive.

The story, which I have called "A Pinch of History" in deference to our culinary theme, is of events and persons whose influences touch our lives in some way, somewhere, every day.

Janet Matthews - 1983

FARE BY THE SEA offers culinary excitement captured in a blend of recipes and menus designed for the most casual to the most elegant of occasions.

Reflective of Sarasota in Southwest Florida where the atmosphere shifts from gulf breeze beach picnics by gliding sailboats to patio parties overlooking the mirrored evening sunsets to family gatherings in the country kitchens or to tuxedo and evening gown soirees just for the taste of it, FARE BY THE SEA has a scent and flavor for every palate.

While experiencing its gastronomical offerings, the discerning chef will also enjoy a pictorial presentation of a series of original drawings showing many scenes and landmarks that hallmark Sarasota.

The cultural heritage of Sarasota is depicted in renderings of John Ringling's majestic mansion known as the Ca'D'Zan and the nationally known Asolo Theater that adjoins the famed Ringling Museum. The reader is further shown the unique Van Wezel Performing Arts Hall, inspired by Frank Lloyd Wright, where performers worldwide come to express their talents.

Accentuating the vacation wonderland attraction that is Sarasota, the artist has captured an inviting beach scene while also contrasting the mirthful spirit of the area's heritage as expressed by a circus clown representing the Ringling Barnum and Bailey Circus.

Both the "cookbook tourist" and the actual visitor to Sarasota will marvel at the etchings of the famed St. Armands Shopping Center where people gather in leisure gaiety just moments away from sailboats lined ashore on the bayfront.

The etching of the prominent Selby Home will remind the natives and visitors alike of the internationally known Selby Botanical Gardens and the continuing philanthropic contributions by the Selby Foundation to this seaside community. Finally, the Oak Tree will ever remind the Sarasotan of the historical site of "The Oaks at Spanish Point".

FARE BY THE SEA beckons all to come and visit, and most of all, to taste and savor the finest.

A PINCH OF HISTORY
© 1983 Janet Snyder Matthews

Ca' D' Zan

Sarasota enjoys her reputation as a unique city of cultural amenities. Along Florida's west coast, the strength and diversity of the city's arts continue to increase and multiply. The origin of Sarasota's cultural base has often been credited to one of her most prominent twentieth century developers — John Ringling, the circus magnate whose career incorporated diverse promotions in the southern coastal city adopted by John and his wife, Mable. It was home over a 25-year span of his life. For those visitors and residents who recognize Ringling's definitive importance, an occasional tour of the house John and Mable built by the bay they loved is a must.

During the "boom" year of 1926, John and Mable were constructing their version of a Venetian palace, "Ca' d' Zan" or "House of John," a thirty-room house oriented around a two-storied Great Hall, a building designed by New York architect Dwight James Baum expressly to combine the facade of Palazzo Ducale in Venice and the tower of the old Madison Square Garden in New York. The colorful residence was designed with elegant access to the bay across a marble terrace 8,000 feet square, confined within a terra cotta balustrade. By descending a stairway, the Ringlings reached their bayside dock where John moored his 125-foot yacht **Zalophus**, along with Mable's authentic Venetian gondola.

But all that was only the setting, the domestic backdrop, for a circus king whose promoter instincts were to shape the character and destiny of a modern-day city.

COCKTAIL BUFFET

Stone Crab Claws with
* Green Mayonnaise

* Seviche

* Chicken Wings Chinoise

* Quiche Stuffed Mushrooms

* John's Antipasto

* Water Chestnut Spread with
* Homemade Melba Toast

* Smoked Salmon Mousse

Virginia Ham with
* Sweet and Sour Mustard Sauce

* Stuffed Kumquats — Salted Nuts

Appetizers & Beverages

Brandied Cheddar Cheese
Elegant cocktail party dip

Chill 1 week   Serves 10 to 12

1 pound sharp Cheddar cheese,   ½ teaspoon dry mustard
  shredded   ½ cup brandy
2 tablespoons butter   Dash cayenne pepper
1 teaspoon sugar

All ingredients should be at room temperature. Combine all but ¼ cup brandy; beat until smooth with mixer or in food processor using steel blade. Add remaining brandy gradually and continue beating until smooth. Store in covered crocks in refrigerator. Should be made at least a week in advance. Can be served in cabbage shell for extra pizzazz.

Chicken Liver Mousse
Great for summer entertaining

Chill   Serves 50

2 pounds chicken livers   2 hard-boiled egg yolks, chopped
½ cup onion, chopped   ⅔ cup whipping cream
2 cloves garlic, minced   ⅛ teaspoon nutmeg
½ cup butter, softened   Salt and pepper to taste
2 tablespoons oil   2 to 4 tablespoons cognac or brandy

Wash livers. Remove fat and tendons. Dry thoroughly. Sauté onion and garlic in 2 tablespoons butter and 1 tablespoon oil until tender. Remove to platter. Add 2 tablespoons more butter and remaining tablespoon oil to skillet. Over high heat quickly sauté chicken livers until tender but still slightly pink in center. Transfer to platter to cool. Purée onion-liver mixture in processor or blender. Add egg yolks. Mix in remaining butter. Blend in cream, nutmeg, salt and pepper. Add cognac or brandy as desired. Place paté in 6-cup mold. Chill thoroughly, preferably overnight. Unmold onto platter. Serve with cucumber slices, melba rounds or plain crackers.

Tip: Create floral design with carrots, beets or egg whites and branches
    of parsley or chives. Edge mousse with chopped egg white, parsley
    or chives.

Appetizers

Chicken Liver Paté
Favorite of men

Chill

Serves 6

½ pound chicken livers
¼ pound mushrooms
1 medium onion, chopped
6 tablespoons butter
1½ teaspoons salt

Dash red pepper
1½ teaspoons Worcestershire sauce
1 tablespoon lemon juice
2 tablespoons brandy

Sauté livers, mushrooms and onion in butter until onion is golden. Add remaining ingredients and purée in blender. Chill. Serve with crackers.

Chicken Wings Chinoise
Oriental magic

Preheat oven 350°

Serves 4

½ cup water
¾ cup soy sauce
2 tablespoons sugar

2 star anise seeds
2 tablespoons medium dry sherry
8 chicken wings

Combine all ingredients except chicken in sauté pan and bring to boil. Simmer briefly. Cut tips off chicken wings. Place wings and sauce in shallow baking dish. Roast 1 hour or until tender. Turn and baste periodically. Cool to room temperature and serve.

Crystallized Orange Nuts
Great Christmas gift

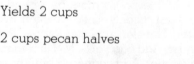

Microwave, medium-high

Yields 2 cups

¼ cup orange juice
1 cup sugar

2 cups pecan halves

Combine orange juice and sugar in 2 quart, 12 x 7-inch glass baking dish; mix well. Stir in pecans. Microwave 6 minutes on medium-high. Stir and continue cooking 4 to 6 minutes on medium-high, or until syrup crystallizes. Spread, separate and cool glazed nuts on buttered cookie sheet. Flavor improves with aging.

Chilled Artichokes with Vinaigrette Sauce
Artichokes are always fun to eat

Chill

4 artichokes
Lemon juice
Water, salted

Serves 4

¼ cup olive oil
4 cloves garlic; peeled and crushed
2 lemon slices

Wash artichokes. With sharp knife cut off 1 inch of top and stem. With kitchen scissors cut off tips of leaves. Brush cut edges with lemon juice. Place artichokes in small amount of boiling salted water. Add olive oil, garlic and lemon slices. Cover and simmer 25 to 30 minutes or until leaf pulls out easily. Drain. Remove fibrous choke with spoon. Wrap in plastic wrap and chill.

Vinaigrette Sauce

¼ teaspoon salt
⅛ teaspoon pepper
1 tablespoon wine or herb flavored
   vinegar or lemon juice
3 to 5 tablespoons olive or
   vegetable oil

⅛ teaspoon dry mustard
1 clove garlic, crushed
1 tablespoon herbs, chopped (parsley,
   tarragon, chives and chervil)

Put all ingredients into screw top jar and shake vigorously ½ minute. Chill.

Tip: Serve artichokes in individual bowls with individual sauce at the side. A great first course as well as hors d'oeurve.

Homemade Melba Toast
White, wheat or rye

Preheat oven 250°

1 loaf bread, sliced ⅛-inch thick

Serves 8 to 10

Butter, melted

Trim crust of bread and cut into assorted shapes. Lightly brush with butter. Arrange on baking sheet. Bake 25 minutes or until crisp and evenly browned. Keep in tightly sealed container.

Appetizers

Glazed Shrimp
Spectacular seafood array

Chill

Serves 6 to 8

2 tablespoons unflavored gelatin
$1/3$ cup white wine
1 cup creamy French dressing
1 tablespoon lemon juice
$1/4$ teaspoon salt

Dash pepper
1 teaspoon Worcestershire sauce
1 teaspoon horseradish
2 pounds large shrimp, cooked,
    peeled, deveined and chilled

Soften gelatin in wine. Add dressing, lemon juice, salt, pepper, Worcestershire sauce and horseradish. Place over low heat, stirring constantly until gelatin is dissolved. Cool until mixture starts to thicken. Dip shrimp to coat. When partially set, repeat dipping. Prepare several hours before serving and keep chilled. Serve on cocktail picks stuck in large orange or grapefruit, which has been sliced flat on bottom.

John's Antipasto
Doubles as a relish tray

Chill 24 hours

Serves 8 to 10

3 celery stalks, sliced diagonally
    $1/2$ inch long
3 carrots, sliced diagonally
    $1/2$ inch long
1 head cauliflower, cut in flowerets
1 green or red pepper, thinly sliced
12 whole mushrooms
2 14-ounce cans artichoke hearts,
    quartered

$1/2$ cup white wine vinegar
1 cup olive oil
3 green onions, white part only, sliced
1 tablespoon parsley, chopped
1 heaping tablespoon oregano
3 large cloves garlic, mashed
$1/2$ teaspoon salt
2 teaspoons sugar
$1/8$ teaspoon freshly ground pepper

Boil celery, carrots, cauliflower and pepper until tender but firm. Add mushrooms and cook 3 minutes. Drain vegetables; add artichoke hearts. Mix remaining ingredients in saucepan and bring to boil. Pour mixture over vegetables. Put vegetables into large glass jar or bowl; refrigerate at least 24 hours. Antipasto should reach room temperature before serving. Serve on large platter with crackers.

Beer Cheese
Spiked cheese

Yields 2 cups

10 ounces sharp Cheddar cheese
¼ cup mayonnaise
¼ teaspoon red pepper

1 teaspoon Worcestershire sauce
½ cup beer
¼ teaspoon salt

Process all ingredients in food processor with steel blade. Serve in crock with crackers.

Nan's Cheese Roll
For those who like it hot

Chill

Yields 2 rolls

1 pound sharp Cheddar cheese,
  grated
8 ounces cream cheese
1 tablespoon mayonnaise
3 teaspoons ketchup
2 teaspoons prepared mustard

2 teaspoons steak sauce
2 shakes Tabasco
½ teaspoon soy sauce
½ teaspoon hot pepper sauce
1 ounce chili powder
Dash red pepper

Mix first 9 ingredients until smooth in large bowl or food processor using steel blade. Divide mixture in half. Mix chili powder and red pepper on waxed paper. Roll ½ cheese mixture on waxed paper until it makes a log and is completely covered with chili powder and pepper. Wrap log in waxed paper and aluminum foil. Repeat with second half of mixture. Refrigerate 2 hours. Serve with crackers.

Raw vegetables used for dips should be soaked in water.

Appetizers

Pickled Shrimp
Tangy elegance

Chill 5 days

Serves 12

2 cups salad oil
1 cup garlic flavored wine vinegar
1 10½-ounce bottle ketchup
Juice of 2 lemons
3 tablespoons Worcestershire sauce
3 tablespoons A-1 sauce
1 clove garlic

Dash Tabasco
Salt and pepper to taste
3 pounds shrimp, cooked, peeled
  and deveined
3 large white onions, thinly sliced
2 lemons, thinly sliced
Leaf lettuce

In bowl or blender mix salad oil, vinegar, ketchup, lemon juice, Worcestershire sauce, A-1 sauce, garlic, Tabasco, salt and pepper. Arrange alternate layers of shrimp, onion and lemon in large bowl or jar. Pour sauce over layers; cover and refrigerate at least 5 days. To serve, drain excess liquid from shrimp and place on bed of leaf lettuce.

Salmon Party Log
Colorful and tasty

Chill

Serves 12

1 1-pound can salmon
8 ounces cream cheese, softened
1 tablespoon lemon juice
2 teaspoons onion, grated
1 teaspoon prepared horseradish

¼ teaspoon salt
¼ teaspoon liquid smoke
½ cup pecans, chopped
3 tablespoons fresh parsley, snipped

Drain and flake salmon, removing skin and bone. Combine salmon with next 6 ingredients and mix thoroughly. Combine pecans and parsley. Shape salmon mixture in 8 x 2-inch log; roll in nut mixture. Chill well. Serve with crackers or melba toast.

Seviche
Serve at your most elegant party

Chill   Serves 8

1 to 1½ pounds raw white fish, cut
   in small bite-size pieces
Juice of 10 to 15 limes
2 tomatoes, skinned, seeded and
   minced
2 onions, minced
2 to 4 chili peppers, minced

1 to 1½ green peppers, minced
4 cloves garlic, minced
2 tablespoons fresh parsley, chopped
2 tablespoons pepper juice
6 teaspoons Tabasco
Salt and pepper

Mix all ingredients. Adjust hot seasonings to taste. Chill at least 6 hours or overnight. Serve with crackers.

Shrimp Mold
Requires no last minute preparation

Chill overnight   Serves 8

½ cup shrimp, cooked, peeled,
   deveined and sliced
¾ cup celery, diced
1 small onion, chopped
2 hard-boiled eggs, chopped
12 stuffed green olives, sliced
1 envelope unflavored gelatin

4 tablespoons cold water
3 tablespoons lemon juice
   (1 lemon)
¾ cup mayonnaise, at room
   temperature
Pinch salt

Grease pint mold with oil and set aside. Combine first 5 ingredients in large bowl. Place gelatin and cold water in small glass. Allow to set; put glass in pan of hot water to soften gelatin. Add lemon juice. Before gelatin congeals, add to mayonnaise and salt in small bowl. Gently add mixture to chopped ingredients and place in mold to jell in refrigerator overnight.

Tip: Serve with crackers or cut into wedges and serve as a salad.

Appetizers

Shrimp Ball
Make for patio party

Chill

Yields 1 large ball

2 4½-ounce cans baby shrimp, drained
2 8-ounce packages cream cheese, softened
2 tablespoons horseradish

1 teaspoon Worcestershire sauce
2 tablespoons milk
4 tablespoons onion, chopped
1 cup pecans, chopped or crushed

Rinse shrimp; add to cream cheese. Add horseradish, Worcestershire sauce, milk and onion to shrimp mixture; mix well. Form into ball. Roll in pecans to coat. Chill. Serve with crackers.

Smoked Salmon Mousse
Ancient gourmet delight

Chill

Serves 8 to 10

½ pound kippered White King salmon
3 tablespoons fresh lemon juice
½ cup butter, melted
½ cup sour cream

½ teaspoon dried dill weed or 2 teaspoons fresh dill weed
Freshly ground white pepper
⅛ pound Nova Scotia salmon, sliced

Remove kippered salmon from skin and crumble into food processor. Add lemon juice. Purée mixture while simultaneously adding butter through feed tube in thin, steady stream. Continue the process until smooth. Transfer purée to bowl and fold in sour cream and seasonings. Line 2-cup fish mold with plastic wrap. Fill evenly with mousse. Cover surface of mold and gently press to eliminate bubbles and gaps. Refrigerate mold until firm, 1 hour or more. Cut strips of Nova Scotia salmon with tear drop shape hors d'oeuvre cutter. Set aside. Unmold mousse and use sliced salmon to create scales on fish. Garnish additionally as desired. Serve with thinly sliced black bread, melba crackers or other plain firm cracker.

Tip: Additional garnishes: Sliced stuffed green olives, egg white, English cucumber slices, lemon slices, watercress or parsley.

Shrimp Roll
Some unlikely combinations

Chill   Serves 15 to 20

2 8-ounce packages cream cheese,   ½ cup salted peanuts, chopped
  softened   1 teaspoon curry powder
1 onion, finely chopped   2 hard-boiled eggs, chopped
1 green pepper, finely chopped   Salt to taste
2 celery stalks, finely chopped   Lettuce
2 6½-ounce cans shrimp, drained   Major Grey's Chutney
  and finely chopped

Mix cream cheese with next 8 ingredients. Roll in shape of log. Wrap in foil;
chill at least 4 hours. Serve on lettuce bed with chutney on top.

Artichoke Nibbles
You will want more than a nibble

Preheat oven 325°   Yields 4 dozen

2 6-ounce jars marinated   ¼ teaspoon salt
  artichoke hearts   ⅛ teaspoon pepper
1 small onion, chopped   ⅛ teaspoon oregano
1 clove garlic, minced   ⅛ teaspoon hot pepper seasoning
4 eggs, beaten   2 cups Cheddar cheese, shredded
¼ cup fine bread crumbs   2 tablespoons parsley, chopped

Drain marinade from 1 jar artichokes into medium skillet. Drain and discard
marinade from 2nd jar. Chop artichokes and set aside. Heat marinade. Add
onion and garlic; sauté until onion is limp, about 5 minutes. Combine eggs,
bread, salt, pepper, oregano and seasoning. Fold in cheese and parsley. Add
onion and artichokes; blend well. Pour into 9-inch square baking dish. Bake 30
minutes. Cool slightly; cut into 1-inch squares. Serve hot or cold.

Tip: Can be made a day ahead and reheated.

19

Appetizers

Stuffed Kumquats
Special for Florida entertaining

Chill

2 dozen kumquats

Yields 48 kumquats

½ pound orange cheese, softened

Split kumquats in half lengthwise. Scoop out soft centers with demi-tasse spoon and discard. Stuff each half with cheese. Chill.

Tip: Any flavor cream cheese may be substituted for orange cheese.

Cheese Wafers
Brunch brightener

Preheat oven 350°

¼ pound sharp Cheddar cheese
½ cup butter, softened
1 cup flour

Yields 36 wafers

1 teaspoon sugar
Dash cayenne pepper
Powdered sugar

Grate cheese in food processor with steel blade. Add butter, flour, sugar and pepper to cheese. Process until smooth. Place mixture in refrigerator 30 minutes. Remove and shape into a long roll. Refrigerate again. Cut into ⅛ inch wafers. Place on cookie sheet. Bake 10 minutes. Sprinkle with powdered sugar while hot. Cool.

Crabmeat Royale
Elegant first course, any season

Preheat oven 400°

1 pound crabmeat, well drained
4 tablespoons butter, melted
½ cup heavy cream
½ teaspoon dry mustard
1¼ teaspoons salt

Serves 6

¼ teaspoon white pepper
Dash cayenne pepper
1 teaspoon Worcestershire sauce
½ cup Parmesan cheese, grated
3 tablespoons bread crumbs

Flake crabmeat, removing any cartilage. Drain well. Mix with butter, cream, mustard, salt, pepper, cayenne pepper, Worcestershire sauce and 4 tablespoons cheese. Toss lightly. Divide among 6 crab shells or any small, individual oven-proof serving dishes. Sprinkle with remaining cheese and bread crumbs. Bake 10 minutes or until browned. Serve immediately.

Crabmeat Spectacular
Eye catching

Preheat oven 350°   Serves 6

1 pound crabmeat
4 ounces lemon juice
Salt and pepper to taste
¼ cup celery, chopped
½ cup onion, finely chopped
¼ cup green pepper, chopped
1 hard-boiled egg, finely chopped
1 2-ounce jar pimiento, chopped
2 to 3 tablespoons cooking sherry

1 egg, beaten
¼ to ½ cup mayonnaise
¼ to ½ cup fine bread crumbs
2 tablespoons prepared mustard
Dash Worcestershire sauce
Dash cayenne pepper
Parsley
Lemon wedges

Remove shell from crabmeat. Pour lemon juice over crabmeat. Salt and pepper to taste. Add celery, onion, green pepper, boiled egg, pimiento, sherry and raw egg. Mix well. Add mayonnaise, being careful not to leave mixture too dry or too moist. Add bread crumbs, being careful to keep a casserole consistency. Add mustard, Worcestershire sauce and cayenne pepper. Place in 2-quart greased baking dish. Bake 40 minutes. Serve hot, alone or over toast points for first course. Garnish with parsley and lemon wedges.

Clam Coquille
Guest applause

Preheat oven broil   Serves 6

4 tablespoons butter
4 tablespoons flour
¼ teaspoon dry mustard
¾ cup milk
1 teaspoon salt
Dash pepper
1 teaspoon onion juice

¾ cup sharp Cheddar cheese, grated
1 egg yolk, slightly beaten
½ cup dry stuffing
½ teaspoon parsley, chopped
1 7½-ounce can clams,
    drained and minced

Over low heat combine first 4 ingredients, stirring constantly until thickened. Add salt, pepper and onion juice. Add cheese and stir until melted. Remove from heat; stir in egg yolk, stuffing and parsley. Add clams to sauce. Place in 6 baking shells. Broil on top rack of oven 4 minutes or until tops brown and hors d'oeuvres are heated through. May be made ahead, stored in refrigerator, and heated just before serving.

Appetizers

Ham Balls
Spicy

Yields 8 dozen

2 pounds lean ground ham
½ pound ground pork
1 cup rolled oats, uncooked
2 tablespoons brown sugar
3 large eggs, beaten

¼ teaspoon ground cloves
1 teaspoon dry mustard
½ small onion, chopped
Shortening, melted

Combine first 8 ingredients; mix well. Shape into firm, bite-size balls. Sauté balls in shortening until browned. Turn balls carefully.

Sauce

2½ cups pineapple juice
1½ cups water
1 cup brown sugar

¼ cup lemon juice
2½ tablespoons cornstarch
20 whole cloves

Combine all ingredients in 3-quart pan; mix well. Add ham balls and simmer 1 hour. Serve hot in chafing dish.

Party Reubens
Hearty appetizer

Preheat oven 375°

Serves 36

1 package refrigerated crescent
   rolls
1¼ cups Thousand Island dressing
9 thin slices corned beef, cooked
   and cut into thirds

1 8-ounce can sauerkraut, well
   drained
3 slices Swiss cheese, cut into
   ¼-inch strips

Cut dough into triangles. Brush small amount of dressing on dough. Place corned beef across wide end of each triangle. Layer 1 teaspoon sauerkraut and 1 teaspoon dressing on corned beef. Top with 2 to 3 strips of cheese. Roll, starting at wide end of triangle. Bake on ungreased cookie sheet 10 minutes. Serve hot. May be made in advance, refrigerated and baked just before serving.

Quiche Stuffed Mushrooms
Cocktail party pleaser

Preheat oven 350°   Yields 24 mushrooms

2 pounds large fresh   2 eggs, beaten
  mushrooms (24)   1 cup heavy cream
4 slices bacon   ½ cup Swiss cheese, shredded
6 tablespoons butter   ½ teaspoon salt
2 tablespoons onion, minced

Rinse, pat dry and remove stems from mushrooms. Chop stems. Sauté bacon and crumble. Discard bacon fat. Brush outside of mushroom caps with 4 tablespoons melted butter. Place in shallow baking pan. Sauté onion in remaining butter 2 minutes. Add stems; sauté 2 minutes. In separate bowl add remaining ingredients. Stir in bacon and mushroom mixture. Spoon into caps. Bake 30 minutes.

Spinach Balls
Bite-size

Preheat oven 325°   Yields 11 dozen

2 10-ounce packages frozen   ¾ cup butter, melted
  spinach, chopped   ½ cup Parmesan cheese, grated
3 cups herb-seasoned stuffing mix   1 tablespoon pepper
1 large onion, finely chopped   1½ teaspoons garlic salt
6 eggs, well beaten   ½ teaspoon thyme

Cook spinach according to package directions; drain well and squeeze to remove excess moisture. Combine spinach and remaining ingredients; mix well. Shape spinach mixture into ¾-inch balls and place on lightly greased cookie sheet. Bake 15 to 20 minutes. Serve warm.

Tip: Spinach balls may be made ahead and frozen. Thaw completely on cookie sheet before baking.

Salmon Quiche
Unique crust

Preheat oven 400°   Serves 6

Crust

1 cup flour
2/3 cup sharp Cheddar cheese,
  shredded
1/4 cup almonds, finely chopped

1/2 teaspoon salt
1/4 teaspoon paprika
6 tablespoons corn oil

Combine first 5 ingredients in bowl. Stir in oil. Set aside 1/2 cup of crust mixture. Press remaining mixture into bottom and sides of 9 or 10-inch pie pan. Bake crust 10 minutes. Remove from oven.

Filling

1 15½-ounce can salmon,
  drain and reserve liquid
3 eggs, beaten
1 cup sour cream
1/4 cup mayonnaise

1/2 cup sharp Cheddar cheese,
  shredded
1 tablespoon onion, grated
1/4 teaspoon dried dill weed

Reduce oven temperature to 325°. Add water to reserved salmon liquid if necessary to make 1/2 cup. Flake salmon, removing skin. Set aside. In bowl blend remaining ingredients and salmon liquid. Stir in salmon. Spoon filling into crust. Sprinkle with reserved crust mixture. Bake 45 to 50 minutes or until quiche is well set. Cool slightly before serving.

Sugared Bacon
Delicious at a morning coffee

Preheat oven 250°   Serves 8

1½ pounds bacon, thickly sliced   2 pounds dark brown sugar

Lay full strips of bacon on baking sheet or large broiler pan and bake about 1 hour. Turn bacon over and drain grease from pan. Sift brown sugar over bacon until lightly coated. Bake until sugar has melted. Remove from oven and cut each strip into 3 pieces. Turn to unsugared side and sift more sugar over strips and again bake until sugar is melted and bacon is crisp. Remember to pour grease off before coating each side with sifted brown sugar.

Burrito Dip
Peck of pickled peppers

Chill overnight

Serves 6 to 8

2 15½-ounce cans red kidney
  beans, drain and reserve juice
1 4-ounce can green chilies,
  undrained
1 7-ounce can jalapeno relish
2 tablespoons onion, minced

1 clove garlic
1 teaspoon salt
½ cup butter
1 pound Monterey Jack cheese,
  grated

Put beans, chilies, relish, onion, garlic and salt in blender and blend until smooth. Melt butter in 2-quart saucepan or chafing dish. Add bean mixture and cheese. Heat on low temperature until cheese has melted, stirring constantly. Reserved bean juice may be added, in small amounts, if thinner consistency is desired. Prepare dip ahead, a few hours or overnight, to allow flavors to meld. It will keep several days in refrigerator and can be reheated. Serve from chafing dish with corn chips for dipping.

Chipped Beef and Mushroom Dip
A distinctive rich taste

Yields 2 cups

¼ cup onion, chopped
1 tablespoon butter
1 cup milk
8 ounces cream cheese
1 cup dried beef, chopped

2 3-ounce cans mushrooms,
  drained and sliced
¼ cup Parmesan cheese, grated
1 tablespoon parsley, chopped
Dash Tabasco

Cook onion in butter until tender. Add milk and cream cheese. Cook until cream cheese is melted. Add dried beef, mushrooms, Parmesan cheese, parsley and Tabasco. Mix well. Keep warm in chafing dish. Serve with crackers.

Appetizers

Mexican Mess
A crowd pleaser for all ages

Serves 6 to 8

2 large avocados, pitted and mashed
1½ tablespoons lemon or lime juice
1 teaspoon salt
1 cup sour cream
¼ to ½ teaspoon taco seasoning
1 cup Monterey Jack cheese, grated

1 cup sharp Cheddar cheese, grated
1 cup tomatoes, chopped
¼ cup green onion with tops, chopped
1 2½-ounce can pitted black olives,
   sliced or chopped

Mix avocados with juice and salt. Mix sour cream and taco seasoning with avocado mixture. Layer in following order: avocado mixture, Monterey Jack cheese, Cheddar cheese, tomatoes, onion and olives. Serve with tortilla chips.

Emerald Sun Dip
Great with raw vegetables

Chill

Yields 2 cups

1 cup spinach leaves, washed
1 tablespoon lemon juice
½ teaspoon Worcestershire sauce
2 tablespoons water
1 cup mayonnaise

3 ounces cream cheese
$1/3$ cup instant non-fat dry milk
½ teaspoon salt
¼ cup scallions, minced

Measure spinach leaves by pressing firmly into measuring cup. Place liquids in blender. Add mayonnaise, cream cheese, dry milk, salt and scallions. Add spinach. Purée . Carefully push ingredients down the sides of blender. Chill at least 2 hours. Stir before serving. Use with raw vegetables, chunks of chicken or ham.

Dill Dip
Vegetarian party delight

Chill

Yields 2 cups

1 cup sour cream
1 cup mayonnaise
1 tablespoon plus 1 teaspoon
   green onion flakes

1 tablespoon plus 1 teaspoon
   parsley flakes
1¹/₃ teaspoons seasoned salt
1¹/₃ teaspoons dill weed

Blend sour cream and mayonnaise. Add onion flakes, parsley flakes, seasoned salt and dill weed. Mix well. Chill. Serve with raw vegetables.

Fresh Mushroom Dip
Microwave

Microwave, medium-high

Yields 2 cups

2 cups fresh mushrooms, chopped
½ cup onion, chopped
2 tablespoons butter, melted
¼ cup flour

¾ cup heavy cream
1 tablespoon parsley flakes
½ teaspoon salt
Dash cayenne pepper

Place mushrooms, onion and butter in 1-quart bowl. Cook on medium-high 3 to 4 minutes or until onion is tender. Stir in flour; blend well. Gradually stir in cream and remaining ingredients. Cook on medium-high 3 minutes or until thickened. Stir once or twice during cooking time.

Tip: Serve with crisp crackers or celery. If desired, let dip cool; drop rounded spoonfuls onto crackers. Heat 12 to 15 crackers on a plate on medium-high 1½ to 2 minutes.

Water Chestnut Spread
A taste of old world elegance

Chill

Serves 16

8 ounces sour cream
1 cup mayonnaise
2 8-ounce cans water chestnuts,
   drained and chopped

¼ cup onion, finely chopped
¼ cup parsley, finely chopped
¾ teaspoon soy sauce
½ teaspoon salt

Blend all ingredients. Cover and chill. Will keep for several weeks. Serve with crackers.

Spicy Bloody Mary
Great with or without spirits

Serves 4

1 46-ounce can clamato juice
¼ to ¹⁄₃ cup Worcestershire sauce
2 teaspoons salt

Juice of ½ fresh lime (or to taste)
Vodka or gin as desired
Dash Tabasco

Mix ingredients thoroughly. Allow flavors to blend before serving.

Escapee Punch
Happy New Year!

Chill   Serves 10 to 12

3 ounces Cointreau
3 ounces brandy
8 ounces orange juice

3 ounces Grand Marnier
2 25.4-ounce bottles champagne
4 ounces fresh lemon juice

Mix all ingredients. Chill. Serve in punch bowl with ice.

Gluhwein
Famous German "concoction" for a cold evening

Serves 9

1 liter dry red wine
Juice of 1 lemon
Several whole cloves

5 to 8 teaspoons sugar
3 cinnamon sticks
Lemon slices

Pour dry red wine in pot and heat (do not boil). Add remaining ingredients except lemon slices and heat about 1 hour. The longer this "concoction" steeps, the better it is. Put slice of lemon in each mug or heat resistant glass. Pour in wine.

Kahlua

Better with age

Yields 3 quarts

3¾ cups sugar
4 cups boiling water
2 ounces instant coffee

1 fifth vodka
1 whole vanilla bean

Dissolve sugar in 3 cups water. Dissolve coffee in 1 cup water. Mix sugar and coffee mixture in large pot. Add bourbon. Pour into three 1-quart bottles. Suspend ⅓ vanilla bean in each bottle.

Sangria

Dangerously delicious

Chill

Serves 24

1 gallon burgundy
3 ounces brandy
2 ounces Triple Sec
1 cup orange juice
1 cup lemon juice
1½ cups sugar

2 cups water
2 quarts 7-Up
Oranges, sliced
Lemons, sliced
Limes, sliced
1 4-ounce jar maraschino cherries

Mix first 5 ingredients. Dissolve sugar in water and add to mixture. Mix should be kept in refrigerator until ready to serve. Add 7-Up, oranges, lemons, limes and cherries to mixture when served.

Sangria Slush

Alcoholic icee

Freeze

Serves 10

1 8-ounce can crushed pineapple
2½ cups dry red wine
½ cup sugar

1½ cups orange juice
½ cup lemon juice
2 tablespoons lemon peel

Put all ingredients in blender. Blend at high speed. Freeze.

Sangria with a Kick
A must with paella

Chill

Serves 6

½ cup water
1 cup sugar
¼ teaspoon cinnamon
2 bananas, peeled and sliced

1 lemon, peeled and sliced
1 orange, peeled and sliced
1 quart red wine
¼ cup vodka

Gently boil water, sugar and cinnamon 5 minutes. Cool. Combine fruit and cover with cooled syrup. Chill several hours. Put ice in glass pitcher and add fruit, ½ cup syrup, red wine and vodka. Serve sangria in well chilled tumblers, garnishing each glass with sliced fruit.

Tip: May use any available fresh fruit.

Whispers
True Sarasota drink

Chill

Serves 4 to 6

1 quart coffee ice cream
½ ounce brandy

½ ounce creme de cocoa

Pack blender ¾ full with coffee ice cream. Pour brandy and creme de cocoa over top of ice cream. Blend until mixture liquefies. Put in freezer to chill. Serve in small glasses.

Champagne Punch
Not your ordinary punch

Chill

Serves 20

1 fifth Southern Comfort
2 quarts champagne
1 quart sparkling water

8 ounces cranberry juice
6 ounces lemon juice
Dash bitters

Have all ingredients cold before combining. Mix well.

Mulled Cider
Great on Halloween

Serves 21

1 gallon cider
½ cup brown sugar
2 cinnamon sticks
1 tablespoon cinnamon
½ tablespoon nutmeg

1 tablespoon whole cloves
1 tablespoon allspice
Orange and lemon slices
 (optional)
Rum (optional)

Bring cider to gentle boil in pot with brown sugar and spices. Simmer 20 minutes. Orange and lemon slices may be floated on cider when served. Keep warm. Rum may be added if desired.

Tip: A little dry ice will add to the "spirit" of things on Halloween.

Mulled Holiday Punch
Serve hot on cold winter nights

Serves 14

1 14-ounce can pink pineapple-
 grapefruit juice
4 cups cranberry juice cocktail
1 cup water

½ cup brown sugar, firmly packed
⅛ teaspoon salt
2 teaspoons whole cloves
2 cinnamon sticks, broken in pieces

Combine juices, water, brown sugar and salt in large saucepan. Place cloves and cinnamon pieces in cheesecloth and tie. Add to juice mixture. Heat to boiling and simmer 15 to 20 minutes. Remove spices. Serve hot or iced.

Russian Tea
Delicious hot drink to serve on a cold night

Serves 12

1 18-ounce jar Tang
1 cup sugar
¾ teaspoon cinnamon
Pinch ginger

½ cup instant tea (not
 freeze dried)
½ teaspoon ground cloves

Combine all ingredients and keep in airtight container. To prepare, place 2 heaping teaspoons of tea mixture in 1 cup boiling water.

Spiced Coffee
Café fiesta

Serves 4 to 6

3½ cups water
1 cinnamon stick
7 whole cloves

3½ teaspoons instant coffee
¼ cup sugar
Whipped cream

Combine water, cinnamon stick, cloves and coffee in 1-quart pot. Cover and heat to boiling point. Remove from heat. Let stand 7 to 10 minutes. Strain. Add sugar and stir. Serve hot or cold (over ice) with whipped cream.

Three Fruit Punch
Serve at your next special occasion

Serves 32

1 6-ounce can frozen lemonade
   concentrate
1 8-ounce can crushed pineapple

1 10-ounce package frozen
   strawberries, thawed
3 quarts ginger ale, chilled
Crushed ice or ice mold

Put lemonade concentrate, pineapple and strawberries in blender and mix until completely smooth. Add ginger ale. Pour over ice in punch bowl.

Tip: Fruit mixture can be made in advance and stored in covered jar in refrigerator. Combine with ginger ale just before serving.

January Committee Cup
Serve when committee is tired of coffee

Serves 10 to 12

8 cups water
3 cups grape juice
6 ounces frozen orange juice
   concentrate

6 ounces frozen lemonade
   concentrate
¼ cup sugar (optional)
1 4-inch cinnamon stick
6 whole cloves

Combine liquids and sugar in 3-quart saucepan. Add spices (using tea ball, if desired). Simmer 15 to 20 minutes. Remove spices. Serve hot or iced.

Orange Julius
When there is no time for breakfast

Serves 4 to 6

1 cup milk
1 6-ounce can frozen orange juice
   concentrate
¼ cup sugar

1 teaspoon vanilla
12 to 14 ice cubes
2 raw eggs (optional)

Combine all ingredients in blender. Mix until thick and foamy. Eggs can be added for nutritious quick breakfast drink.

Shrub
A citrus delight

Chill

Serves 14

1 quart orange juice
1 pint pineapple juice

1 46-ounce can apricot nectar
1 quart orange sherbet

Mix first 3 ingredients. Place scoop of orange sherbet in small juice glass and add shrub mixture.

If a sweet punch is desired, mix equal parts of cranberry juice and 7-Up. For a tart punch, mix equal parts of cranberry juice and ginger ale. A cup of white wine would add spirit to either.

John and Mable Ringling
Museum of Art

John Ringling has been described by those who knew him well as "flamboyant," "daring," "a big, handsome fellow... [whose] very presence inspired men and excited women." He was the youngest of the five Ringling brothers who created and owned the circus (two more brothers rounded out the family total of seven sons and one daughter). John was the front man, the gambler, the operator, and the brother whose alternate extravagance and pettiness created a multi-hued personal legend. Though his acquaintances included detractors as well as admirers, few would argue the merits of Ringling's gifts to Sarasota. And one of the prime gifts was to be the John and Mable Ringling Museum of Art.

During routine circus-related business travels to Europe during the depressed post-World War I era, John and Mable acquired statuary, paintings, furnishings, and building materials — at first for personal enjoyment and construction projects. Ultimately, as John became a self-starting connoisseur of Baroque art, the Ringlings' purpose was to construct an art museum to house the growing collection — specifically as a legacy to the people of Sarasota and the State of Florida. Ringling's entire collection and museum were to be conceived, acquired, and completed between 1925 and 1931.

During Florida's "boom" period, John Ringling hired New York architect John Henry Phillips, who had participated in the design for the Metropolitan Museum of Art. The land for which Phillips designed the Ringlings' museum lay along the bayfront, between Ca' d' Zan and the home of Ellen and Ralph Caples, general agent for the New York Central Railroad. To the north of their house lay the magnificent residence of John's brother, Charles Ringling, and his wife, Edith. The land in which the Caples-Ringling complex lay was within a plat called "Shell Beach Subdivision," laid out by Charles N. Thompson, another circus entrepreneur and former manager of the famed Forepaugh-Sells Circus. In fact, Thompson's own home became John and Mable's first home at Sarasota Bay. The Thompson home, built expansively of white frame and spacious porches, had access to deepwater navigation by means of a 1,660 foot dock extending out into the bay.

The John and Mable Ringling Museum of Art which Phillips designed was completed in 1930, amid a national depression at a cost of $1,500,000. That same year, Mable Ringling died.

In accordance with John Ringling's bequest, the museum is open without charge one day each week. On December 15th of 1982, the Caples-Ringling estates were listed in **The National Register of Historic Places** under the U.S. Department of Interior.

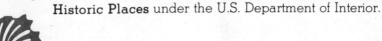

LADY'S LUNCHEON

* Vichyssoise Café L'Europe

* Chutney Chicken Salad on a Bed of Lettuce

* Buffet Broccoli

* Carrot Muffins

* Mocha Torte

  Wine Spritzer

Salads

Cauliflower Salad
Unusual taste

Chill

Serves 10 to 12

1 head lettuce, chopped
1 head cauliflower, chopped
1 pound bacon, cooked and
    chopped

1 large onion, chopped
¼ cup sugar
2 cups salad dressing
½ cup Parmesan cheese, grated

Layer first 4 ingredients in large bowl. In separate bowl, combine remaining ingredients and spread over lettuce mixture. Cover and refrigerate 24 hours. Toss before serving.

Caesar Salad
Prepare at table for special effect

Serves 8

1 clove garlic
2 medium heads Romaine lettuce
½ teaspoon salt
¼ teaspoon dry mustard
¼ teaspoon black pepper
½ cup Parmesan cheese, grated

6 tablespoons olive oil
Juice of 2 lemons
1 anchovy fillet, chopped
2 eggs, coddled
2 cups garlic croutons

Rub salad bowl with garlic. Tear lettuce into medium-sized pieces and put in bowl. Add salt, mustard, pepper and cheese. Sprinkle mixture with oil, lemon juice and anchovy fillet. Break eggs in greens. Toss salad gently but thoroughly until no trace of egg is seen and lettuce is well coated. Taste for seasoning. Add croutons and toss again.

Gazpacho Relish Salad
Colorful accompaniment

Serves 4 to 6

⅓ cup Italian dressing
¼ cup tomato sauce
1 medium green pepper, cut into
    thin strips

1 cup celery, bias cut
4 scallions, finely chopped
1 medium cucumber, sliced
2 medium tomatoes, cut into wedges

Mix all ingredients in 1-quart jar. Serve on lettuce.

Green Salad with Chinese Noodles
Unusual

Preheat oven 200°   Serves 8

3 tablespoons butter, melted   2 to 3 tablespoons Italian dressing
1 teaspoon Worcestershire sauce   ½ cup mayonnaise
1 teaspoon curry powder   Variety of greens, torn in pieces
1 teaspoon garlic salt   Ripe olives, sliced (optional)
1 3-ounce can chow mein noodles   Cauliflower flowerets (optional)

Combine butter and seasonings. Add noodles. Bake 15 minutes, stirring 3 times. Mix Italian dressing and mayonnaise. Toss with greens in salad bowl and add seasoned noodles. Add olives and cauliflower. Serve immediately.

Rice Salad à la Kermess
Refreshing

Chill   Serves 12

3¼ cups chicken stock   ⅜ teaspoon sugar
¾ tablespoon unsalted sweet butter   ¼ teaspoon freshly ground white
1¼ teaspoons salt   pepper
1⅝ cups long grain brown rice   1 cup orange sections, pared and cut
⅝ cup peanut oil   into ¾- inch pieces
⅜ cup fresh lime juice   ⅜ cup green onions with tops, sliced
1 tablespoon tarragon white wine   ⅜ cup pecans, toasted and coarsely
   vinegar   chopped
1 tablespoon fresh chives, minced   ¼ cup radishes, thinly sliced

Heat stock, butter and ⅜ teaspoon salt in Dutch oven to boiling; stir in rice. Cover and cook over medium-low heat until rice is tender, about 55 minutes. Cool to room temperature. Combine oil, lime juice, vinegar, chives, remaining salt, sugar and pepper. Whisk until blended. Stir dressing into cooled rice with fork. Cover and refrigerate 2 hours or overnight. Before serving, gently stir in oranges, green onions, pecans and radishes.

Peanut Crunch Slaw
Crunchy cole slaw

Chill   Serves 4 to 6

2 cups cabbage, shredded
½ cup celery, finely chopped
¼ cup sour cream
¼ cup mayonnaise
2 tablespoons scallions, chopped

2 tablespoons green pepper, chopped
¼ cup cucumber, chopped
½ teaspoon salt
¼ cup salted peanuts, chopped

Mix cabbage and celery. Chill. Mix next 6 ingredients. Chill. Just before serving, toss 2 mixtures together. Top with peanuts.

Seoul Salad
Korean

Serves 8 to 10

10 ounces fresh spinach, torn in
   pieces
1 8-ounce can bamboo shoots,
   drained and rinsed
1 8-ounce can water chestnuts,
   drained, rinsed and halved
6 green scallions, sliced
¼ cup parsley, minced
3 hard-boiled eggs, sliced

3 slices bacon, cooked and
   crumbled
1 cup peanut oil
¼ cup rice vinegar
⅓ cup tomato purée
2 teaspoons honey
1 teaspoon sea salt
1 teaspoon Worcestershire sauce

Combine first 7 ingredients in large serving bowl. Heat remaining ingredients and pour over tossed vegetables. Serve immediately. May be served chilled.

Greens that are torn rather than cut are less likely to turn brown.

Salads

Spinach Salad
Popeye's delight

Chill

Serves 4 to 6

10 ounces fresh spinach, washed
  and dried
8 slices bacon, cooked and
  crumbled
½ cup water chestnuts, thinly sliced
4 hard-boiled eggs, chopped

1 cup oil
½ cup sugar
⅓ cup vinegar
1 teaspoon Worcestershire sauce
1 medium onion, grated
⅓ cup ketchup

Combine spinach with bacon, water chestnuts and eggs. Chill. In separate bowl, combine remaining ingredients. Chill. Before serving, thinly coat salad with dressing.

Tip: Substitute ½ cup Jerusalem artichokes for water chestnuts.

Wilted Spinach Salad
For adults only

Serves 4

3 cups fresh spinach
4 slices red onion
3 large mushrooms, sliced
1 tablespoon Parmesan cheese,
  grated
1 tablespoon butter, melted
½ tablespoon Dijon mustard

Juice of ½ lemon
1 ounce brandy
1 ounce Cointreau
¼ cup oil
¼ cup vinegar
½ tablespoon shallots, chopped
4 strips bacon, cooked
Salt and pepper to taste

Toss first 4 ingredients and set aside. Combine butter, mustard and lemon juice. Add brandy and Cointreau. Flame liquor to burn off alcohol. Combine remaining ingredients and add to mustard mixture. Cook 3 minutes. Pour over spinach mixture.

Tabouli
Wheat garden salad

Serves 6

1 cup cracked wheat
1 bunch scallions, finely chopped
2 bunches parsley, finely chopped
4 tomatoes, finely chopped

Juice of 4 lemons
½ cup olive oil
Salt and pepper to taste

Soak wheat in water for a few minutes. Squeeze dry by pressing between palms. Add remaining ingredients. Mix well. Serve with fresh lettuce leaves and pita bread.

Avocado Salad
Dieter's delight

Serves 6

1 large avocado, peeled and cubed
2 cups fresh tomatoes, cubed
1 small purple onion, sliced
1½ tablespoons olive oil

1 teaspoon salt
⅛ teaspoon pepper
⅓ cup cottage cheese
1 tablespoon lemon juice

Combine all ingredients.

Mandarin Orange-Avocado Salad
Fruity green salad

Serves 6

1 head fresh leaf lettuce, torn
  in pieces
1 11-ounce can mandarin oranges,
  drained
1 large avocado, diced
½ cup salad oil

2 tablespoons lemon juice
1 teaspoon orange rind, grated
½ cup orange juice, freshly squeezed
2 tablespoons sugar
¼ teaspoon salt
¼ teaspoon dry mustard

Toss lettuce, oranges and avocado in large salad bowl. Mix remaining ingredients and pour over lettuce mixture.

Salads

Broccoli Rice Salad
Colorful

Serves 6

1 cup long grain rice
¼ cup wild rice
½ pound broccoli
½ red bell pepper, cored and diced
½ cup pitted black olives, sliced
¼ cup red onion, chopped
½ of 15½-ounce can garbanzo
   beans, drained

⅓ cup vegetable oil
¼ cup white wine or tarragon vinegar
1 tablespoon Dijon mustard
1 teaspoon dried oregano
Few dashes hot pepper sauce
Salt and pepper to taste
Parsley
Lemon wedges

Cook rices according to package directions. Cool slightly. Cut broccoli stalks into small pieces and separate flowerets into small pieces. Cook in boiling, salted water 4 minutes. Rinse under cold water. Mix warm rice with broccoli, red pepper, olives, onion and garbanzo beans. Mix oil, vinegar, mustard, oregano, hot pepper sauce, salt and pepper in small container. Pour over salad, toss to coat. Garnish with parsley and lemon wedges. Serve cold or room temperature.

Carrot Colada Salad
Holiday carrots

Chill

Serves 12

⅓ cup dates, chopped
⅓ cup raisins
1 8-ounce can crushed pineapple,
   drain and reserve juice

2 pounds carrots, peeled and shredded
⅓ cup nuts, chopped
¼ cup mayonnaise
½ cup coconut, shredded

Soak dates and raisins in reserved pineapple juice until plump. In large bowl, combine carrots, nuts, pineapple, raisins and dates with enough reserved pineapple juice to moisten mixture. Add mayonnaise. Toss coconut in lightly. Chill 2 hours.

Cauliflower Orange Salad
With lemon dressing

Serves 6 to 8

1 medium cauliflower, divided into flowerets
2 cups orange wedges, cut in pieces

¼ cup green pepper, finely chopped
1 teaspoon onion juice

Mix cauliflower, orange pieces, green pepper and onion juice in large salad bowl. Set aside.

Lemon Dressing

1 tablespoon salad oil
2 tablespoons flour
½ cup water
1 egg yolk
½ teaspoon salt

½ teaspoon dry mustard
¼ teaspoon paprika
2 tablespoons lemon juice
¼ cup salad oil

Blend salad oil with flour and water. Bring to boil, stirring constantly. Boil 1 minute. Remove from heat. Blend in remaining ingredients. Beat until smooth. Pour over cauliflower-orange mixture. Serve on greens.

Chilled Broccoli Salad
For warm summer nights

Chill

Serves 6 to 8

1 bunch fresh broccoli, flowerets only
3 to 4 celery stalks, chopped
⅓ cup green olives, chopped
3 hard-cooked eggs, chopped

1 tablespoon lemon juice
Dash Tabasco
Dash Worcestershire sauce
2 tablespoons mayonnaise

Cut broccoli flowerets into 1-inch pieces. Add next 6 ingredients. Spoon mayonnaise through mixture carefully. Chill.

Tip: Broccoli may be blanched if desired.

Salads

Cucumber Onion Salad
Dilly of a salad

Chill
Serves 8

2 large cucumbers, peeled and thinly sliced
1 medium yellow onion, thinly sliced
2 tablespoons white wine vinegar

¼ teaspoon white pepper
4 tablespoons sour cream
1 teaspoon salt
1 to 2 tablespoons fresh dill, chopped

Combine all ingredients except dill. Chill several hours. Sprinkle with dill before serving.

Four Bean Salad
Nice for a picnic

Chill
Serves 8

1 1-pound can green beans, drained
1 1-pound can yellow wax beans, drained
1 1-pound can red kidney beans, drained
1 1-pound can lima beans, drained
1 medium green pepper, thinly sliced
1 medium onion, thinly sliced

½ cup sugar
½ cup wine vinegar
½ cup salad oil
1 teaspoon salt
½ teaspoon dried tarragon
½ teaspoon dry mustard
½ teaspoon basil leaves
2 teaspoons parsley, shredded

Mix all vegetables in bowl. Combine remaining ingredients. Add to vegetables. Marinate in refrigerator overnight, stirring once after about 1 hour. To serve, mix well and drain.

To make salad cool and crisp, place torn, washed lettuce in salad bowl and cover with paper towel until time to serve. Add tomatoes and dressing just before serving.

Green Bean Salad Mimosa
Excellent with pasta

Serves 6

1½ pounds green beans
6 tablespoons olive oil
2 tablespoons red wine vinegar
1 large shallot, minced
1 teaspoon salt
Freshly ground pepper

½ pound mushrooms, sliced
¾ cup Wesphalian or prosciutto ham,
cut in julienne strips
2 tomatoes, cut in 8 wedges or 12
cherry tomatoes, halved
1 hard-boiled egg, grated

Snap beans into 1½-inch lengths. Cook 5 to 8 minutes in boiling, salted water. Drain and rinse with cold water until cool. Dry thoroughly. Chill. Combine oil, vinegar, shallot, salt and pepper in jar. Shake well. Toss green beans, mushrooms and dressing. Marinate 30 minutes. Add ham and tomatoes. Top with grated egg.

Herbed Tomatoes
Simple, light summer salad

Chill

Serves 6

6 ripe tomatoes, peeled and sliced
1 teaspoon salt
¼ teaspoon coarse black pepper
½ teaspoon dried thyme or
marjoram

¼ cup parsley, snipped
¼ cup chives, snipped
⅔ cup salad oil
¼ cup tarragon vinegar

Place tomatoes in bowl, sprinkle with seasonings and herbs. Combine oil and vinegar; pour over tomatoes. Cover and chill 1 hour, stirring occasionally. Drain dressing and serve on side. Garnish with additional parsley or chives.

Never boil gelatin and never add fresh pineapple.

Salads

Insalata di Fontina
Pepper and Fontina cheese salad

Chill

Serves 4 to 6

6 yellow sweet peppers
½ pound Fontina cheese, diced
¼ cup green olives, pitted
3 tablespoons olive oil

1 teaspoon prepared mustard
Salt and pepper to taste
2 to 3 tablespoons cream

Cut peppers in half, discarding cores and seeds. Bake at 450° or broil until skins blacken and blister. When cool, pull off thin, outer skin and cut flesh into thin, long, even strips. In salad bowl, mix pepper strips, cheese and olives. Combine remaining ingredients and pour over pepper mixture. Stir well and chill 2 hours.

Layered Salad Deluxe
Excellent for a buffet

Chill

Serves 12 to 15

1 pound fresh spinach, torn in pieces
1 medium head lettuce, torn in
  pieces
6 hard-cooked eggs, sliced
1 pound bacon, cooked and
  crumbled
1 8-ounce can water chestnuts,
  drained and sliced

1 10-ounce package frozen English
  peas, thawed
1 cup salad dressing or mayonnaise
½ cup sour cream
1 4-ounce package buttermilk
  mayonnaise dressing mix
Fresh parsley, chopped

Layer first 6 ingredients in large salad bowl. Combine salad dressing, sour cream and dressing mix. Mix well. Spread over vegetables, sealing to edge of bowl. Garnish with parsley. Cover tightly and refrigerate 3 hours or overnight. Toss gently before serving.

Salade Frappant
Beautiful salad

Serves 6

¼ pound snow pea pods
2 quarts water
Salt
1 pint fresh strawberries, sliced
⅛ pound Westphalian ham, cut
   in julienne strips
1 small honeydew melon, cut in
   julienne strips

2 tablespoons strawberry, raspberry or
   red wine vinegar
½ tablespoon fresh lime juice
6 tablespoons light olive oil
½ teaspoon salt
Freshly ground white pepper to taste
1 head Bibb lettuce

String snow peas and soak in cold water. Bring 2 quarts water to boil, add salt and snow pea pods. Blanch 1 minute, then refresh pods in ice water until completely cool. Drain and cut into thin strips. In large bowl, combine snow peas, strawberries, ham and melon. Set aside. Combine vinegar and lime juice in bowl; slowly whisk in oil. Add salt and pepper. Before serving, toss pea pod mixture with enough salad dressing to moisten and flavor. With slotted spoon, transfer salad to Bibb lettuce cups and serve.

Spanish Rice Salad
Serve with your backyard barbeque

Chill

Serves 8

1 10-ounce package Spanish yellow
   rice
½ large green pepper, finely
   chopped
12 pimiento stuffed olives, sliced
1 4-ounce can mushrooms, drained
   and sliced

1 12-ounce jar marinated artichoke
   hearts, drained, halved, and
   reserve marinade
½ teaspoon curry powder
⅓ cup mayonnaise
Salt and pepper to taste

Cook rice according to directions on package, omitting butter. Cool. Add pepper, olives and mushrooms. Combine reserved marinade, curry powder and mayonnaise. Add artichokes to rice mixture. Season to taste. Add mayonnaise mixture and chill several hours.

Salads

Northern Potato Salad
Great for picnic

Serves 6 to 8

3 pounds small, new potatoes, boiled
1 pound bacon, diced and cooked
1 pound fresh green beans, cooked
½ cup salad oil
½ cup scallions, chopped
1 teaspoon salt
½ teaspoon tarragon

Pepper to taste
¼ cup chicken consommé
¼ cup fresh parsley, chopped
½ teaspoon basil
1 teaspoon dry mustard
¼ cup tarragon vinegar
1 clove garlic, crushed

Slice unpeeled potatoes into ¼-inch slices and combine with bacon and green beans. In jar, shake together remaining ingredients. Pour dressing over potatoes and beans. Marinate at room temperature 2 to 3 hours.

Peas Pizzicato
Gives peas crunch and color

Serves 6 to 8

2 10-ounce packages frozen peas,
  thawed
½ cup scallions, chopped
½ cup celery, chopped
½ cup sour cream

Salt and pepper to taste
Garlic to taste, chopped
1 pound bacon, cooked and crumbled
¾ cup cashews
Pimiento (optional)

Mix first 6 ingredients. Cover and refrigerate. Before serving, add bacon, nuts and pimiento.

Zucchini Artichoke Salad
Serve with your most elegant meal

Serves 4 to 6

1 14-ounce can artichoke hearts, drained and halved
2 cups mushrooms, thinly sliced
2 small zucchini squash, quartered and sliced
1/4 cup red wine vinegar
2 teaspoons Dijon mustard

1/4 cup vegetable oil
1 teaspoon garlic, minced
1 teaspoon dried dill
Salt and pepper to taste
1 cup half and half
1/2 cup blanched almonds, sliced and lightly toasted

In non-metal bowl, combine artichoke hearts, mushrooms and zucchini. In separate bowl, combine vinegar, mustard, oil, garlic, dill, salt and pepper. Slowly add half and half, whisking until well combined. Toss vegetables with dressing and almonds. Serve on plates lined with lettuce.

Chop Suey Salad
Simple meal

Serves 8

1 cup ripe olives, sliced
1 medium green pepper, sliced in 1-inch strips
4 cups mixed salad greens, torn in pieces
1 cup canned bean sprouts, rinsed and drained
1 8-ounce can water chestnuts, drained and sliced

1 cup scallions, sliced
3/4 cup celery, chopped
1 cup chicken, cooked and thinly sliced
1 tablespoon mayonnaise
2 tablespoons lemon juice
1 tablespoon vegetable oil
1/3 cup soy sauce
4 slices bacon, cooked and crumbled

Combine first 8 ingredients in salad bowl. Mix remaining ingredients except bacon. Pour dressing over salad just before serving. Top with bacon.

Salads

Sweet and Sour Carrots
Children love this one

Chill

Serves 12 to 15

2 pounds carrots, sliced
1 10¾-ounce can tomato soup
⅓ cup salad oil
¾ cup sugar
¾ cup wine vinegar

⅛ teaspoon salt
⅛ teaspoon Worcestershire sauce
1 green pepper, finely chopped
1 medium onion, finely chopped

Cook carrots until just barely tender. Drain. Combine remaining ingredients in saucepan and cook until ready to boil. Remove from heat. Pour over drained carrots and marinate in refrigerator overnight. Serve hot or cold.

Warm Mushroom Salad
Serve with your favorite steak

Serves 4

1 head leaf or red leaf lettuce, torn
   in pieces
½ cup olive oil
Juice of 1 lemon

Salt to taste
¼ teaspoon freshly ground pepper
¼ pound fresh mushrooms, thinly
   sliced

Place lettuce in serving bowl. Combine oil, lemon juice, salt and pepper in saucepan over medium heat. Heat until oil is very warm. Add mushrooms and cook for 1 to 2 minutes. Pour over lettuce and toss well. Serve immediately on hot plates.

Mexican Salad
Barbeque favorite

Chill

Serves 6

1 large head lettuce, shredded
2 medium tomatoes, diced
1 tablespoon onion, finely chopped
1 pound Cheddar cheese, grated

1 15-ounce can ranch style beans
6 ounces Catalina salad dressing
12 ounces corn chips

Mix first 5 ingredients in large salad bowl. Pour salad dressing over salad. Stir in corn chips. Chill.

Hearty Tuna Salad
Unique

Chill   Serves 4

1 10-ounce package frozen Italian   ½ cup mayonnaise
  green beans   1 tablespoon lemon juice
1 6½-ounce can tuna, drained and   1½ teaspoons soy sauce
  flaked   Dash garlic powder
1 cup celery, thinly sliced   1 cup chow mein noodles

Cook green beans as directed on package. Drain and cool. Combine beans, tuna, celery, mayonnaise, lemon juice, soy sauce and garlic powder. Mix gently. Chill. Before serving, add chow mein noodles; toss lightly. Serve in lettuce cups.

Curried Chicken Salad
For ladies luncheon

Chill   Serves 6

2 to 3 cups chicken or turkey,   1 cup celery, finely chopped
  cooked and cubed   1 cup mayonnaise
1 8-ounce can water chestnuts,   1 teaspoon curry powder
  drained and sliced   2 teaspoons soy sauce
½ pound seedless grapes, halved,   2 teaspoons lemon juice
  or 1 11-ounce can mandarin   Salt to taste
  oranges, drained

Combine chicken, water chestnuts, grapes or mandarin oranges and celery. Mix remaining ingredients. Add to chicken mixture and toss well. Chill several hours. Serve on Bibb lettuce.

Chutney Chicken Salad
Unusual

Chill   Serves 8

1 cup raisins
1 cup salted peanuts
1 cup mango chutney
1 cup coconut flakes
2 bananas, sliced

1 teaspoon lemon juice
Salt and pepper to taste
1½ cups mayonnaise
2 to 3 pounds chicken, cooked and
  cubed

Soak raisins in warm water 15 minutes. Drain and combine with remaining ingredients. Chill 6 hours.

Cold Pasta Chicken Primavera
Serve for dinner on hot summer night

Chill   Serves 6 to 8

½ pound vermicelli or spaghetti
1 cup garlic vinaigrette dressing
10 fresh mushrooms, sliced
1 cup broccoli flowerets, blanched
1 cup fresh green peas, blanched

12 to 14 cherry tomatoes
2 cups chicken, boiled, boned, skinned
  and cubed
⅓ cup fresh basil, chopped
⅓ cup pine nuts

Cook pasta according to package directions. Drain and place in mixing bowl. Add ⅓ cup vinaigrette dressing, toss and cool. Chill 3 hours. In separate mixing bowl, place vegetables and remaining vinaigrette dressing, toss to coat. Before serving, combine pasta, vegetables, chicken, basil and nuts.

Japanese Chicken Salad
Nice lunch

Serves 6 to 8

2 whole chicken breasts, cooked,
  boned and cubed
1 head lettuce, torn in pieces
3 green onions, sliced
1 3-ounce can chow mein noodles
4 ounces slivered almonds, toasted

¼ cup poppy seed
2 tablespoons sugar
1 teaspoon salt
½ teaspoon pepper
4 tablespoons vinegar
½ cup salad oil

Mix chicken, lettuce and onions. Add noodles, almonds and poppy seed. Combine remaining ingredients in blender or shaker. Pour over salad. Serve immediately.

Lobster Salad
Ladies lunch

Chill

Serves 4 to 6

1 envelope unflavored gelatin
½ cup water
½ teaspoon salt
2 tablespoons lemon juice
¼ teaspoon Tabasco
1 cup mayonnaise

1 teaspoon onion, minced
½ cup celery, diced
¼ cup green pepper, chopped
¼ cup pimiento, chopped
1 cup lobster, cooked and chopped

Sprinkle gelatin on water to soften. Place over low heat and stir until dissolved. Remove from heat and stir in salt, lemon juice and Tabasco. Cool. Stir gelatin mixture into mayonnaise. Chill to unbeaten egg-white consistency. Fold in remaining ingredients. Place in 3-cup mold or individual molds and chill until firm. Unmold on serving platter with salad greens.

Salads

Winter Fruit Salad
Sweet

Freeze

Serves 6

1 tablespoon mayonnaise
3 ounces cream cheese, softened
⅛ teaspoon salt
1 cup heavy cream
2 teaspoons sugar
½ cup dates, chopped

½ cup crushed pineapple, drained
½ cup purple or red grapes, seeded
   and sliced
½ cup maraschino cherries, halved
½ cup pecan pieces

Cream mayonnaise and cream cheese until soft and smooth. Add salt. Whip cream, adding sugar, and fold into mixture. Add remaining ingredients except nuts. Pour into loaf pan. Sprinkle with nuts. Cover and freeze until firm. Slice and serve on lettuce.

Cherry Soufflé Mold
Doubles as salad or dessert

Chill

Serves 6 to 8

1 envelope unflavored gelatin
1¼ cups water
⅓ cup sugar
1 16-ounce can dark sweet cherries,
   drain, chop and reserve juice

2 tablespoons lemon juice
½ cup sour cream
1 8¼-ounce can crushed pineapple,
   drained
¼ cup pecans, chopped

Soften gelatin in ¼ cup water. Combine remaining water, gelatin and sugar. Heat until dissolved. Pour in bowl and add ½ cup reserved cherry juice, lemon juice and sour cream. Beat with mixer until blended. Chill until set around edges. Beat until light and frothy. Fold in cherries, pineapple and pecans. Pour into 6 x 12-inch dish. Chill. Cut into squares.

Rap head of lettuce on counter top; the core can then be removed without cutting.

Suncoast Pita Pocket Salad
Great for the beach

Serves 8

Pita pocket bread
1 pound ham, slivered
½ pound Swiss cheese, slivered
Lettuce, shredded
2 tomatoes, chopped

1 onion, chopped
Green or ripe olives, chopped
1 bunch bean sprouts
Italian dressing

Cut pocket bread in half. Fill each half with ham and Swiss cheese. Wrap in foil or place in airtight container. When ready to serve, add condiments. Top with Italian dressing.

Summer Fruit Salad
Use fresh fruit

Serves 6 to 8

4 bananas, cut in large pieces
2 oranges, sliced
½ pineapple, cut into spears
½ cantaloupe, sliced
1 cup blueberries
½ cup strawberries, sliced
¼ small watermelon, cut in wedges

⅓ cup sour cream
⅓ cup mayonnaise
2 bananas, peeled and mashed
1 tablespoon honey
2 tablespoons almonds, toasted and
finely chopped

Arrange fruit on plate. Combine remaining ingredients and serve with fruit.

Tomato Carlos
Different crab salad

Serves 2

2 tomatoes, peeled
1 teaspoon dressing mix
½ cup mayonnaise
1 cup apple, diced

1 cup celery, diced
6 ounces crabmeat
2 lemon wedges
Lettuce

Prepare tomatoes for stuffing. Combine dressing mix and mayonnaise. Add next 3 ingredients. Put crabmeat mixture into tomatoes. Serve with lemon wedges on lettuce.

Salads

Mandarin Orange Mold
Refreshing

Chill

Serves 8

2 11-ounce cans mandarin oranges
2 3-ounce packages orange flavored
 gelatin
1 pint orange sherbet

1 13½-ounce can crushed pineapple,
 undrained
Watercress
Strawberries

Drain 1 can oranges and reserve syrup. Add enough water to syrup to make 1½ cups liquid. Pour into saucepan and bring to boil. Remove from heat; add gelatin and stir until dissolved. Add sherbet and stir until melted. Chill until mixture is the consistency of unbeaten egg white. Fold in 1 can oranges and pineapple. Pour into 2-quart mold and chill several hours until firm. Unmold on serving plate. Garnish with watercress, remaining oranges and strawberries.

Party Grapefruit Salad
Not dessert sweet

Chill

Serves 16

4 grapefruit, halved
2 3-ounce packages lemon jello

9 ounces cream cheese
½ cup salad dressing
Henri's Tastee Dressing

Remove fruit carefully from 2 grapefruit and shred. Reserve juice. Squeeze juice from remaining grapefuit. Combine all juice and add enough water to make 3 cups liquid. Bring liquid to boil; pour over jello. Stir until dissolved. Blend cream cheese with salad dressing. Add ⅓ jello mixture. Pour remaining jello mixture over shredded grapefruit. Clean insides of grapefruit halves thoroughly, removing all pulp. Fill grapefruit shells ⅓ full with grapefruit mixture. Refrigerate until partially jelled. Add cheese mixture and refrigerate until partially jelled. Pour remaining grapefruit mixture over cheese. Jell in refrigerator. Quarter each half. Serve on lettuce with Henri's Tastee Dressing.

Cole Slaw Soufflé
Different

Chill   Serves 6

1 3-ounce package orange flavored   1 cup cabbage, finely shredded
  gelatin   1 cup carrot, shredded
¾ cup boiling water   ½ cup raisins
1 8-ounce can crushed pineapple,   ½ cup walnuts, chopped
  drain and reserve liquid   3 egg whites, stiffly beaten
¾ cup mayonnaise

Tape aluminum foil firmly around top of 1-quart soufflé dish. Dissolve gelatin in
water. Add reserved pineapple liquid. Beat in mayonnaise. Place in loaf pan
and freeze until firm 1 inch from edge, but soft in center, about 20 minutes. In
large bowl, beat mixture until fluffy. Fold in pineapple and remaining
ingredients. Pour into soufflé dish. Chill until set.

Cranberry Fruit Mold
Serve with turkey

Chill   Serves 12

3 cups fresh cranberries, chopped   1 envelope unflavored gelatin
½ to 1 cup sugar   ¾ cup celery, chopped
1 20-ounce can crushed pineapple,   1 cup apples, unpeeled and chopped
  drain and reserve liquid   ½ cup walnuts, chopped
                                           Sour cream (optional)

Mix cranberries and sugar. Let stand 15 minutes. Combine reserved
pineapple liquid and gelatin in small pan. Heat until gelatin is dissolved. Add
celery, apple, nuts and pineapple to cranberries. Add gelatin mixture. Pour
into 6-cup ring mold. Chill. Serve with sour cream.

Salads

Tomato Aspic
Zippy flavor

Chill   Serves 10 to 12

4 packages unflavored gelatin   ¼ cup lemon juice
½ cup cold water   2 tablespoons Worcestershire sauce
1 46-ounce can Sacramento Plus   1 teaspoon onion, minced
   tomato juice (no substitute)   ½ cup salad olives, chopped
½ cup sugar   1 teaspoon horseradish
1 teaspoon salt   1 teaspoon prepared mustard
¼ cup white vinegar

Soften gelatin in water. Heat tomato juice. Add gelatin and stir until dissolved.
Stir in remaining ingredients. Pour into lightly greased mold or 12-inch pyrex
pan. Refrigerate until congealed. Invert on serving plate if using mold. Use
side dish of mayonnaise or other dressing if desired.

Two Toned Salad
A rainbow meal

Chill   Serves 8

1 envelope unflavored gelatin   1 cup celery, chopped
¼ cup cold water   1 tablespoon onion, minced
½ cup boiling water   1 cup salad dressing or mayonnaise
2 cups chicken, cooked and cubed   1 8-ounce can cranberry jelly
   or 2 6½-ounce cans tuna, drained   1 3-ounce package lemon jello
2 hard-boiled eggs, chopped   ¾ cup boiling water
½ cup stuffed olives, chopped   ½ cup orange juice

Mix gelatin into cold water. Add ½ cup boiling water and stir until dissolved.
Set aside. Mix next 6 ingredients. Add to gelatin mixture. Pour into 9 x 7-inch
pan. Refrigerate until set. Beat cranberry jelly. Add lemon jello that has been
dissolved in ¾ cup boiling water. Add orange juice. Mix well. Cool. Pour over
first layer and refrigerate until well set. Cut in squares and serve on lettuce.

Supreme Vegetable Aspic
Serve with herbed mayonnaise

Chill   Serves 8 to 10

3 envelopes unflavored gelatin   2 teaspoons dill weed
5½ cups tomato juice   1 teaspoon basil
⅓ cup lemon juice   1 teaspoon oregano
1 teaspoon onion, grated   1 bay leaf, finely crushed
1 clove garlic, crushed   1 14-ounce can artichoke hearts,
2 teaspoons salt   drained and halved
                                          1 ripe avocado, sliced

Soften gelatin in ½ cup tomato juice. Set aside. Combine remaining ingredients except artichokes and avocado. Simmer 10 minutes, stirring occasionally. Remove from heat and strain through cheesecloth. Add gelatin to hot
juice mixture; stir until dissolved. Cool. Place artichokes and avocado in 9 x 13-
inch pyrex dish. Add tomato mixture. Refrigerate until set or overnight. Cut in
squares.

Herbed Mayonnaise

                                          Yields 1½ cups

1 cup mayonnaise   1 clove garlic, minced
½ teaspoon lemon juice   1 tablespoon chives, chopped
¼ teaspoon salt   ⅛ teaspoon curry powder
¼ teaspoon paprika   ½ teaspoon Worcestershire sauce
1 teaspoon salad herbs   ½ cup sour cream

Mix all ingredients. Chill.

Tip: May also be used as seafood or vegetable dip.

To unmold salad easily, set in warm water for moment,
then shake gently onto serving plate.

Salad Dressings

Honey Garlic Salad Dressing

Yields 1¼ cups

1 tablespoon Parmesan cheese, grated
¼ teaspoon black pepper
½ teaspoon salt
2 cloves garlic, crushed
1 tablespoon honey

Dash cayenne pepper
⅔ cup olive oil
⅓ cup red wine vinegar
1 teaspoon lemon juice
1 teaspoon leaf oregano

Place all ingredients in quart jar. Shake vigorously until smoothly blended.

Lemon Mustard Salad Dressing
Tart and tangy

Yields 1¼ cups

2 tablespoons Dijon mustard
¾ cup olive oil
3 teaspoons fresh lemon juice
5 teaspoons white vinegar
¼ teaspoon garlic, pressed

¼ teaspoon salad herbs
⅛ teaspoon tarragon
¼ teaspoon salt
Pinch sugar

Combine all ingredients and shake until thoroughly mixed.

Light Lemon Salad Dressing
Serve on fresh mushrooms

Yields ½ cup

½ teaspoon coarse salt
¼ teaspoon freshly ground pepper
1 clove garlic, chopped (optional)

2 tablespoons lemon juice
6 tablespoons oil

Combine salt and pepper in bowl. Add garlic and mash into salt and pepper. Add lemon juice and mix. Remove pieces of garlic. Add oil and beat until combined.

Creamy French
Very spicy

Yields 3 cups

2 cloves garlic, crushed
1 cup mayonnaise
½ cup chili sauce
½ cup salad oil
½ cup ketchup
1 teaspoon prepared mustard

1 tablespoon Worcestershire sauce
1 teaspoon horseradish
2 tablespoons water
½ teaspoon black pepper
Dash Tabasco
Juice of 1 onion
Juice of 1 lemon

Mix all ingredients. Place in tightly covered container.

Creamy Vinaigrette Salad Dressing
Use with any green salad

Chill

Yields 2 cups

½ cup oil
½ cup half and half
1 egg, lightly beaten
1 clove garlic, minced
5 tablespoons tarragon vinegar
2 tablespoons olive oil
Juice of ½ lemon

2 teaspoons salt
1 teaspoon freshly ground white
  pepper
½ teaspoon freshly ground black
  pepper
¼ teaspoon sugar
½ teaspoon dry mustard

Combine all ingredients in jar and shake well. Refrigerate at least 2 hours. Shake before using.

French Dressing
Sweet and sour

Yields 1½ cups

1 cup oil
4 tablespoons wine vinegar
1 medium onion, chopped
1 teaspoon salt

1 teaspoon dry mustard
1 teaspoon celery seed
6 tablespoons sugar
1 teaspoon paprika

Blend all ingredients.

Salad Dressings

Real French Salad Dressing
Guaranteed to please

Yields ¼ cup

1 clove garlic, mashed
1 tablespoon red wine vinegar
1 teaspoon Dijon mustard

3 tablespoons olive oil
Freshly ground pepper

In wooden bowl, blend garlic, vinegar and mustard. Add olive oil. Mix well.
Add ground pepper.

Red Barn Famous Dressing
Spicy

Chill

Yields 4 cups

2 cups mayonnaise
1 avocado, finely mashed
6 scallions, finely chopped
1 ounce anchovies, finely chopped
4 tablespoons buttermilk
1 teaspoon Tabasco
¼ teaspoon dry mustard
¼ teaspoon white pepper

¼ teaspoon Accent
1½ tablespoons Worcestershire sauce
1½ tablespoons soy sauce
1½ teaspoons wine vinegar
1 tablespoon lemon juice
¼ teaspoon celery seed
¼ teaspoon oregano
¼ teaspoon garlic powder

Mix all ingredients thoroughly and chill. Excellent on all salad greens.

Spicy Thousand Island

Yields 4 cups

1 small onion, chopped
1 cup mayonnaise
⅓ cup salad oil
¼ cup ketchup
2 tablespoons sugar
2 tablespoons wine vinegar

1 teaspoon mustard
½ teaspoon salt
½ teaspoon paprika
¼ teaspoon celery seed
Dash pepper

Put all ingredients in blender. Process.

Tip: Add 4 ounces Roquefort cheese for variation.

Mayfair Caesar Dressing

Chill   Yields 3½ cups

5 cloves garlic, chopped   Juice of 2 small lemons
1 tablespoon salt   1½ tablespoons freshly ground pepper
2 eggs, beaten   ¾ cup Parmesan cheese, grated
2 cups oil   1½ tablespoons Worcestershire sauce

Pulverize garlic in salt. Combine eggs and ¼ cup oil. Alternately add remaining oil and lemon juice. Stir in pepper, cheese, Worcestershire and garlic mixture. Chill. Serve on Romaine lettuce with toasted croutons.

Mayfair Dressing

Chill   Yields 4 cups

1 clove garlic, peeled and sliced   ½ teaspoon sugar
1 celery stalk, scraped, peeled and 2 tablespoons salad mustard
  sliced   1 tablespoon lemon juice
4 tablespoons green onion, chopped 3 eggs
1 2-ounce can flat anchovies   2 cups salad oil
1 teaspoon freshly ground pepper
1 teaspoon Accent

Place all ingredients except eggs and oil in blender and whirl 2 seconds. Add eggs 1 at a time, blending 2 seconds after each. Add salad oil gradually, blending until well mixed. Chill. Serve on lettuce salads.

Sour Cream Dressing

                                    Yields 2 cups

1 cup sour cream   ¼ large onion, juiced
1 cup mayonnaise   ⅓ cup buttermilk
Juice of 1 lemon   Salt to taste

Mix ingredients with wire wisk. Place in covered jar in refrigerator.

Asolo Theater

After his death in 1936 at seventy, John Ringling's legacy to Sarasota was enriched by a succession of further acquisitions. One of the important ones — a theater — followed his death by fourteen years.

An 18th century Italian theater was destined to become part of the John and Mable Ringling Museum of Art. The tiny theater, of the hill town of Asolo north of Venice, had stood for nearly 150 years as part of a castle, once home for a Renaissance queen. It had been constructed in the town between 1796 and 1798, in memory of the renowned Caterina Cornaro, a 15th century Queen of Cyprus and a creative patron of the arts.

In 1930, the theater at the city of Asolo was replaced by a modern building designed to accommodate the twentieth century's motion pictures. Dismantled and purchased by a Venetian antique collector, the theater was ultimately removed from storage in 1950, when it was acquired for the John and Mable Ringling Museum of Art by the State of Florida under the authorization of the Florida State Board of Control. When early plans fell through for a new museum wing to house the acquisition, museum director A. Everett Austin Jr. installed the theater in the museum's lecture room.

Thus, its arrival anticipated, the little European theater made its entrance in summer of 1950, shipped to New Orleans and Tampa, then trucked from Tampa to Sarasota. Reconstruction began in February of 1951 and was complete by the following February when it was opened to the public.

The Asolo, as a professional repertory theater, is the original state theater of Florida. The Asolo State Theater performs in repertoire at Sarasota during its annual season, additionally preparing as many as three touring companies per season to perform throughout Florida. The Asolo housed the Asolo Opera Company and its winter season for more than twenty years. In conjunction with Florida State University, the Asolo State Theater is the location for that institution's Master of Fine Arts degree program for practicing theatre artists.

EASY ENTERTAINING

* Spinach Bisque with Crabmeat

* India Chicken Curry with Condiments

* Mango Chutney

  Parsley Buttered Rice

* Lavash

* Rainbow Fruit Pie

  White Wine: Aveleda

Soups

Cold Cream of Cucumber Soup
Serve on hot summer night

Chill

Serves 4

2 large cucumbers
1 medium onion, chopped
1 cup chicken broth
2 tablespoons flour

¼ teaspoon white pepper
½ teaspoon salt
1 cup sour cream
Fresh dill

Pare, seed and chop cucumbers. Place all ingredients except sour cream and dill in bowl of food processor. Blend until smooth. Add sour cream and chill 2 hours. Serve with fresh dill on top.

Creme Senegalese
Elegant cold curried cream of chicken soup

Chill

Serves 8 to 12

6 leeks
1 pound potatoes, peeled and
    thinly sliced
1 tart green apple, peeled and cored
4 tablespoons butter
¾ cup onion, finely chopped
½ teaspoon garlic, chopped

2 tablespoons curry powder or to taste
6 cups rich chicken broth
Salt and freshly ground pepper
1 cup heavy cream or half and half
Tabasco
½ cup breast of chicken, cooked and
    finely diced

Trim and discard ends of leeks. Split lengthwise and chop. Cover potatoes with cold water. Cut apple into ½-inch cubes. Heat butter in soup kettle. Add leeks, apple, onion and garlic. Cook until leeks are limp. Sprinkle with curry powder. Cook, stirring, about 5 minutes. Drain potatoes and add to mixture. Cook, stirring, about 3 minutes. Add chicken broth. Simmer 45 minutes. Add salt and pepper to taste. Purée soup in blender or food processor, ⅓ at a time. Soup should be smooth and creamy. Chill thoroughly. When ready to serve, add cream and Tabasco to taste. Mix well. Add chicken. Serve thoroughly chilled.

Refrigerate broth or stock overnight for ease in removing fat the following day. Skim fat off with metal spoon.

Soups

Gazpacho
A Florida favorite

Chill   Serves 8

1 cucumber, peeled and cut
   in chunks
½ green pepper, seeded and cut
   in chunks
1 small onion, cut in chunks
2 tomatoes, peeled

½ ripe avocado, peeled
4 cups tomato juice
3 tablespoons olive oil
2 tablespoons wine vinegar
½ teaspoon oregano
Salt to taste

Using steel blade of food processor, coarsely chop cucumber. Transfer to bowl. Process green pepper and onion until finely chopped. Add to cucumber. Cut tomatoes into ¼-inch cubes. Cut avocado in ½-inch cubes. Add tomatoes and avocado to cucumber along with remaining ingredients. Chill at least 2 hours.

Zucchini Soup
For hot Florida nights

Chill   Serves 6

5 medium zucchini squash, cut
   into small pieces
1 large onion, sliced
1½ teaspoons curry powder

3 cups chicken broth
1½ cups cream
Salt and pepper to taste
Chives, chopped

Place zucchini in saucepan with onion and curry powder. Stir to coat pieces. Add chicken broth and bring to boil. Reduce heat and simmer 45 minutes. Put mixture, a small amount at a time, in blender and purée. Add cream, salt and pepper to taste. Chill thoroughly. Serve with chives sprinkled on top.

Vegetables should be added to soups during last half hour of cooking. A well washed, unpeeled, yellow onion adds color to stock or soup.

Anastasia's Soup
Florida garden soup

Serves 14

2 leeks, chopped
2 large carrots, finely chopped
5 tablespoons butter
6 cups chicken broth
1 heaping tablespoon fresh dill, chopped
2 teaspoons salt

Dash pepper
1 bay leaf
5 cups potatoes, peeled and finely diced
1 pound fresh mushrooms, sliced
2 tablespoons flour
1 cup half and half

In large kettle sauté leeks and carrots in 3 tablespoons butter until soft. Stir in broth, dill, salt, pepper, bay leaf and potatoes. Bring to boil; reduce heat and simmer 20 minutes or until vegetables are just tender. Remove bay leaf. In large skillet melt remaining 2 tablespoons butter and sauté mushrooms 5 minutes. Add flour and stir 1 minute. Add cream and stir until thickened. Add mixture to soup and stir until thickened. Bring to boil.

Black Bean Soup
Southwest Florida tradition

Serves 6 to 8

1 12-ounce package dry black beans
8 cups water
1 large onion, chopped
2 green peppers, chopped
2 cloves garlic, minced
½ cup olive oil

1 ham hock
2 bay leaves
1 tablespoon salt
1 ounce white bacon
½ cup vinegar
Rice, cooked
Onion, chopped

Wash beans thoroughly and soak in water overnight. Fry onion, green peppers and garlic in olive oil. Add bean mixture. Add next 4 ingredients. Bring to boil. Skim off foam. Reduce heat. Cover and cook slowly 2 to 3 hours. Add vinegar and cook 2 minutes. Serve with rice; top with chopped onion.

For strong meat broth, allow 2 cups water to each pound of meat, fat and bone.

Soups

Cedar Key Clam Chowder
Sarasota favorite

Serves 6

1 quart Quahog clams, drain
  and reserve juice
3 medium potatoes, peeled and
  diced
1 clove garlic, chopped
3 medium onions, cut in small pieces

4 teaspoons bacon fat
4 teaspoons olive oil
2 quarts water
¼ cup cornmeal
2 tablespoons Worcestershire sauce
1 tablespoon ketchup
Salt and pepper to taste

Chop or grind fresh clams. Put potatoes, garlic, onions, bacon fat and olive oil in 10-inch frying pan. Cover and steam-fry until potatoes are done. Mash with spoon. This gives chowder a creamy texture. Mix part of water with cornmeal. Pour remaining water, Worcestershire sauce, ketchup and juice from clams into potato mixture. Pour into large pot. Bring to boil and slowly add cornmeal. Cook 15 to 20 minutes. Add clams and cook about 20 minutes longer. Add salt and pepper to taste.

Cold Night Cheddar Cheese Soup
Hearty soup for a casual supper

Serves 8

¼ cup butter
½ cup onion, finely chopped
½ cup carrot, finely chopped
½ cup celery, finely chopped
¼ cup flour
1½ tablespoons cornstarch

1 quart chicken stock
1 quart half and half
⅛ teaspoon baking soda
2½ cups sharp Cheddar cheese, cubed
Salt and white pepper
2 tablespoons parsley, finely chopped

Melt butter in large heavy saucepan. Add onion, carrot and celery and sauté until soft. Slowly stir in flour and cornstarch. Gradually add chicken stock and half and half, stirring constantly over low heat until smooth and thickened. Add soda. Stir in cheese until melted. Season with salt and pepper. Serve in individual bowls garnished with parsley for color. Do not overcook.

Conch Chowder
Key West specialty

Serves 6 to 8

2 large onions, finely diced
2 green peppers, finely diced
¼ pound salt pork, ground
1 32-ounce can tomato purée
½ teaspoon black pepper
2 cups water
1 bay leaf
3 cloves garlic, crushed

1 tablespoon wine vinegar
2 tablespoons dark sugar
½ tablespoon poultry seasoning
½ teaspoon oregano
¾ teaspoon salt
¼ cup butter
1 pound potatoes, finely diced
1 pound conch meat

Sauté onions, peppers and salt pork until well done. Add remaining ingredients except potatoes and conch. Heat thoroughly and simmer on low heat approximately 2 hours. Add potatoes and conch; cook 30 minutes or until potatoes are done.

Tip: Soup may be prepared the day before without potatoes and conch. Before serving, reheat, and add potatoes and conch.

Corn Chowder
Creamy

Serves 6 to 8

6 slices bacon
1 medium onion, thinly sliced
2 cups water
2 cups potatoes, diced

Salt and pepper to taste
2 17-ounce cans cream style corn
2 cups half and half
1 tablespoon butter (optional)

Partially cook bacon in frying pan. Add onion; cook until bacon is crisp and onion is lightly browned. Drain and remove bacon. Add water, potatoes, salt and pepper to onion. Cover and simmer 20 minutes. Add corn and cream; simmer 5 minutes. Just before serving, add butter and crumbled bacon.

Simmer soup and stews; do not boil.

Soups

Cream of Broccoli Soup
A refreshing lunch

Serves 3 to 4

1 10-ounce package frozen broccoli, chopped
1 cup chicken broth

2 pinches nutmeg
Salt and white pepper to taste
1 cup heavy cream
Almonds, slivered (optional)

Combine broccoli and chicken broth. Boil 3 to 5 minutes until broccoli is tender. Add seasonings. Mixture can be processed if a smoother texture is desired. Add cream and heat. Serve immediately. Top with almonds if desired.

Tip: Substitute asparagus for broccoli to make cream of asparagus soup.

Cream of Cauliflower Soup
Unusual soup

Serves 6

1 large head cauliflower, broken into flowerets
Water or milk
2 tablespoons onion, chopped
3 celery stalks, finely chopped
¼ cup butter, melted
¼ cup flour

4 cups chicken stock
2 cups milk or cream, scalded
Nutmeg
Salt
Paprika
Sharp Cheddar cheese, grated

Cook cauliflower in 1 inch milk or water 15 minutes or until tender. Drain, reserving liquid. Set aside ⅓ of cauliflower flowerets. Put remaining ⅔ in blender and purée. Sauté onion and celery in butter until tender. Blend in flour. Slowly add chicken stock. Bring to boil and cook until thickened. Add puréed cauliflower, reserved liquid, cream, flowerets, nutmeg, salt and paprika to taste. Garnish with cheese.

Always add salt to water in cooking meat stock soup.
Salt draws out more meat flavor.

Fantastic Fish Chowder
A terrific family supper

Serves 8 to 12

2 medium onions, chopped
4 carrots, thinly sliced
¼ cup parsley, minced
4 medium potatoes, diced
3 cloves garlic, minced
¼ cup vegetable oil
½ teaspoon pepper

1 teaspoon salt
2 8-ounce cans tomato sauce
4 cups hot water
2 7-ounce cans whole baby clams, undrained
2 pounds fish fillets, cut in 1-inch pieces

In 5-quart Dutch oven sauté onions, carrots, parsley, potatoes and garlic in hot oil until onions are soft. Add pepper, salt, tomato sauce and hot water. Bring to boil. Add clams and fish. Cover and simmer about 30 minutes.

Tip: 2 5½-ounce cans minced clams may be substituted for whole clams.

Minestrone
Vegetable treat

Serves 12

¼ cup olive oil
1 clove garlic, minced
1 small onion, minced
1 tablespoon parsley, chopped
2 teaspoons dried thyme
1 tablespoon tomato paste
¼ cup water
1 16-ounce can tomatoes
3 celery stalks, chopped
2 carrots, diced

2 potatoes, diced
½ small cabbage, shredded
2 zucchini squash, diced
4 cups beef stock
4 cups water
Salt and pepper
⅓ cup rice, uncooked
1 16-ounce can garbanzo beans, drained
Fresh Parmesan cheese, grated

In large pot heat olive oil. Add garlic, onion, parsley and thyme. Cook until soft. Add tomato paste thinned with ¼ cup water; cook 5 minutes. Add remaining ingredients except rice, beans and cheese. Simmer 1 hour. Bring to boil. Add rice and simmer until soft. Add beans and heat. Serve with Parmesan cheese sprinkled on top.

Soups

Mushroom Soup
Easy and delicious

Serves 4 to 6

2 cups onions, chopped
4 tablespoons butter
1 pound fresh mushrooms, chopped
1 teaspoon fresh dill
2 cups water
1 tablespoon soy sauce
1 teaspoon paprika

3 tablespoons flour
1 cup milk
1 teaspoon salt
Freshly ground pepper to taste
2 teaspoons lemon juice
½ cup sour cream
Chopped parsley

Sauté onions in 2 tablespoons butter. Add mushrooms, dill, ½ cup water, soy sauce and paprika. Cover and simmer 15 minutes. Melt remaining butter in large pan. Wisk in flour. Add milk. Cook, stirring frequently, over low heat until thick. Stir in mushroom mixture and remaining water. Cover and simmer 10 minutes. Just before serving, add salt, pepper, lemon juice and sour cream. Garnish with fresh parsley.

Pasta Fasuli
Italian bean soup

Serves 4

1 15-ounce can red kidney beans
1½ cups tomato purée
3 tablespoons butter
1 clove garlic, chopped
2 tablespoons dried parsley
2 teaspoons oregano

2 teaspoons thyme
1 tablespoon dried minced onion
2 teaspoons salt
½ teaspoon pepper
6 cups cold water
¼ cup tubetti

Put all ingredients, except tubetti, in large saucepan. Cover and simmer 1 hour. Add tubetti and cook 30 minutes, stirring occasionally to keep pasta from sticking. If it becomes necessary to add more water, add hot water as cold will cause beans to split.

Tip: Macaroni can be substituted for tubetti.

Potage Portugaise
Wonderful complement for pasta supper

Serves 6

6 tablespoons butter
2 tablespoons olive oil
3 large onions, thinly sliced
1 teaspoon thyme
1 teaspoon basil
Salt and pepper to taste
2 1-pound 12-ounce cans Italian
    tomatoes

3 tablespoons tomato paste
½ cup flour
3½ cups chicken broth
1 teaspoon sugar
3½ cups water
Parsley, chopped
Sour cream

Heat butter and oil in large heavy saucepan. Add onions, thyme, basil, salt and pepper. Sauté, stirring until onions are soft but not browned. Add tomatoes and tomato paste; blend well. Simmer 10 minutes. Put flour in small mixing bowl and add 2 cups broth. Mix until smooth. Add to tomato mixture, along with remaining broth, sugar and water. Bring to boil; simmer 30 minutes, stirring frequently to prevent mixture from sticking. Remove from heat. Cool slightly. Purée in blender, filling no more than ½ full each time. Reheat and serve with parsley or a dollop of sour cream.

Tip: Soup is better if made 1 day before serving.

Rockefeller Bisque
For oyster lovers

Serves 6

1 pint oysters, drain and
    reserve liquid
3 tablespoons butter
1 10-ounce package frozen spinach
½ cup water
¼ teaspoon white pepper

¼ teaspoon garlic salt
1 teaspoon salt
⅛ teaspoon allspice
4 tablespoons lemon juice
1 pint cream

Cook oysters in butter just until they curl or shrink slightly. Cook spinach in water 3 minutes. Place oysters and spinach with all their liquids in blender. Add remaining ingredients except cream and purée. Heat soup to boiling point and add cream. Heat again, but do not boil.

Soups

Spinach Bisque with Crabmeat
Incredibly elegant

Serves 8 to 10

4 slices white onion
2 10½-ounce packages frozen
   spinach, chopped
6 cups chicken broth
6 tablespoons butter

2 tablespoons flour
Salt and white pepper to taste
2 cups half and half
1 cup fresh crabmeat
½ teaspoon nutmeg

Add onion to spinach and cook according to directions on spinach package. Drain thoroughly. Combine with 2 cups chicken broth and blend until puréed. Melt butter in large saucepan. Stir in flour, salt and white pepper until blended. Gradually stir in remaining 4 cups chicken broth and bring to boil, stirring constantly. Add puréed spinach mixture; cook over low heat 10 minutes. Stir in half and half and crabmeat. Heat, but do not boil. Add nutmeg. Taste for seasoning.

Terri's Onion Soup Nonpareil
Showy first course

Preheat oven 350°

Serves 4

2 celery stalks with leaves, chopped
2 carrots, chopped
2½ cups beef stock
½ cup sherry
2 large onions, thinly sliced
3 cloves garlic, minced

¼ cup butter
¼ cup olive oil
4 1-inch slices crusty French bread
¼ pound sharp Cheddar cheese,
   in chunks
½ pound Swiss cheese, sliced
   (Jarlsberg or Dofeno)

Cook celery and carrots in beef stock until softened. Strain broth from vegetables and reserve. Purée vegetables and return to broth. Add sherry; set aside. Combine onions, garlic, butter and oil. Sauté until softened. Remove onions and garlic; set aside. In same butter and oil, sauté both sides of bread. Do not saturate. Toast bread lightly in oven for crispness. Butter individual oven-proof soup crocks. In equal amounts, place sharp cheese on bottom of crocks. Cover with onions and garlic; pour in broth mixture. Place bread slice on each portion; cover thickly with Swiss cheese. Bake 1 hour until browned and puffed.

Won Ton Soup
Wonderful with stir-fry dinners

Serves 6 to 8

3 13¾-ounce cans chicken broth
1¾ cups cold water
1½ teaspoons celery salt

¾ teaspoon onion salt
Carrots
Parsley sprigs

In medium saucepan, combine chicken broth, water, celery salt and onion salt. Bring to boil. Reduce heat and simmer 5 minutes. Garnish with carrots and parsley sprigs.

Tip: For garnish, pare 3 thick carrots. Cut into circles and shape into flowers.

Garnishes for Soups
Avocado slices
Slivered almonds
Chopped walnuts
Sliced or chopped hard-cooked eggs
Finely chopped fresh herbs: parsley, basil, chives or dill
Strips of green pepper, green onion, mushrooms or pimiento
Grated or crumbled cheese
Sour cream or whipped cream
Croutons

If soup is too salty, add ½ peeled, raw potato. If still too salty, add other half. Remove before serving.

The Circle at St. Armands

The shopping district called St. Armands Circle was part of one of John Ringling's diverse developments. Initiated during the heyday of Florida's real estate boom, St. Armands was a division of a development called John Ringling Estates. The development project was one of those undertaken by Ringling in conjunction with Owen Burns, downtown real estate developer and Vice President of John Ringling Estates. This diverse Ringling enterprise envisioned resorts, a casino, subdivisions, and shopping areas. The total development, called Ringling Isles, encompassed the chain of islands nearest the city — Bird Key, St. Armands, Lido, and holdings on Longboat. Owen Burns, a native Marylander who had acquired lands held by the city's 19th century development company, shared Ringling's entrepreneurial enthusiasm for the future of the coastal area.

The first requirement for such development was, of course, construction of a bridge from the mainland across the bay, then from key to key. Even as Ca' d' Zan was underway under Burns' direction and Ringling was in the midst of his art acquisition period, Burns had begun Ringling's Causeway from the city to Bird Key by 1926.

The name "St. Armands" which the developers applied to the island shopping district was a departure in style. It was, uncharacteristically, not that of some known New York or Mediterranean entity, but that of the homesteader of the island. The name, mispelled in the course of title transfers, was that of Charles St. Amand. St. Amand, a native of Louisiana, had settled the island long before bridges, in the fall of 1885. The homesteader had built a house, cleared an acre, and officially claimed his land — all 130 acres of it — for thirteen dollars. The native treeline was low (before the importation of Australian pines) and consisted of cedars and palms.

Though the subdivision and central park and bandstand were laid out and Ringling's imported statuary in place, St. Armands Circle and the John Ringling Isles, designed by Ohio architect John J. Watson and Sarasota engineer Leon Pickett, were subjected to the same slump that struck all Florida during the depression following the collapse of the real estate "boom." For years, St. Armands Key and its subdivision lay amid sandspurs and miles of concrete curbings, sidewalks, and street lamps with clustered bulbs. Lido Beach, essentially deserted, lay to the west. On the north across the "New Pass," Ringling's golf course and Ritz-Carlton hotel, halted in mid-construction, rose up on south Longboat with a promise of grandeur that was not to be. Unlike the Ritz-Carlton, St. Armands and John Ringling Estates thrived, as planned, when the fiscal health of the country was ultimately restored.

BRUNCH

Freshly Squeezed Orange Juice

* Spicy Bloody Mary

* Vegetable Quiche

* Breakfast Soufflé

* Apricot Bread with Honey-Whipped Cream
Cheese Spread

* Spiced Fruit Compote

* Orange Marmalade

Croissants — Butter Curls

Coffee — Tea

Eggs & Cheese

New Year's Brunch Eggs
What could be easier the morning after

Serves 8 to 10

12 eggs
⅔ cup milk or light cream
6 ounces cream cheese, softened

1 teaspoon dill
1 tablespoon dried onion, minced

Beat all ingredients in large mixing bowl. Pour into hot, buttered frying pan. Scramble till done to your taste. Serve with sausage or bacon.

Bonitza
An old Bulgarian recipe

Preheat oven 350°

Serves 8 to 10

5 eggs
15 ounces dry cottage cheese
½ pound Feta cheese, crumbled

1 pound phyllo dough leaves
1 cup butter, melted

Fold eggs into cheese. Unfold phyllo and brush each layer with butter (3 sheets in a layer). Put 3 tablespoons filling at end and roll. Place in 13 x 9-inch baking pan. Bake 1 hour.

Tip: Keep damp cloth on phyllo while working to prevent drying.

Breakfast Soufflé
Nice for teenage slumber party

Preheat oven 350°

Serves 10

1½ pounds sausage
9 eggs, slightly beaten
3 cups milk
1½ teaspoons prepared mustard
1 teaspoon salt

3 slices white bread, cut
  in ¼-inch cubes
1½ cups sharp Cheddar cheese,
  grated

Brown crumbled sausage; drain well. Mix eggs, milk, mustard and salt. Stir in bread, sausage and cheese. Put in 9 x 13-inch pan. Cover and refrigerate overnight. Bake 1 hour.

Eggs & Cheese

Breakfast Casserole
Pizza for breakfast

Preheat oven 350°

Serves 6

6 to 8 slices bread
1 pound sausage, cooked and
   drained
½ cup Swiss cheese, shredded
½ cup sharp Cheddar cheese,
   shredded
½ cup mushrooms, sliced

¾ cup light cream
1¼ cups milk
5 eggs, slightly beaten
1 teaspoon Worcestershire sauce
1 teaspoon prepared mustard
Salt and pepper to taste

Grease 13 x 9-inch pan. Cube bread after removing crust and line bottom of pan. Sprinkle sausage over bread. Add cheese and mushrooms. Add cream and milk to eggs. Stir in seasonings; pour over casserole ingredients. Refrigerate overnight. Bake 35 to 40 minutes.

Avocado and Crabmeat Quiche
A true Florida quiche

Preheat oven 375°

Serves 6 to 8

Pastry for single crust 9-inch pie
1 avocado, peeled and thinly sliced
2 teaspoons lemon juice
¼ teaspoon salt
Dash Tabasco
1 6½-ounce can crabmeat, drained

4 eggs
1½ cups half and half or heavy cream
¼ cup dry white wine
Pinch salt
Pinch nutmeg
Freshly ground pepper

Roll out pastry; line 9-inch tart pan or deep pie plate. Partially bake, but do not brown pastry. Arrange avocado slices in pin wheel fashion in pastry shell. Sprinkle with lemon juice and salt. Add Tabasco to crabmeat and arrange on top. Blend remaining ingredients. Pour custard over all and bake 40 to 45 minutes. Cool 5 minutes before removing from pan.

Eggs should be fresh. Old eggs can have exposed yolks, wispy whites and very unpresentable results.

Crab Quiche

Complete the meal with a spinach salad

Preheat oven 350°   Serves 6 to 8

½ cup mayonnaise
2 tablespoons flour
2 eggs, well beaten
½ cup milk
1 6½-ounce can crabmeat, drained

8 ounces Swiss cheese, grated
⅓ cup green onion, tops included,
   chopped
1 9-inch pie shell, unbaked

Combine mayonnaise, flour, eggs and milk. Mix until well blended. Stir in crab, cheese and onion. Pour into pie shell and bake 45 minutes or until set.

Jef's Quiche

Serve hot or cold

Preheat oven 375°   Serves 6

½ cup butter
3 ounces cream cheese
1 cup flour
½ pound bacon, crisply fried
1 5-ounce jar mushrooms, drained
   and chopped

5 ounces Swiss cheese, diced
3 eggs
1 13-ounce can regular condensed
   milk
5 ounces sweetened condensed milk
Dash nutmeg

Cream butter and cream cheese; add flour. Spread in quiche or 9-inch pie pan. Layer bacon and mushrooms on crust; top with cheese. Mix eggs, condensed milk, sweetened condensed milk and nutmeg. Pour over cheese. Bake 30 minutes. Let stand 10 minutes before serving.

Leftover hard cheeses like Cheddar, Swiss, and Parmesan can be grated and frozen in a plastic bag for future use.

Eggs Poached in Tomato Sauce
Serve to your Italian friends

Serves 6

4 tablespoons olive oil
½ onion, finely chopped
1 clove garlic, finely chopped
2 cups canned Italian tomatoes

2 teaspoons parsley, chopped
½ teaspoon salt
Pinch red pepper flakes
6 eggs

Heat olive oil in 12-inch skillet; add onion. When onion is soft and golden, add garlic, tomatoes, parsley, salt and red pepper. Simmer 20 minutes. Break eggs, 1 at a time and slip with care into sauce. Cover pan and cook eggs over low heat 3 to 5 minutes or until whites are set. Serve at once.

Oeufs Cressoniere
Unique deviled eggs

Serves 4

1 bunch watercress
2 sprigs dill
1 large shallot
3 tablespoons heavy cream
½ cup mayonnaise

Salt and pepper to taste
Dash cayenne pepper
6 hard-boiled eggs, quartered
    lengthwise
Watercress sprigs

Chop watercress, dill and shallot to a fine paste. Gradually stir in cream. Mix with mayonnaise. Season to taste. Arrange eggs on serving dish and cover each quarter with green mayonnaise. Garnish with sprigs of watercress.

Bread crumbs added to scrambled eggs will improve the flavor and increase the portions.

French Scrambled Eggs
Perfect for Sunday brunch with champagne

Serves 4 to 6

4 to 6 slices white bread,
  lightly toasted
3 cloves garlic, peeled
7 tablespoons unsalted butter,
  softened
2 red bell peppers, halved
  lengthwise
1 tablespoon olive oil

10 anchovy fillets, drained
  and chopped
12 eggs, well beaten
20 cured French black olives,
  pitted and minced
3 tablespoons fresh chives,
  chopped
Freshly ground pepper

Rub 1 side of each piece of toast with garlic clove. Spread toast with ½ the butter, dividing evenly. Mince remaining 2 cloves garlic; reserve. Add peppers to small saucepan of boiling water. Boil until skin begins to loosen, about 6 minutes. Drain; run under cold water until cool enough to handle. Cut into ¼-inch slices. Heat remaining butter and oil in large heavy skillet over medium heat until butter is foamy. Add minced garlic and anchovies; cook until garlic is fragrant, about 1 minute. Add ½ red peppers; sauté until softened, about 3 minutes. Reduce heat to low. Pour eggs over sautéed mixture in skillet. Cook, stirring frequently, until mixture congeals but is still soft and creamy, about 15 minutes. Fold olives into egg mixture until blended. Fold in remaining red peppers and chives. Spoon egg mixture over toast. Sprinkle with freshly ground pepper.

Grits South of the Border
For a southern brunch

Preheat oven 325°

Serves 6 to 8

3½ cups water
1 cup quick grits
4 ounces garlic cheese, shredded
1 egg, beaten

½ cup milk
4 drops Tabasco
¾ cup Cheddar cheese,
  grated

Heat water until boiling; add grits. Turn heat to low and cook grits until water is absorbed. Add garlic cheese and stir until cheese is melted. Combine egg, milk and Tabasco. Add to grits and mix well. Pour into well-greased 1-quart casserole. Top with Cheddar cheese. Bake 30 minutes.

Eggs & Cheese

Omelette Bayonnaise
A mushroom omelet

Serves 2

¼ pound mushrooms, sliced
2 tablespoons butter
½ cup ham, cooked and diced
1 tablespoon sour cream

Pinch tarragon
4 large eggs
2 tablespoons cold water
Salt and pepper to taste

Sauté mushrooms in 1 tablespoon butter. Add ham, sour cream and tarragon. Set aside. Beat eggs in bowl with water, salt and pepper until well mixed but not too foamy. Heat omelet pan; melt remaining butter over entire surface of pan. Pour in eggs. Cook a few minutes, until center is slightly moist. Fill with mushroom and ham mixture. Fold over and serve.

Oyako Domburi or Mother and Child in a Bowl
A Japanese chicken and egg omelet

Preheat oven 250°

Serves 2

2 cups cooked rice
4 fresh mushrooms, sliced
2 green onions, including 2
   inches of stems, sliced
1 chicken breast half, boned,
   skinned, and cut in bite-size
   pieces
2 tablespoons chicken broth

2 tablespoons dry sherry
2 tablespoons cream sherry
2 tablespoons soy sauce
1 teaspoon ginger
2 tablespoons oil
4 eggs, beaten
Green onion, sliced
Sesame seeds

Place 1 cup hot rice in each of 2 serving bowls. Cover and keep warm. Using 2 separate small bowls divide mushrooms, onions and chicken evenly. In 2-cup measuring cup combine broth, dry sherry, cream sherry, soy sauce and ginger. Mix well; pour over chicken, dividing evenly. Heat 1 tablespoon oil in small skillet. Pour ingredients from bowl into pan and bring to boil over high heat. Reduce heat and cover pan. Cook about 2 minutes. Add ½ beaten eggs to bubbling sauce. Cover. Cook 2 to 3 minutes until eggs are lightly set. With spatula slide omelet on top of 1 bowl of rice. Garnish with onion and sesame seeds. Keep warm in oven. Repeat process for second omelet.

Tip: May place all ingredients in 1½-quart casserole instead of individual bowls.

Mexican Omelet
Hot and spicy

Preheat oven 325°   Serves 4 to 6

¾ cup avocado, chopped   Dash Tabasco
¼ cup sour cream   2 tablespoons butter
2 tablespoons green chilies, chopped   1 corn tortilla, torn in small pieces
1 tablespoon green onion, chopped   6 eggs, beaten
1 teaspoon lemon juice   1 cup Monterey Jack cheese,
¼ teaspoon salt   shredded

Combine first 7 ingredients; set aside. Melt butter in 10-inch oven-proof skillet. Add tortilla pieces and cook until softened, 1 to 2 minutes. Pour in eggs. Cook 3 to 5 minutes, lifting eggs to allow uncooked mixture to flow under. Remove from heat. Sprinkle with cheese and bake about 4 minutes or until cheese melts. Spread avocado mixture on ½ the omelet. Return to oven 5 minutes. Fold in half and serve.

Lobster Supper Pie
A complete meal

Preheat oven 325°   Serves 6

1 cup Gruyere cheese, grated   1 cup coffee cream
1 9-inch pastry shell, unbaked   ½ teaspoon salt
3 scallions, tops included, sliced Freshly ground white pepper
8 to 10-ounces fresh or frozen lobster   ½ teaspoon lemon peel, grated
  meat, cooked and slivered   ¼ teaspoon dry mustard
3 eggs, beaten   ⅓ cup almonds, sliced

Sprinkle cheese evenly over bottom of pastry shell. Add scallions; top with lobster meat. Combine eggs, cream, salt, pepper, lemon peel and mustard. Pour over lobster. Top with almonds. Bake 45 to 60 minutes or until set. Let stand 10 minutes before serving.

Eggs & Cheese

Top Hat Cheese Soufflé
Great for hot summer nights

Preheat oven 300°

Serves 6

1/3 cup butter, melted
1/3 cup flour
1½ cups milk
1 teaspoon salt

Dash cayenne pepper
2 ounces sharp Cheddar cheese,
   grated
6 eggs, separated

In 2-quart saucepan, combine butter and flour. Add milk, salt and pepper, stirring constantly until thickened. Add cheese; stir until melted. Remove from heat and gradually add beaten egg yolks. Cool. Beat egg whites until stiff; fold into cheese mixture. Pour into 2-quart soufflé dish. Bake 1¼ hours.

Zucchini Frittata
Unique omelet

Serves 4

1 cup yellow onion, thinly sliced
¼ cup vegetable oil
3 medium zucchini squash, washed
   and sliced ¼-inch thick
½ teaspoon salt
4 extra large eggs, beaten

2/3 cup fresh Parmesan cheese, grated
8 twists of pepper mill
1 tablespoon parsley, minced
¼ teaspoon basil
3 tablespoons butter

Sauté onion in oil in medium skillet over low heat until wilted and rich golden brown color. Add zucchini and salt. Cook over medium heat until lightly browned. Remove vegetables with slotted spoon to cool. Combine eggs, cheese and vegetables in bowl. Add pepper, parsley and basil; beat well. Melt butter in 10-inch skillet over medium heat. When butter begins to foam, add egg mixture; turn heat down as low as possible. When eggs have set and thickened and only top surface is runny, about 10 to 12 minutes, place skillet under broiler 30 seconds to 1 minute or until surface is set. Loosen with spatula and slide onto warm platter. Cut into 4 pie shaped wedges to serve.

Hamburger Quiche
Excellent luncheon

Preheat oven 350°   Serves 6 to 8

1 pound ground beef   ½ pound sharp Cheddar cheese,
1 9-inch pie shell, unbaked   shredded
½ cup mayonnaise   ½ cup onion, chopped
1 tablespoon cornstarch   Salt and pepper to taste
2 eggs, beaten   2 teaspoons dried parsley
½ cup milk   2 teaspoons oregano

Brown meat and drain. Put into pie shell. Mix mayonnaise and cornstarch. Add eggs and milk; blend. Add cheese, onion, salt, pepper, parsley and oregano. Pour over beef. Bake 30 minutes. Let set for 5 to 10 minutes before cutting.

Mexican Chorizo and Chili Quiche
From south of the border

Preheat oven 425°   Serves 6

Pastry for a single crust 10-inch pie   4 eggs
12 ounces chorizo sausage   1 cup sour cream
¼ cup green onion, sliced   ¼ teaspoon ground cumin
¼ cup bottled green taco sauce   ⅛ teaspoon liquid hot pepper
1 4-ounce can green chilies, drained   seasoning
  and diced   1½ cups Monterey Jack or Muenster
1 2¼-ounce can ripe olives, drained   cheese, shredded
  and sliced

Fit pastry into 11-inch quiche pan or 10-inch pie pan; trim or flute edge. Bake 10 minutes or until golden brown. Reduce oven temperature to 350°. Crumble sausage into frying pan over medium-high heat. Cook, stirring until meat browns. Remove meat with slotted spoon and set aside. Discard all but 1 tablespoon drippings. Add green onion to drippings and cook, stirring, 1 minute. Remove from heat. Mix in sausage, taco sauce, chilies and olives; set aside. Beat eggs, sour cream, cumin and hot pepper seasoning until blended. Gently stir in sausage mixture and cheese; pour into pre-baked crust. Bake 35 to 40 minutes or until center appears set when dish is gently shaken.

Eggs & Cheese _____

Quickie Spinach Quiche
They will think you worked most of the day

Preheat oven 375°   Serves 6 to 8

8 ounces sharp Cheddar cheese,   1 3-ounce can mushrooms, drained
  shredded   and sliced
1 9-inch deep dish pie crust,   1 to 2 tablespoons butter
  unbaked   3 eggs
1 pound fresh spinach, cooked,   1 cup half and half
  drained and finely chopped   Dash salt and pepper
1 small onion, chopped   Bacon bits

Spread 4 ounces cheese on bottom of pie crust. Spread spinach on cheese.
Sauté onion and mushrooms in butter, put on top of spinach. Add remainder
of cheese. Blender beat eggs, half and half, salt and pepper. Pour into pie
shell. Sprinkle bacon bits on top. Bake 30 to 45 minutes until knife in center
comes out clean.

Sausage Quiche
Spicy taste

Preheat oven 375°   Serves 6

1½ cups Cheddar cheese, grated   1 cup evaporated milk
1 9-inch deep dish pie shell,   1 tablespoon flour
  unbaked   1 tablespoon parsley
1 pound sausage, crumbled   ¾ teaspoon seasoned salt
½ cup onion, chopped   ¼ teaspoon pepper
⅓ cup green pepper, chopped   ¼ teaspoon garlic salt
2 eggs

Place ½ the cheese on bottom of pie shell. Lightly brown sausage; add onion
and green pepper. Drain mixture thoroughly. Mix remaining ingredients into
sausage mixture. Pour into pie shell. Bake 35 minutes. Let stand 15 minutes
before serving.

Vegetable Quiche
Sunday brunch dish

Preheat oven 425°

Serves 6 to 8

½ cup green onion, chopped
1 clove garlic, minced
2 tablespoons butter
1 pound fresh spinach, cooked,
   drained and finely chopped
1½ cups Swiss cheese, shredded
   (6 ounces)
3 eggs, lightly beaten
¾ cup milk

1 teaspoon salt
1 teaspoon basil leaves, crumbled
½ teaspoon celery salt
1 9-inch deep dish pie crust, unbaked
2 medium tomatoes, thinly sliced
1 tablespoon bread crumbs
1 tablespoon Parmesan cheese,
   grated

Sauté onion and garlic in butter in medium skillet until golden. Add spinach; cook over medium heat, stirring constantly, until excess moisture evaporates. Combine spinach mixture, Swiss cheese, eggs, milk, salt, basil and celery salt in large bowl; stir well. Pour into pie crust. Arrange tomatoes around outer edge. Bake 15 minutes. Reduce heat to 350° and bake 10 minutes. Combine bread crumbs and Parmesan cheese in small bowl. Sprinkle over tomato slices. Bake until top is puffy and center moves slightly, about 10 minutes. Let stand 10 minutes before serving.

To preserve left-over egg yolks for future use, place them into a small bowl; add a small amount of salad oil and refrigerate. The egg yolks will remain soft and fresh.

Clowns

"Where are the Clowns?" The popularity of that contemporary song reminds us again of the traditional paradox of the clown, that artistic character who inspires joy and underlines sorrow, treading in his oversized shoes the fine line between *pathos* and *Eros*. The sentimental path of both today's song and today's clown is well worn and old. But in twentieth century America, the path of the clown has frequently led south to Sarasota.

The origin of Sarasota's clowns dates back to the bitter-sweet year of 1927, when Florida's real estate boom had begun to decline from its loudest, grand volume of the prosperous twenties, and only two years before the stock market crash of 1929 signalled widespread financial ruin. It was in the spring of 1927, the year following Charles Ringling's death, that John Ringling announced the circus would accept Sarasota's offer to host the winter home of Ringling Brothers and Barnum and Bailey Circus. Instead of its routine return to Bridgeport, Connecticut that summer, the circus headed South to Sarasota's vacated former fairgrounds site (the area extending within the northwest quadrant of Fruitville Road and Oriente [Beneva] Avenue intersection). With the circus came elephants, gorillas, tigers, lions, bareback riders, midgets, aerialists, daredevils, acrobats, roustabouts — and the clowns. For many of the circus folk, Sarasota became home.

Over the years, Sarasota County has been home base for some of the nation's best-known clowns — men and women whose stylized antics include the likes of the famed Emmet Kelly, the great "tramp clown" Otto Griebling, the great "august clown" Lou Jacobs, and the great "white face clowns" Charlie Bell as well as Felix Adler, who was called "King of Clowns."

The clown spirit continues to grow. Ten years after the circus transferred its winter quarters to Venice in 1959, a notable clown named Danny Chapman with Mel Miller, former curator of the Ringling Circus Museum, helped establish the first Ringling Brothers and Barnum and Bailey "Clown College." The training program, which opened in the fall of 1968, operates at Venice circus quarters several months prior to the annual circus season, and has produced a class of clown "graduates" each year.

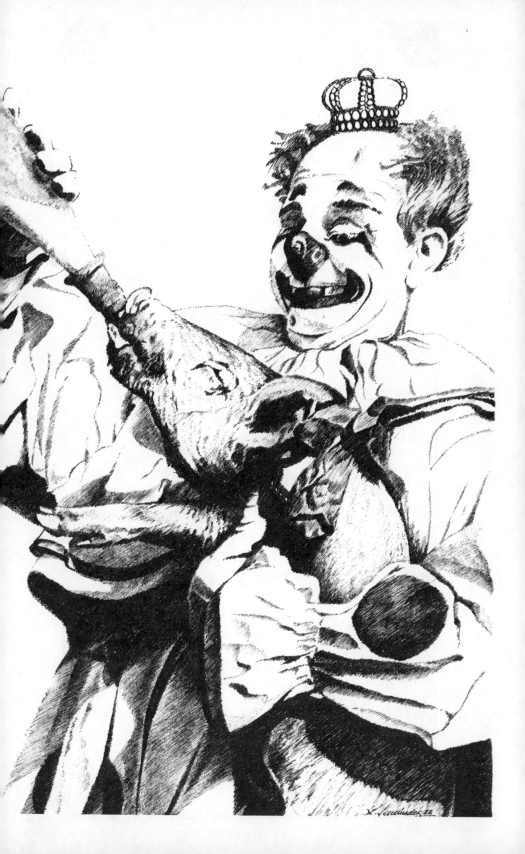

PASTA PARTY

* Potage Portugaise

* Carbonara

* Carciofi Ripieni di Ricotta

* Caesar Salad

  Italian Bread

* Cold Lime Soufflé

  Wine: Chianti

Rice & Pasta

Herb Rice
Spicy

Serves 4

1 cup rice, uncooked
2 beef bouillon cubes
½ teaspoon salt
½ teaspoon rosemary
½ teaspoon marjoram

½ teaspoon thyme leaves
1 teaspoon dried onion flakes
¼ cup butter
2 cups cold water

Mix first 7 ingredients in 2-quart saucepan. Add butter and water. Bring to boil. Reduce heat. Cover and simmer until all liquid is absorbed. Stir once with fork.

Javanese Fried Rice
A taste of the old country

Serves 4 to 6

1 cup rice, uncooked
1½ cups water
¾ cup peanut oil
2 medium onions, finely chopped
1 clove garlic, crushed

1 fresh chili, cut in strips
½ pound pork or veal, diced
½ cup canned shrimp
Salt to taste
3 eggs

Cook rice in water 10 minutes. Spread on large dish to cool. Heat oil in large heavy skillet. Fry onions, garlic and chili. Add meat and fry 2 minutes, stirring constantly. Add rice and shrimp. Increase heat, adding more oil if necessary and fry all ingredients together until rice is golden in color. Season with salt. Prepare omelet separately and cut into thin strips. Add strips of egg to rice and stir. Serve hot.

Perfectly cooked rice is dry and fluffy, with every grain separate. If the core is hard like a grain of sand, cook rice a moment longer. If the kernals appear soft and flat, the rice has been cooked too long.

Rice

Pecan Rice
Rice at its best

Preheat oven 400°   Serves 6

¾ cup long grain rice, uncooked   1 4-ounce can mushrooms, drained
1¹⁄₃ cups beef consommé   and sliced
½ cup water   ¼ cup butter
1 small onion, chopped   ¼ cup pecans, chopped
1 2-ounce jar pimientos, sliced   Salt, pepper and paprika to taste

Combine all ingredients in greased 2-quart casserole. Cover and bake 45 minutes.

Rice Croquettes
Serve with stuffed artichokes

                                                    Yields 10 croquettes

5 cups cooked white rice   ¹⁄₃ cup celery leaves, chopped
¾ cup fresh Parmesan cheese,   1 teaspoon salt
   grated   3 medium eggs, beaten
1 cup ham, cooked and chopped   ¼ cup flour
2 cups Mozarella cheese, shredded   1 cup olive oil
¹⁄₃ cup parsley, chopped

After cooking, drain rice in colander 30 minutes or more. (Do not refrigerate). Combine Parmesan cheese, ham, Mozarella cheese, rice, parsley, celery leaves, salt and eggs. Roll in the shape of large eggs. Coat with flour. Place in oil and cook until brown, turning occasionally. Drain on absorbent paper and serve.

Risi E Bisi
Venetian rice and peas

Serves 4 to 5

1 tablespoon olive oil
¼ cup butter
1 small onion, chopped
1 slice bacon, diced
2 cups green peas, freshly shelled

¾ cup rice, uncooked
1¾ cups chicken stock
Salt and pepper to taste
1 tablespoon Parmesan cheese, grated

Heat olive oil and butter in saucepan. Add onion and bacon; brown. Add peas and cook 5 minutes, stirring frequently. Add rice and cook 3 minutes longer, stirring often until grains are well coated with oil and butter. Add chicken stock, salt and pepper. Cover and cook over low heat 15 to 20 minutes. The rice should absorb all liquid and be tender, not mushy. Toss with cheese and serve.

Regal Rice Casserole
Always get compliments

Preheat oven 350°

Serves 4

2 12-ounce packages rice, peas and
  mushrooms in cooking pouch
8 slices bacon, crisply fried and
  crumbled

⅓ cup green onion, chopped
½ cup sour cream
½ cup Cheddar cheese, shredded
Paprika

Place pouches in boiling water; bring to second boil and cook 15 minutes. Do not cover. Combine cooked rice mixture, bacon and onion in 1½-quart casserole. Mix sour cream throughout mixture. Top with cheese. Cover and bake 35 minutes. Sprinkle with paprika.

Tip: **If fresh vegetables are preferred, substitute ¾ cup uncooked rice, 12 ounces green peas and 8 ounces mushrooms.**

Sausage and Wild Rice
Great company dish

Preheat oven 350°

Serves 20

1 pound wild rice, uncooked
½ pound hot bulk sausage
½ pound fresh mushrooms, sliced
6 to 8 green onions, tops included, sliced
1 large green pepper, finely chopped

6 celery stalks, sliced
2 10¾-ounce cans cream of mushroom soup, undiluted
2 tablespoons dry white wine
2 teaspoons salt
½ cup almonds, toasted and slivered

Prepare rice according to package directions. Fry sausage, crumbling and stirring. Drain and set aside. In fat remaining from sausage, sauté mushrooms, onions, green pepper and celery. Combine rice, sausage, sautéed vegetables, soup, wine, salt and almonds. Fold together thoroughly. Divide mixture into two 2-quart buttered casseroles. Cover and bake 30 to 45 minutes or until heated through.

Tip: Casserole may be frozen before baking. Thaw completely and uncover during last half of baking time.

South African Yellow Rice
Excellent served with Bobotie, a South African beef dish

Serves 5 to 6

1 cup rice, uncooked
2 cups water
1 teaspoon salt
½ teaspoon turmeric

1 tablespoon raisins
1 teaspoon butter
1 tablespoon sugar

Cover rice with water. Add remaining ingredients. Bring to boil, stirring frequently. Reduce heat. Cover and simmer 20 minutes. Remove from heat and let stand 5 minutes. Place cooked rice in colander and steam over boiling water 10 minutes.

Risotta Alla Milanese
Serve with your most elegant dinner

Serves 10 to 12

½ cup onion, minced
½ cup olive oil
1 cup mushrooms, sliced
2 cups rice, uncooked
¼ teaspoon powdered saffron

2 quarts chicken broth
Salt and pepper
1 tablespoon butter
1 cup fresh Parmesan cheese,
   grated

Brown onion in olive oil in large skillet. When lightly brown, add mushrooms and cook over low heat for about 10 minutes. Add rice and continue cooking for 15 minutes, stirring constantly. Dissolve saffron in ½ cup chicken broth. Add ½ the remaining broth, 1 cup at a time, to rice mixture, stirring well. Add saffron, salt and pepper and continue to cook, adding broth as needed and stirring constantly. When rice reaches the chewy state, remove from heat; stir in butter. Top with grated cheese and serve immediately.

Noodles au Tim
Hearty

Preheat oven 350°

Serves 6

8 ounces medium noodles
2 cups cottage cheese
2 cups sour cream
¼ cup onion, chopped
1 teaspoon Worcestershire sauce

Dash Tabasco
¼ cup butter, melted
1 clove garlic, minced
¼ cup Parmesan cheese, grated

Cook noodles 10 minutes; drain and rinse. Combine noodles and remaining ingredients except Parmesan cheese. Bake in buttered 2-quart casserole 45 minutes. Serve with grated cheese sprinkled over top.

Fill a 6-quart kettle with at least 4 quarts water. Add 1 teaspoon salt and 1 tablespoon olive oil; bring to a boil. Drop pasta into rapidly boiling water. Return to boiling and cook, uncovered, on high heat for about 2 to 3 minutes or until al dente (tender to bite). Drain in colander.

Tagliatelle Ferdinando
Comes from the Piedmont region of Italy

Preheat oven 400°

Serves 4

¾ pound tagliatelle or egg noodles
2 tablespoons foie gras, diced
½ cup sweetbreads, cooked and
   diced
¾ cup chicken, cooked and diced
2 tablespoons butter

1½ tablespoons flour
2 cups light cream
½ teaspoon curry powder
¼ cup fresh Parmesan cheese, grated
¼ cup butter
1 teaspoon paprika

Cook tagliatelle according to package directions. Drain ½ and place in bottom of buttered 13 x 9-inch baking dish. Sprinkle foie gras, sweetbreads and chicken over top. In saucepan melt butter. Stir in flour and cream. Flavor with curry powder. Heat until mixture thickens, stirring constantly. Pour ½ sauce over mixture in baking dish. Add rest of tagliatelle; pour on remaining sauce. Sprinkle with cheese, ¼ cup butter and paprika; brown lightly in oven 10 minutes.

Manicotti
Well worth the effort

Preheat oven 350°

Serves 8

8 ounces manicotti noodles
1 pound ricotta cheese
1 pound cottage cheese
8 ounces Mozarella cheese,
   shredded
⅓ cup Parmesan cheese, grated
2 eggs, slightly beaten
1 tablespoon parsley, chopped

1 teaspoon salt
¼ teaspoon pepper
1 pound ground beef
1 onion, chopped
1 green pepper, chopped
Garlic powder to taste
1 32-ounce jar spaghetti sauce
3 slices Mozarella cheese, cut in half

Cook manicotti according to package directions. Combine ricotta cheese, cottage cheese, shredded Mozarella cheese, Parmesan cheese, eggs, parsley, salt and pepper. Blend well and stuff manicotti shells. Sauté ground beef, onion, green pepper and garlic powder until green pepper is tender. Add spaghetti sauce. Pour ½ meat sauce in 9 x 13-inch pyrex pan; arrange manicotti shells on top. Pour remaining sauce over all and top with slices of Mozarella cheese. Bake uncovered 30 minutes.

Angel Pasta
Colorful

Serves 6

½ pound carrots, cut in thin
  julienne strips
½ pound fresh asparagus, cut in thin
  julienne strips
12 oil cured black Greek olives,
  pitted

3 cups heavy cream
1 pound angel hair pasta
1 tablespoon salt
1 tablespoon olive oil
Salt and freshly ground pepper
⅓ cup fresh Parmesan cheese,
  grated

Cook carrot strips in boiling water 2 minutes. Refresh in cold water; drain and set aside. Dip asparagus in boiling water and remove immediately. Refresh in cold water; drain and set aside. Cut olives in long slivers; set aside. Pour cream into 4-quart saucepan; simmer over low heat until it is ½ original volume and thickened. Keep warm. Boil pasta rapidly in boiling water with 1 tablespoon salt and olive oil. Cook 30 seconds to 1½ minutes only. Add carrots, asparagus and olives to cream. Salt and pepper to taste. Drain pasta; return to kettle. Toss with sauce. Serve immediately with cheese.

Carbonara
Cheesy spaghetti

Serves 4 to 6

5 slices bacon
1 medium onion, chopped
2 cloves garlic, minced
2 cups Parmesan cheese, grated

2 eggs
2 tablespoons black pepper
1 1-pound box spaghetti, cooked

Fry bacon. Remove from frying pan and drain on paper towel. Sauté onion and garlic in bacon drippings. Add crumbled bacon. In large bowl mix cheese, eggs and pepper. Add bacon mixture. Mix thoroughly. Pour hot spaghetti over mixture; blend until spaghetti is coated with cheese.

Pasta

Chicken and Asparagus Pasta
Northern Italian pasta

Serves 4

1 1-pound chicken breast, skinned
 and boned
1 pound fresh asparagus spears
¾ pound linguine or fettucine
2 tablespoons butter
Salt and freshly ground pepper
 to taste
3 tablespoons shallots, finely
 chopped

1 cup heavy cream
⅛ teaspoon dry red pepper
⅛ teaspoon nutmeg
¼ pound Gorgonzola cheese, broken
 into small pieces
2 tablespoons tarragon
½ cup fresh Parmesan cheese, grated

Cut chicken into strips about 1½ inches long. Peel and trim asparagus. Cut asparagus on bias into 1½-inch lengths. Drop pieces into boiling water 3 minutes; drain and set aside. Cook pasta according to package directions. Heat butter in 10-inch skillet. Add chicken and cook, stirring to separate the pieces quickly. Add salt and pepper to taste. Cook 30 seconds or just until chicken changes color. Add asparagus and shallots; cook 30 seconds. Add cream, red pepper and nutmeg; stir. Add Gorgonzola cheese; cook just until cheese melts. Add a generous grinding of black pepper and tarragon. Drain pasta and add sauce. Toss well. Serve Parmesan cheese on side.

Count Pietro's Brussels Rottini
Complete the meal with Italian bread, salad and bottle of Chianti

Serves 4

2 tablespoons olive oil
2 large cloves garlic, minced
1 onion, finely chopped
1 28-ounce can Italian tomatoes,
 peeled
1 large sprig fresh basil, chopped
1 large sprig fresh parsley, chopped

½ teaspoon oregano
Salt and pepper to taste
10 ounces Brussels sprouts, sliced
 in half
1 pound rottini
½ cup Parmesan cheese, grated

Heat oil in pan; sauté garlic and onion until slightly yellow. Add tomatoes, basil, parsley, oregano, salt, pepper and Brussels sprouts. Break up tomatoes with wooden spoon and cook gently over low heat 15 minutes. Cook pasta according to package directions. Add ½ of cheese to sauce. Serve sauce warm over pasta. Use remaining cheese for topping.

Chicken-Spinach Stuffed Shells
Not your basic stuffed shells

Preheat oven 375°   Serves 5

20 jumbo macaroni shells
1 tablespoon salt
3 quarts boiling water
4 large ripe tomatoes, chopped
1 28-ounce can tomatoes, crushed
1½ cups fresh spinach with stems
    removed, chopped

3 tablespoons scallions, chopped
¾ teaspoon oregano
½ teaspoon salt
¼ teaspoon pepper
1½ cups chicken, cooked and
    diced

Gradually add shells and salt to rapidly boiling water so that water continues to boil. Cook uncovered, stirring occasionally, 8 minutes or until tender; drain. Combine all tomatoes, spinach, scallions, oregano, salt and pepper. Cover and cook over medium heat 10 minutes. Measure 1 cup sauce; stir into chicken. Spoon 1 tablespoon chicken mixture into each shell. Set in single layer in shallow 13 x 9-inch baking pan. Spoon remaining sauce over and around shells. Cover and bake 25 minutes or until heated through.

Fungi Mushroom Linguine
A treat for the penniless gourmet

Serves 6

½ cup butter
1 cup olive oil
2 cloves garlic, chopped
1 pound fresh mushrooms, thinly
    sliced
1 teaspoon oregano

1 teaspoon dried sweet basil
½ teaspoon thyme
1 pound linguine, cooked
Salt and pepper to taste
¼ cup fresh parsley, chopped
¼ cup fresh Parmesan cheese, grated

Melt butter gently in oil. Add garlic and sauté 5 minutes. Add mushrooms, oregano, basil and thyme. Sauté 10 minutes or until mushrooms are tender. Serve over cooked linguine. Toss with salt, pepper, parsley and cheese.

Guido's Garden Pasta
Anchovies eliminate the need for salt

Serves 6

1 head fresh broccoli, chopped into
  flowerets
2 whole fresh tomatoes, chopped
  into ½-inch pieces
2 cloves garlic, minced

4 anchovy fillets
1 cup olive oil
¼ teaspoon pepper
1 pound rigatoni, cooked
½ cup fresh Parmesan cheese, grated

Steam broccoli until tender without losing color. Remove and set aside to cool. Sauté tomatoes, garlic and whole anchovies in oil 10 minutes over medium heat. Add broccoli flowerets; reduce heat and simmer 5 minutes. Add pepper. Toss with cooked rigatoni and cheese.

Linguine with Shrimp and Clams
Seafood pasta de Count Pietro

Serves 4

2 large cloves garlic, minced
1 ounce anchovies, chopped
¼ cup imported olive oil
1 teaspoon oregano
½ teaspoon dried basil
1 teaspoon ground pepper
1 pound large shrimp, peeled
  and deveined

2 6-ounce cans clams with liquid,
  chopped
Juice of 1 lemon
¼ cup dry white wine
¼ cup Pecorino or Romano cheese,
  grated
½ cup parsley, chopped
1 pound imported linguine, cooked

Sauté garlic and anchovies in oil. Add oregano, basil and pepper. Add shrimp and clams. Cook 3 minutes, turning shrimp. Add lemon juice and wine. Simmer 5 minutes. Sprinkle with cheese and parsley to taste. Serve steaming hot over linguine.

Pasta Pietro
Spicy

Preheat oven 350°   Serves 8 to 12

1 pound vermicelli   2 tablespoons Worcestershire sauce
½ pound bacon, fried and diced   Dash Tabasco
3 cups cottage cheese   4 teaspoons salt
3 cups sour cream   3 tablespoons horseradish
2 cloves garlic, crushed   1 cup Cheddar cheese, grated
2 medium onions, chopped   (optional)

Cook vermicelli according to package directions. Blend all ingredients except
Cheddar cheese and put in 3½-quart casserole. Bake 30 minutes. Add grated
cheese and cook 10 minutes more.

Rolli Lasagne
Serve to any Italian food lover

Preheat oven 350°   Serves 8

¼ cup olive oil   1 12-ounce can tomato paste
½ cup onion, diced   ½ pound lasagne noodles
1 clove garlic, minced   1 pound Mozarella cheese,
1 pound ground beef   chopped
1 tablespoon oregano   12 ounces ricotta cheese
1 teaspoon salt   2½ ounces Parmesan cheese,
1 teaspoon pepper   grated
1 28-ounce can Italian tomatoes

Heat oil in large heavy skillet. Add onion and garlic and sauté 2 minutes.
Crumble in ground beef. Blend and sauté until meat is brown. Add oregano,
salt, pepper, tomatoes and tomato paste. Cover and simmer 40 minutes. Cook
lasagne noodles in salted boiling water. Drain noodles, rinse in cold water and
separate. Arrange noodles in layers in 13 x 9 x 2-inch baking dish, alternately
with meat sauce, Mozarella and ricotta, ending with meat sauce. Top with
Parmesan cheese; bake 30 minutes. Let stand 15 minutes before serving.

Tip: For a change, substitute 4 ounces raw spinach for ground beef.

Selby Gardens

Marie and Bill Selby moved to Sarasota Bay soon after they married in 1908. Before their wedding in the Presbyterian Church of his and Marie's Ohio hometown of Marietta, Bill had come to Sarasota seasonally for hunting and fishing, staying in the old Belle Haven Hotel at the foot of Main Street. Selby's father, Frank, an Ohio farm boy, had become an oil driller and founded Selby Oil Company. Selby interests owned wells in Oklahoma and Texas and maintained a business office in Tulsa. Ultimately, the company was to acquire substantial holdings in Standard Oil of California, Standard Oil of New Jersey, and Texas Oil Company — later Texaco.

During the mid-twenties at Sarasota, the Selbys constructed a bayfront house on five acres located on the secluded north side of the mouth of historic Hudson's Bayou. Along the bayou they docked their boat, a series of motor launches named *Bilma*, for Bill and Marie. The Selbys acquired a ranch where they raised purebred Angus cattle. Mrs. Selby herself had some ranching enthusiasm and owned riding horses, which she rode regularly throughout most of her life.

Bill Selby, a six-foot sportsman, routinely dressed in rough cowboy clothes complete with hat and boots and frequented Roth's newsstand and Badger's Drug Store at downtown Five Points — a daily pastime for Sarasotans of his day. The Selbys enjoyed hunting and fishing trips together, and he continued a lifelong pattern of fishing excursions north in summer, hunting and fishing at Okeechobee in winter. Marie, a strawberry blonde who also dressed plainly and remained retiring, was interested in her gardens and music, and maintained a low profile. During their Sarasota years, the couple did not take part in organized political or civic groups. They lived frugally and quietly.

A year before Selby's death from leukemia in 1956, he instituted a charitable trust funded from his estate, which amounted to assets in excess of ten million dollars. Mrs. Selby played an active role in the trust, called the William G. and Marie Selby Foundation. In the implementation of the terms of the foundation, the Selby profile was transformed from low to high. The Selbys' foundation has underwritten hundreds of local and statewide bequests for institutions which include Sarasota's Selby Library, New College, YMCA, Boys and Girls Clubs, Sarasota Welfare Home, Ringling Redskins, Sarasota Memorial Hospital, Sailor Circus, scholarship grants of $400,000 to more than 500 students a year, and distribution of an annual total in excess of a million dollars.

When Marie Selby died in 1971 at 86, she bequeathed and endowed with assets of $2 million in Texaco stock and cash, their bayfront home and acreage in trust for a botanical garden envisioned for the landscaped grounds which she had developed and enthusiastically maintained over the years. Marie Selby Botanical Gardens has been opened to the public since 1975, and includes acquisition of the house adjacent to the Selby home, a two-story brick and columned house constructed during the depression by Christy Payne, son of C.N. Payne, a Sarasota benefactor and an oilman like Selby. The Payne family home, pictured here, has been adapted for a museum within the Marie Selby Botanical Gardens complex.

FLORIDA SUMMER SUPPER

* Summer Fruit Salad

* Cold Cream of Cucumber Soup

* Fresh Vegetable Sauté with
* Horseradish Sauce

* Stone Ground Wheat Bread

* Calamondin Cake

  Iced Tea

Vegetables

Carciofi Ripieni di Ricotta
Artichokes stuffed with ricotta

Preheat oven 325°   Serves 6

6 tender young artichokes   1 egg, slightly beaten
Juice of 1 lemon   ¼ cup Pecorino or Parmesan cheese,
Salt to taste   grated
5 tablespoons butter   ¼ pound Italian salami, diced
½ pound ricotta cheese   1 to 2 tablespoons soft bread crumbs

Remove hard outer leaves from artichokes and scrape stalks. Cut each one in half lengthwise and soak in bowl of water mixed with lemon juice. Wash carefully in same water, then cook in pan of boiling salted water for 10 minutes. Drain. Place in well-buttered 13 x 9-inch baking dish, cut side up. Work ricotta with wooden spoon until soft. Add egg, grated cheese, salami and salt to taste. Mound cheese mixture on top of each artichoke half. Sprinkle with bread crumbs; dot with remaining butter. Bake for 20 minutes. Serve hot or cold.

Tip: Encase artichokes in foil while baking to avoid over browning.

Asparagus à la Polonaise
Asparagus never had it so good

Preheat oven 350°   Serves 6

3 tablespoons butter   ¼ teaspoon salt
2 tablespoons flour   2 15-ounce cans asparagus spears
1 cup milk   4 hard-cooked eggs, sliced
1 cup Cheddar cheese, grated   ½ cup almonds, toasted and chopped
Tabasco   Buttered bread crumbs

Melt butter in saucepan. Blend in flour and add milk, stirring constantly until thick. Add cheese and seasonings to sauce and cook until blended. In greased 9 x 13-inch casserole, alternate layers of asparagus, eggs, sauce and almonds to make 2 layers. Top with bread crumbs. Bake for 30 minutes.

Selected artichokes should feel heavy and compact and have tightly closed petals of bright green color.

Vegetables

Chinese Beets
Delicious hot or cold

Serves 10

1 cup white vinegar
1 cup sugar
5 tablespoons ketchup
2 tablespoons cornstarch
3 tablespoons oil

1 small onion, grated
1 teaspoon vanilla
¼ teaspoon ground cloves
3 16-ounce cans beets, slice,
   drain and reserve juice

Mix vinegar, sugar, ketchup, cornstarch, oil, onion, vanilla and cloves in large saucepan. Add beets and 1½ cups reserved juice. Cook over medium heat, stirring constantly, until mixture thickens. Serve hot or cold.

East Indies Broccoli
An unusual combination of flavors

Preheat oven 350°

Serves 6

1 large head fresh broccoli
1 cup mayonnaise
1 tablespoon lemon juice
1 tablespoon soy sauce
1 tablespoon curry powder

2 tablespoons butter, melted
1¼ cups whole wheat bread crumbs
¼ teaspoon garlic powder
¼ cup sunflower seeds, toasted

Trim broccoli. Cut into flowerets. Rinse in cold water. Bring 1 cup water to boiling; add broccoli. Cover with tight lid and remove from heat. Let broccoli steam for 12 minutes. Drain and place in shallow 8 x 8-inch baking dish. Blend mayonnaise, lemon juice, soy sauce and curry powder. Pour mixture over broccoli. Add butter to bread crumbs and garlic powder. Sprinkle bread crumb mixture and sunflower seeds over broccoli. Bake for 10 minutes.

Broccoli should have firm, dark green, compact clusters with small, crisp leaves and no yellow flowers visible inside buds.

Brussels Sprouts Scallop
For Brussels sprouts lovers and those in doubt

Preheat oven 350°   Serves 6 to 8

2 10-ounce packages frozen   ¼ cup milk
   Brussels sprouts   1 10¾-ounce can cream of
3 hard boiled eggs, sliced   mushroom soup
4 ounces American cheese,   ½ cup corn flake crumbs
   shredded   2 tablespoons butter, melted

Cook sprouts, omitting salt, according to package directions. Drain. Arrange sprouts in 13 x 9-inch baking dish. Place eggs on top of sprouts and cover with cheese. Blend milk and soup; pour over sprouts. Combine crumbs with butter and sprinkle over top. Bake for 25 minutes.

Buffet Broccoli
Vary by adding whole cherry tomatoes

Chill 24 hours   Serves 10 to 12

3 heads fresh broccoli   1 teaspoon pepper
1 cup cider vinegar   1½ cups vegetable oil
1 tablespoon sugar   1 tablespoon dried or fresh dill weed
1 teaspoon salt   1 teaspoon garlic salt

Trim large leaves of broccoli. Remove stalks. Separate broccoli into flowerets and wash thoroughly. Drain and place in large shallow container; set aside. Combine next 7 ingredients, mixing well. Pour over broccoli. Toss gently to coat. Chill at least 24 hours, stirring several times.

Dress freshly cooked or frozen asparagus with twist of lime and melted butter. For tender asparagus stalks, use vegetable peeler to carefully pare stalks, and be sure to wash thoroughly to remove sand.

Vegetables

Glazed Carrots and Parsnips
A simple way to make vegetables special

Serves 6

½ cup unsalted butter
4 to 5 medium carrots, peeled
   and grated

4 to 5 medium parsnips, peeled and
   grated
Salt and pepper to taste
1 to 2 tablespoons light brown sugar

Melt 6 tablespoons butter in large frying pan over medium low heat. Add carrots, parsnips, salt, pepper and brown sugar. Cover and cook, stirring every 2 to 3 minutes until just tender and glazed. Add remaining butter if needed.

Zesty Carrot Sticks
A welcome change

Chill

Serves 6 to 8

1 pound carrots, peeled and cut
   in strips
1 cup water
½ cup oil
½ cup wine vinegar

1 teaspoon sugar
4 cloves garlic, coarsely chopped
1½ teaspoons oregano
Parsley

Combine carrots and water in saucepan and cook until tender. Drain. Mix oil, vinegar, sugar, garlic and oregano. Pour over carrots and refrigerate in tightly covered container several hours or overnight. When ready to serve, drain and garnish with parsley.

Tip: The longer the carrots marinate, the better they are.

Carrots with tops intact are fresher. The brighter the orange color, the more nutritious the carrots.

Cauliflower Celery Royale
A new taste sensation

Preheat oven 350°   Serves 8

1 large head cauliflower, broken
   into flowerets
1 cup celery, chopped
2 10¾-ounce cans cream of
   shrimp soup
¾ cup milk

2 tablespoons pimiento, chopped
1 cup saltine crackers, crushed and
   buttered
1 tablespoon parsley, chopped
1 teaspoon paprika

Parboil cauliflower and celery until tender. Drain well. Place in buttered 2–quart casserole. Mix soup, milk and pimiento and pour over cauliflower and celery. Cover with cracker crumbs. Top with parsley and paprika. Bake for 30 minutes.

Corn Pudding Deluxe
Kids will love this

Preheat oven 350°   Serves 6 to 8

2½ cups milk
½ cup butter
3 10-ounce packages frozen
   cream style corn, thawed
1½ tablespoons sugar

1½ tablespoons flour
6 eggs, beaten
¾ teaspoon salt
Pepper

Scald milk and butter together. Set aside. Combine remaining ingredients. Add milk mixture. Pour into greased, shallow casserole. Place casserole in pan of hot water. Bake 1 hour 15 minutes or until knife inserted comes out clean.

Tip: If desired, add sautéed green pepper, pimiento and/or onion.

Cauliflower heads should be firm, compact and creamy white, with fresh green outer leaves.

Vegetables

Mushrooms Magnifique

Serve instead of potatoes with your favorite beef roast

Preheat oven 450°   Serves 8

6 tablespoons unsalted butter   1½ cups beef stock or bouillon
2 pounds fresh mushrooms, sliced   ½ cup Madeira or dry sherry
Lemon juice   ½ cup cream, heated
Dash soy sauce   1 top pie crust
3 tablespoons flour   1 egg, beaten

Melt 3 tablespoons butter in skillet and add mushrooms. Sprinkle with lemon juice and soy sauce. Cover and cook 5 minutes. Remove mushrooms to buttered 1-quart casserole. In skillet, melt remaining 3 tablespoons butter and blend in flour. Add beef stock and cook until thickened. Stir in Madeira and cream. Pour over mushrooms. Cover with pie crust. Vent crust with favorite design. Brush with egg wash. Bake 15 minutes; reduce temperature to 300° and bake 15 minutes longer.

Okra-Tomato Bake

A change of pace

Preheat oven 350°   Serves 4

1 pound okra   4 tomatoes, skinned and chopped or
4 tablespoons butter   ¼ cup tomato paste plus ½ cup
3 medium onions, chopped   water
1 green pepper, chopped   ½ teaspoon salt
1 clove garlic, minced   ⅛ teaspoon pepper
                                     ⅛ teaspoon cinnamon

Wash okra and trim stems. Melt butter in skillet and slowly sauté onions, pepper and garlic until light golden brown. Add tomatoes or paste mixture and simmer slowly for 10 minutes. Place okra in 9 x 11-inch baking dish. Sprinkle with salt, pepper and cinnamon and cover with sauce. Cover and bake for 30 minutes or until okra is done.

Charcoal Grilled Onions
Star attraction at your next cookout

Grill   Serves 4

4 large onions, thinly sliced   ½ cup butter
Salt and pepper

Place onions on large piece heavy duty foil. Season generously with salt and pepper. Divide butter into sixths and arrange over onions. Tightly seal foil and place on rack over hot coals. Roast for 20 to 25 minutes.

Tip: Sliced cooked potatoes may be added to onions before roasting.

Creamy Baked Onions and Beans
A perfect side dish for your holiday meal

Preheat oven 350°   Serves 6 to 8

2 9-ounce packages frozen green   ¼ cup butter
  beans   3 9-ounce packages frozen small
1½ cups water   onions with cream sauce
½ cup milk   Bread crumbs

Cook beans according to package directions; drain and set aside. Combine water, milk, butter and onions. Bring to boil; stir well. Add beans. Pour into 3-quart casserole and sprinkle top with bread crumbs. Bake for 20 minutes.

In order to have vegetables taste better and to preserve more nutrients, steam them. Put vegetables in steamette and place in pot of boiling water, being careful not to have the water come over the vegetables. Cover and cook. Fresh green beans usually take 4 minutes.

Parsnips Supreme
A tasty combination

Preheat oven 350°   Serves 6

1 pound parsnips
2 tablespoons butter
2 teaspoons cornstarch
1½ cups milk
1 chicken bouillon cube

½ teaspoon sweet basil or marjoram, crushed
⅓ cup Parmesan or Romano cheese, grated
3 tablespoons almonds, chopped

Scrub parsnips and cook in boiling water until tender. Drain, cool, pare and slice. Arrange slices in 1½-quart baking dish. Melt butter in saucepan; remove from heat and stir in cornstarch. Add milk and bouillon cube. Cook over low heat stirring constantly, until thickened and smooth. Stir herbs into sauce. Combine 2 tablespoons cheese with almonds and set aside. Add remaining cheese to sauce. Stir until cheese is melted. Pour over parsnips. Sprinkle with reserved cheese and almond mixture. Bake for 20 minutes.

Incredible Hash Brown Potatoes
Everybody's favorite

Preheat oven 350°   Serves 8 to 10

2 24-ounce packages hash brown potatoes, thawed and drained
16 ounces sharp Cheddar cheese, grated

2 10¾-ounce cans cream of potato soup
1½ cups sour cream
¾ cup Parmesan cheese, grated

Combine first 4 ingredients. Place in 9 x 13–inch baking dish. Top with Parmesan cheese. Bake 1 hour.

Add chives to parsleyed new potatoes or sprinkle new potatoes, cooked in their jackets, with freshly grated Parmesan cheese.

Oven Fried Potatoes
Just like mother used to make

Preheat oven 375°   Serves 10

6 medium white potatoes   ½ cup milk
½ cup butter, melted   1 tablespoon onion, grated
½ pint half and half   Salt and pepper to taste

Cook potatoes in jackets until tender. Cool. Peel potatoes and grate. Mix butter, cream, milk, onion, salt and pepper. Add potatoes. Pour into greased 7 x 11–inch baking dish. Bake 1 hour.

Italian Potato Pie
Daring but different

Preheat oven 425°   Serves 6

2 pounds potatoes, peeled   3 tomatoes, peeled and sliced
¼ cup butter, softened   ½ inch thick
½ cup sour cream   1 teaspoon basil
½ cup chives (optional)   1 teaspoon oregano
Seasoned salt and pepper to taste   ½ cup Parmesan cheese, grated
12 ounces Mozzarella cheese, sliced ¼ cup butter, melted

Cover potatoes with salted water and boil until tender. Drain and mash. Stir in softened butter, sour cream, chives, seasoned salt and pepper. Butter and lightly flour 9½-inch deep pie plate. Spread in mashed potatoes. Arrange 6 ounces Mozzarella cheese on potatoes; top with tomatoes. Sprinkle with basil and oregano. Top with remaining Mozzarella cheese, Parmesan cheese and melted butter. Bake 20 to 25 minutes or until cheese is melted. Cool slightly before cutting.

Add fresh mint or basil to buttered peas.

Vegetables

Elegant Spinach Roll
A dish for a grand occasion

Preheat oven 350°

Serves 8

2 10-ounce packages frozen
spinach, chopped
4 eggs, separated
¼ cup butter, melted
½ teaspoon salt
¼ teaspoon pepper
⅛ teaspoon nutmeg

1 cup fresh mushrooms, sliced
¼ cup scallions, chopped
2 tablespoons butter
Parmesan cheese, grated
2 tomatoes, thickly sliced
Watercress

Cook spinach according to package directions. Drain well and chop again. Lightly beat egg yolks. Stir in spinach, butter, salt, pepper and nutmeg. Beat egg whites until stiff. Fold egg whites into spinach mixture. Line greased jelly roll pan with waxed paper. Grease and lightly flour paper. Spread spinach mixture evenly in pan; bake 15 minutes until firm. Sauté mushrooms and scallions in butter. Invert jelly roll soufflé on waxed paper that has been lightly sprinkled with cheese. Carefully peel paper from back of baked roll. Spread mushroom and scallion mixture evenly over surface and carefully roll. Place seam side down on serving dish. Garnish with tomato slices and watercress.

Florentine Torta
Attractive to serve and tasty to eat

Preheat oven 400°

Serves 10 to 12

3 10-ounce packages fresh spinach
or 2 10-ounce packages frozen
spinach
½ pound Feta cheese, crumbled
1 pound ricotta cheese
4 eggs, beaten

½ cup milk
Salt and pepper to taste
¼ cup Parmesan cheese, grated
(optional)
1 cup butter, melted
1 pound phyllo dough

Cook spinach and drain. Mix with Feta cheese, ricotta cheese, eggs, milk, salt, pepper and Parmesan cheese. Brush bottom of 9 x 13-inch pan with melted butter. Layer pan with 8 sheets of phyllo, brushing with butter between each layer. Pour in spinach mixture. Top with 10 to 12 more sheets of phyllo, buttering between each layer. Brush top with butter and score in squares. Bake 20 to 30 minutes or until golden brown. May layer spinach separately, if desired.

Herbed Squash Imperial
A touch of class

Serves 4

8 small firm yellow squash, thinly
  sliced
3 tablespoons butter
Pinch thyme, rosemary and
  marjoram

2 green onions, chopped
2 tablespoons soy sauce
¼ cup dry white wine
Dash salt and pepper

Sauté squash in butter over medium heat for 10 minutes, until translucent and slightly limp. Add thyme, rosemary, marjoram and green onions. Sauté for another 2 minutes. Add soy sauce and wine. Stir until blended. Add seasonings. Serve immediately.

Skillet Squash au Gratin
Simple, but delicious

Serves 5

¼ cup butter
4 cups zucchini squash, thinly
  sliced
2 onions, sliced
1 teaspoon salt

Dash pepper
1 teaspoon sweet basil
¼ cup water or 2 average tomatoes,
  sliced
1 cup Swiss or Cheddar cheese, grated

Melt butter in skillet. Add squash, onions, salt, pepper, basil and water (or tomatoes). Cover and cook for 10 minutes, or until tender. Remove from heat. Sprinkle with cheese and cover for 10 minutes or until cheese melts.

Zucchini and yellow summer squash should be firm, young and small in size. The larger ones may be too seedy. Zucchini should have dark green, glossy skin; yellow squash should have a glossy, uniform color with no nicks or marks. Gently prod the blossom end (the end opposite the stem end) to make sure it is hard; a soft blossom end is a sign of overripeness.

Vegetables

Squash à la Swiss
For your next buffet dinner

Preheat oven 350°   Serves 12

4 pounds yellow squash, sliced   3 cups milk
2 medium onions, finely chopped   1 teaspoon seasoned salt
2 bay leaves   Dash ground nutmeg
½ teaspoon thyme   Dash Worcestershire sauce
Dash salt   1½ cups Swiss cheese, shredded
6 tablespoons butter   4 egg yolks, beaten
6 tablespoons all purpose flour   Buttered bread crumbs

Cover squash and cook until barely tender in boiling water to which onions, bay leaves, thyme and dash salt have been added. Drain and remove bay leaves. Set aside. In saucepan, combine butter, flour and dash salt; gradually add milk and cook, stirring constantly until thickened. Stir in seasoned salt, nutmeg, Worcestershire sauce and 1 cup cheese. Remove from heat. Add 1 to 2 tablespoons of sauce to egg yolks, then gradually add warmed egg yolks to rest of sauce. Gently combine squash and sauce mixture. Turn into 11¾ x 7½-inch buttered baking dish. Mix remaining cheese with buttered bread crumbs. Sprinkle over squash and bake for 35 minutes or until top is bubbly and brown.

Plantation Sweets
Sweet potatoes with a surprise

Preheat oven 375°   Serves 6

1 1-pound can sweet potatoes,   ⅛ teaspoon cinnamon
  halved lengthwise   1 1-pound can apricot halves,
1¼ cups brown sugar   drain and reserve syrup
1½ teaspoons cornstarch   2 tablespoons butter
¼ teaspoon salt   ½ cup pecan halves

Place sweet potatoes in greased 10 x 16-inch baking dish. In saucepan, combine brown sugar, cornstarch, salt and cinnamon. Stir 1 cup reserved apricot syrup into cornstarch mixture. Cook and stir over medium heat until boiling. Boil 2 minutes. Add apricots, butter and pecans. Pour over sweet potatoes. Bake uncovered for 25 minutes.

Sautéed Cherry Tomatoes
A dish in a dash

Serves 6 to 8

2 to 3 tablespoons butter
  or olive oil
1 pint ripe, firm cherry tomatoes
1 clove garlic or 1 tablespoon green
  onion, finely chopped

1 tablespoon fresh parsley or basil,
  finely chopped
Salt and freshly ground pepper to taste

Heat butter in large skillet. Add tomatoes. Cook over medium-high heat until just heated through, about 2 minutes, to avoid popping tomatoes. Stir in garlic or onion, parsley or basil, salt and pepper. Cook for a few seconds. Serve warm.

Zucchini Custard
Friends will rave

Preheat oven 400°

Serves 4 to 6

1 large zucchini squash, sliced
  ¼-inch thick
1 egg
½ cup sour cream

Dash salt and pepper
1 cup fresh Parmesan cheese, grated
2 tablespoons butter
Paprika or parsley

Steam zucchini 3 to 4 minutes until tender; drain. Put in shallow 8 x 8-inch baking dish. Beat together egg, sour cream, salt, pepper and ½ of cheese. Pour over zucchini. Dot with butter and sprinkle with remaining cheese. Bake for 15 minutes or until set. Garnish with paprika or parsley.

Use herbs to add zest to vegetables: thyme and marjoram, dill and tarragon, basil and oregano.

Zucchini in Dilled Cream
A taste of elegance, quickly prepared

Serves 3 to 4

4 medium zucchini squash, grated
1 teaspoon salt
4 tablespoons butter
¼ cup green onion with tops, thinly
  sliced

2 to 3 sprigs fresh dill, snipped or
  1 teaspoon dried dill weed
Pepper to taste
½ to 1 cup sour cream

Sprinkle zucchini with salt. Let stand 5 minutes. Drain in sieve pressing out as much liquid as possible. Heat butter in heavy skillet. Add onion. Cook and stir 1 minute; add zucchini. Stir and cook until just tender, about 5 minutes. Stir in dill and pepper. Reduce heat and add sour cream.

Tip: Delicious stuffed into baked, seeded tomatoes.

Zucchini Provencale
Easy as 1, 2, 3

Preheat oven 350°

Serves 8

4 medium zucchini squash,
  sliced ¼-inch thick
2 to 3 medium onions, thinly sliced
4 large tomatoes, sliced

½ cup butter
Salt and pepper to taste
Garlic powder to taste
Parmesan cheese, grated

Layer ½ zucchini, ½ onion and ½ tomato in greased 10 x 10-inch baking dish. Slice ¼ cup butter in pats and arrange on top of tomatoes. Sprinkle with salt, pepper, garlic powder and Parmesan cheese. Repeat entire process to form second layer. Bake uncovered for 50 minutes.

Vegetables cooked in the microwave? Of course! Micro vegetables are fast, crunchy, rich in color, low in calories, delicious and nutritious.

Fresh Vegetable Sauté
A vegetarian's delight

Onion
Carrots, celery, cabbage,
  cauliflower, green beans and
  broccoli

Zucchini squash, mushrooms, peppers,
  sweet potatoes and spinach
Oil
Basil, oregano, thyme and marjoram

Cut vegetables in thin bite-size pieces. Separate cut vegetables into 3 groups:
(1) onion, (2) carrots, celery, cabbage, cauliflower, green beans and broccoli
and (3) zucchini squash, mushrooms, peppers, sweet potatoes and spinach.
Over medium heat, pour small amount of oil in heavy skillet. Add onion and
herbs. Sauté until onion is soft. Add group 2; sauté until tender. Add group 3;
stir and sauté until tender. Serve with sour cream horseradish sauce.

Tip: Make your own combinations; 2½ cups raw vegetables per serving.

Sour Cream Horseradish Sauce

Yields 1½ cups

2 egg yolks
1 cup sour cream
1 tablespoon horseradish

½ teaspoon salt
Juice of 1 lemon
Dash sugar

Whisk egg yolks into sour cream. Add remaining ingredients. Heat slowly for 8
to 10 minutes, stirring constantly. Use over vegetables, fish or potatoes.

To microwave corn on the cob, butter each ear generously (salt
after cooking), wrap separately in waxed paper and place on
paper towels. Cook 8 to 10 minutes on high setting for 4 ears.
Turn halfway through cooking.

Vegetables

Steamed Vegetable Bowl
Use your imagination

Preheat oven 300°

Serves 6

1 cup each broccoli spears, yellow or zucchini squash, carrots, mushrooms, cauliflower, celery and/or cabbage

1 cup boiling water
1 package onion soup mix
2 tablespoons cornstarch
1 cup Mozzarella cheese, shredded

Cut vegetables into bite-size pieces. Steam vegetables until tender; drain. In saucepan, combine boiling water and onion soup mix. Stir in cornstarch to thicken. Place vegetables in deep 3-quart casserole. Pour onion soup mixture over vegetables. Top with cheese and bake for 5 minutes or until cheese melts.

Tip: Substitute 1 11-ounce can Cheddar cheese soup for onion soup mix; top with bread crumbs and bake as above.

Savory Vegetable Medley
Rich in color and flavor

Preheat oven 375°

Serves 6 to 8

½ pound mushrooms, sliced
2 tablespoons butter, melted
1 10¾-ounce can cream of mushroom soup
¼ cup light cream
1 teaspoon ground dill weed or dill seed

1 cup fresh green beans, cooked and drained
1 cup lima beans, cooked and drained
½ cup corn, cooked
1 cup carrots, sliced, cooked and drained
¼ cup Parmesan cheese, grated

Add mushrooms to butter and sauté gently until lightly browned. Blend soup, cream and dill. Fold in mushrooms, green beans, lima beans, corn and carrots. Pour into greased 1½-quart casserole. Sprinkle Parmesan cheese on top. Bake for 25 to 30 minutes or until bubbly.

When cooking vegetables in microwave oven, refer to instruction booklet for timing techniques. Normally, add just a splash of water (1 or 2 tablespoons) and cook in covered casserole.

Mediterranean Eggplant
Perfect as a main course

Preheat oven 325°   Serves 12 to 14

1 large eggplant, peeled and cut
   in 1-inch cubes
3 medium onions, peeled and cut
   in 1-inch cubes
2 green bell peppers, cut in 1-inch
   cubes
½ pound fresh mushrooms, sliced
1 10-ounce can stewed tomatoes
1 15½-ounce jar spaghetti sauce

1 12-ounce can tomato paste
1 4-ounce can green chilies, chopped
4 cloves garlic, chopped
1 teaspoon black pepper
1 tablespoon Italian seasoning
1 10-ounce can Parmesan cheese,
   grated
1½ pounds hot Italian sausage,
   browned, drained and sliced

Add eggplant, onions, peppers and mushrooms to 2 quarts boiling water and cook 4 to 5 minutes. Drain well and add tomatoes. For sauce, mix spaghetti sauce, tomato paste, chilies, garlic, pepper, seasoning and ½ cup cheese. Layer sausage, vegetables and sauce in greased 13 x 9-inch baking dish. Top with remaining cheese. Cover with loose foil tent and bake 1 hour.

Mélange of Spring Vegetables
Wholesome summer fare

Preheat oven 375°   Serves 6 to 8

1 pound fresh string beans
1 large head broccoli
1 small head cauliflower

6 tablespoons butter
Salt and pepper to taste
½ cup fresh Parmesan cheese, grated

Trim beans, cut in even 2 inch segments. Cook in boiling water about 8 minutes; drain. Cool beans under cold water, drain, set aside. Cut broccoli into flowerets. Cook in boiling water 3 minutes, drain and cool as for green beans. Cut cauliflower into flowerets. Cook in boiling water 5 minutes, drain and cool as above. Melt butter in 11 x 15-inch pan. Arrange vegetables in pan. Add salt and pepper. Bake 2 minutes, baste once or twice with butter. Sprinkle with Parmesan cheese and bake 5 more minutes.

Tip: Cook all vegetables in same boiling water.

Vegetables

Southern Style Hot Baked Fruit
Unforgettably delicious

Preheat oven 350°   Serves 8

1 1-pound package dried pitted   1 16-ounce can cherry pie filling
  prunes   1½ cups water
5½ ounces dried apricots   ⅓ cup dry sherry
1 13-ounce can pineapple chunks,   ⅓ cup slivered, toasted almonds
  undrained

Place prunes, apricots and pineapple in deep 9–inch round casserole.
Combine pie filling, water and sherry. Pour over fruit, mixing well. Stir in
almonds. Cover and bake for 1½ hours.

Spiced Fruit Compote
Nice accompaniment with ham, pork or turkey

Chill overnight   Serves 12

2 oranges, peeled and cut in large   1 16-ounce can apricot halves, drained
  pieces   2 cups orange juice
1 16-ounce can pear halves, drained   ¼ cup sugar
1 29-ounce can peach halves,   2 to 3 cinnamon sticks
  drained   12 whole cloves
                                      ¼ teaspoon ginger

Peel oranges, reserving 1 peel. In large bowl, combine oranges, reserved peel,
pears, peaches and apricots. In medium saucepan, combine remaining
ingredients and simmer 5 minutes. Pour over fruit; cover bowl and refrigerate
overnight. Remove cinnamon sticks, peel and cloves. Serve in chilled crystal
bowl.

Tip: Add ½ cup maraschino cherries for color.

When cooking vegetables in microwave oven, refer to instruction
booklet for timing techniques. Normally, add just a splash of
water (1 or 2 tablespoons) and cook in covered casserole.

Classic Peaches
A holiday favorite

Preheat oven 350°   Serves 6 to 8

1 29-ounce can peach halves,   Brandy
  drained   Butter
1 20½-ounce can mincemeat

Arrange peach halves in shallow 11 x 8-inch baking dish. Fill each peach half with mincemeat and pour 1 teaspoon brandy over each and dot with butter. Bake for 20 minutes. Serve immediately.

Hot Curried Pears
Turn ordinary canned fruit into a gourmet treat

Preheat oven 300°   Serves 6 to 8

1 29-ounce can pear halves,   2 tablespoons butter, melted
  drain and reserve syrup 1 to 2 tablespoons curry powder
⅓ cup raisins   2 tablespoons brown sugar
1 tablespoon nuts, chopped

Place pears, cut side up, in greased 11 x 8-inch baking dish. Fill centers with raisins and nuts. Combine butter, curry powder, sugar and ¼ cup reserved syrup. Spoon over pears. Bake for 15 minutes.

Lewis and Eugenia Van Wezel
Performing Arts Hall

Sarasota's interest in the arts and her attraction of patrons continues to influence the direction of her path through the twentieth century. One of the more visible landmarks to which that path leads is to the bayfront and the Lewis and Eugenia Van Wezel Performing Arts Hall.

Leaders of the Woman's Club and the Allied Arts Council of Sarasota and Manatee Counties were among those who started the ball rolling for a modern facility in the early sixties. A 1964 city bond referendum was backed and enthusiastically campaigned for by one of Sarasota's devoted art patrons, David Cohen, who at the time was a City Commissioner and Mayor. The referendum, as passed, provided the sum of more than four million dollars to construct three projects — a new city hall, a new beach pavilion at Lido, and earmarked $1,350,000 for a performing arts hall. Though the measure had passed by a margin of three to two, its most controversial item had been the hall.

To develop building plans, city officials adopted a selection committee's recommendation to retain the services of Taliesin Associated Architects of the Frank Lloyd Wright Foundation, commissioning William Wesley Peters as chief architect for the project. A lavender-to-purple color finish was personally selected by Olgivanna Lloyd Wright, the venerated architect's third wife and widow, also associated with Taliesin, based at Wright's former homes.

The project struck a major snag in 1967, when total accumulated construction funds of two and a half million fell $400,000 short. Eventually, administrators of the Van Wezel Foundation of New York agreed to contribute that sum with the stipulation that the hall be named for its benefactors, the late Lewis and Eugenia Van Wezel, former Sarasota residents of Lido Key. Van Wezel, of Dutch-American ancestry, had been a diamond merchant in New York.

In 1968, construction began. On the fifth day of January, 1970, the hall opened with "Fiddler on the Roof." Public objection to the building's lavender-hued finishes initially inspired such derisive nicknames as "Purple People Seater" and "Purple Cow," but the names faded from use as the facility's popularity and civic stature became increasingly apparent.

The 1800-seat Van Wezel Performing Arts Hall thus took its place among other public facilities situated at the Civic Center complex. The VW's income approached the $2 million mark within a dozen years. As many as 250 performances a year attract several hundred thousand patrons to its doors to enjoy opera, Broadway musicals, lectures, concerts, and ballet. The hall has lured to its stage such acclaimed performing artists as Beverly Sills, Isaac Perlman, Vladimir Horowitz, Leonard Bernstein, and Luciano Pavarotti. Its track record and caliber of scheduled performers have earned the hall recognition as one of the country's most successful. Much of the hall's star-studded success has often been credited to the expertise of Curtis Haug, former President and Program Director of Chautauqua Institution, who has been the Van Wezel's managing director since November of 1970.

FORMAL DINNER

* Crabmeat Royale

* Charcoal Broiled Butterflied Leg of Lamb

* Glazed Carrots and Parsnips

  Petit Potatoes with Parsley

  Romaine Leaves with
* Creamy Vinaigrette Salad Dressing

* Sally Lunn Bread

* Frozen Raspberry Pie

  Red Wine: Beaujolais Village

Entrées

Austrian Goulash
Can be prepared in advance

Serves 4

2 pounds beef chuck cubes
Flour
Butter
2 to 3 onions, sliced
Paprika
1¼ cups beef stock

2 bay leaves
2 peppercorns
¼ cup red wine vinegar
1 tablespoon sour cream
1 dill pickle, diced
Egg noodles

Coat meat with flour and brown in butter. Add onion slices; sprinkle generously with paprika. Add beef stock, bay leaves, peppercorns and vinegar. Simmer 2 hours. Remove 1 cup gravy; add sour cream. Return to pot. Add pickle. Serve over egg noodles.

Tip: If necessary, remove 1 cup gravy, thicken with flour and return to pot.

Beer Beef Stew
Beer adds zip

Serves 4 to 6

1 pound beef stew meat, cubed
Flour
3 tablespoons cooking oil
1 large onion, chopped
1 clove garlic, minced
1 teaspoon salt

1 12-ounce bottle beer
½ pound mushrooms, sliced
2 to 3 carrots, sliced
1 bay leaf
3 to 4 potatoes, diced
1 10-ounce package frozen peas
(optional)

Roll beef in flour. Brown in oil in Dutch oven. Add onion, garlic and salt. Sauté. Add beer, mushrooms, carrots and bay leaf. Cover and simmer slowly 2 to 2½ hours. Add potatoes and peas last ½ hour.

Bobotie
South African dish

Preheat oven 350°   Serves 4 to 6

2 medium onions, sliced
2 tablespoons butter
2 pounds 4 ounces lean
   ground beef
1¼ cups milk
3 eggs
2 slices white bread, cubed
¼ cup dried apricots, finely chopped
1 apple, peeled and grated

¼ cup seedless raisins
¼ cup blanched almonds
2 tablespoons sugar or apricot jam
1 tablespoon curry powder
2 tablespoons lemon juice
2 teaspoons salt
¼ teaspoon pepper
6 bay leaves or fresh lemon leaves
¼ teaspoon turmeric

Sauté onions in butter until golden. Add meat and stir until browned. Remove from heat. In large bowl, mix ¼ cup milk, 1 egg and bread, mashing bread with fork. Add apricots, apple, raisins, almonds, sugar or jam, curry, lemon juice, salt and pepper. Mix until well blended. Add onions and beef. Mix lightly. Spread evenly into lightly greased casserole. Press bay or lemon leaves into top of meat mixture. Bake uncovered 30 minutes. Remove from oven. Beat remaining 2 eggs with remaining 1 cup milk and turmeric until just blended. Pour over meat. Bake 10 minutes or until topping has set. Serve with yellow rice and chutney.

Bourbon Steak
Great flavor

Grill   Serves 10

¼ cup oil
¼ cup bourbon
1 teaspoon Worcestershire sauce
1 heaping teaspoon ginger

2 teaspoons soy sauce
1 teaspoon garlic powder
1 tablespoon brown sugar
1 large sirloin, 2½ to 3-inches thick

Combine first 7 ingredients; pour over steak. Cover and marinate in refrigerator at least 4 hours or overnight. Turn meat several times. Remove from refrigerator and let stand until room temperature. Grill about 45 minutes for rare. Slice thin.

Hamburger Pie
Quick delicious main dish

Preheat oven 375°   Serves 4

1 8- or 9-inch frozen pie shell   2 tablespoons flour
1 pound ground chuck   Salt and pepper
1 cup onion, thinly sliced   Seasoned salt
½ cup green pepper, chopped   2 eggs, beaten
3 tablespoons butter   1 cup sour cream
1 8-ounce can mushrooms, drained   Paprika
  and sliced

Partially bake pastry shell according to package directions. Remove from oven. Brown meat; drain. Return to skillet. Add onion, green pepper and butter. Cook until vegetables are tender. Stir in mushrooms, flour and seasonings. Pour into pastry shell. Blend eggs into sour cream. Pour over meat; sprinkle with paprika. Bake 30 minutes or until topping turns golden.

Marinated London Broil
Easy company dish

Preheat oven broil   Serves 8

4 pounds London broil   ½ teaspoon ginger
1 cup dry white wine   ⅓ cup peanut or vegetable oil
1 cup soy sauce   ¼ teaspoon garlic powder

Pierce steak with large fork, and place in 9 x 13-inch pan. Combine remaining ingredients and pour over steak. Cover and marinate 24 hours. Turn steak several times. Broil 20 minutes for rare, 30 minutes for medium. Slice ¼-inch thick and arrange on platter. Warm remaining marinade and serve on side.

Corned Beef von Reuben
Can be prepared ahead

Preheat oven 325°   Serves 8

1 6-ounce package seasoned   8 ounces Swiss cheese, sliced
  croutons   3 eggs, beaten
1 12-ounce can corned beef   2 cups milk
1 16-ounce can sauerkraut,
  drained

Butter 2-quart casserole. Layer ½ croutons, corned beef and sauerkraut. Top
with remaining croutons and cheese. Combine eggs and milk. Pour over
corned beef mixture. Bake 35 minutes.

Reuben in Caraway Pastry
A natural for a party

Preheat oven 425°   Serves 6 to 8

1 cup flour   1 1-pound can corned beef
1 teaspoon baking powder   1 8-ounce can sauerkraut, drained
⅔ cup shortening   1 teaspoon pepper
¾ teaspoon salt   1 cup Swiss or Monterey Jack cheese,
1 egg   grated
¾ cup water   1 to 2 teaspoons caraway seed

Beat flour, baking powder, shortening, salt, egg and water well with mixer.
Pour into 9-inch pie pan. Make 6-inch patty with corned beef and gently place
in center of batter. Arrange sauerkraut over beef and sprinkle with pepper.
Cover with cheese. Sprinkle caraway seed over cheese and pastry. Bake 40 to
45 minutes.

**To prevent splashing when frying meat, sprinkle a little salt into
the pan before adding the oil.**

Eggplant Lasagne
Without the calories of noodles

Preheat oven 350°   Serves 6

2 small eggplants, peeled and sliced   1 28-ounce can Italian tomatoes
Flour   1 6-ounce can tomato paste
2 to 4 tablespoons olive oil   2 tablespoons dried parsley flakes
1 large onion, chopped   1 teaspoon salt
1 large green pepper, chopped   8 ounces Mozzarella cheese, sliced
⅛ teaspoon garlic powder   1 pound ricotta cheese
1 teapoon basil leaves   Parmesan cheese, grated
1 pound ground beef

Dust eggplant with flour and sauté in oil until lightly browned. Set aside. Sauté onion and pepper in oil until soft but not brown. Add garlic powder and basil. Stir in meat and cook until lightly browned. Drain. Add tomatoes, tomato paste, parsley and salt. Simmer 30 minutes. Alternate layers of sauce, eggplant, Mozzarella and ricotta in 9 x 13-inch casserole, ending with sauce. Sprinkle heavily with Parmesan cheese and bake 30 to 40 minutes.

Tip: Partially bake day before so juices will be absorbed.

Polly's Meatloaf
Stuffing adds an interesting change

Preheat oven 350°   Serves 8

1½ pounds ground chuck   1 egg, beaten
½ cup tomato juice   Brown sugar
1 cup herb stuffing   Ketchup
½ onion, chopped   2 strips bacon
Salt and pepper

Combine first 6 ingredients. Shape into loaf and place in 9 x 12-inch pan. Make valley down center of loaf. Sprinkle top with brown sugar and ketchup. Place bacon strips on top. Bake 1 hour.

Beef

Mexican Lasagne
A hearty, satisfying entrée

Preheat oven 350°   Serves 4 to 6

1 pound lean ground beef
1 10-ounce can tomatoes, chopped
1 8-ounce can tomato sauce,
  minus 3 tablespoons
½ of 1.5-ounce package enchilada
  sauce mix
¾ teaspoon salt

Dash pepper
1 egg, beaten
8 ounces small curd cottage cheese
¼ pound Monterey Jack cheese,
  shredded
1 7-ounce package tortilla chips
½ cup Cheddar cheese, shredded

Brown meat; drain. Add tomatoes, tomato sauce, enchilada sauce mix, salt and pepper. Simmer 2 minutes. Combine egg and cottage cheese, stirring well. Add to meat sauce mixture and mix thoroughly. Spread ½ meat sauce in lightly greased 8 x 12-inch casserole. Top with ½ Monterey Jack cheese and ½ tortilla chips. Repeat layers. Sprinkle with Cheddar cheese. Bake 30 minutes.

Judy's Brunswick Stew
Pungent potfull

Preheat oven 250°   Serves 12

2 pounds ground beef
2 8- to 10-ounce cans corned beef
8 smoked sausage links, sliced
2 16-ounce cans whole kernel corn
1 15-ounce can tomato sauce
1 15-ounce can tomato sauce
  with bits

1 16-ounce bottle barbecue sauce
1 8-ounce can kidney beans
1 8-ounce can garbanzo beans
¼ cup lemon juice
Bacon, onion or chicken, cooked
  (optional)

Brown beef and drain. Combine beef with remaining ingredients in large Dutch oven. Cover and bake 2 hours or longer. Longer cooking increases flavor. Serve over rice.

Tip: Ingredients can be varied in amount to suit individual tastes and to stretch the quantity.

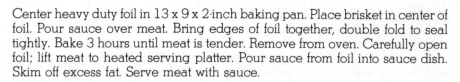

Oven Barbequed Brisket of Beef

Use with zippy barbeque sauce

Preheat oven 350°   Serves 8

1 lean 4- to 5-pound brisket   2 cups zippy barbeque sauce

Center heavy duty foil in 13 x 9 x 2-inch baking pan. Place brisket in center of foil. Pour sauce over meat. Bring edges of foil together, double fold to seal tightly. Bake 3 hours until meat is tender. Remove from oven. Carefully open foil; lift meat to heated serving platter. Pour sauce from foil into sauce dish. Skim off excess fat. Serve meat with sauce.

Zippy Barbeque Sauce

Yields 4½ cups

1 cup onion, finely chopped   ½ cup lemon juice
1 clove garlic, minced   ¼ cup Worcestershire sauce
¼ cup vegetable oil   ⅓ cup brown sugar, firmly packed
2 tablespoons chili powder   2 tablespoons prepared mustard
2 teaspoons cumin seed, crushed   1 tablespoon celery seed, crushed
2 cups ketchup   2 tablespoons butter
1 cup cider or white vinegar

Sauté onion and garlic in oil in large saucepan until golden and tender, about 10 minutes. Stir in chili powder and cook 1 minute. Add remaining ingredients except butter; bring to boil. Reduce heat. Simmer uncovered, stirring often, 30 minutes. Stir in butter.

Liver Birds

Delicious

Preheat oven 350°   Serves 3 to 4

6 to 8 slices baby beef or   6 to 8 strips bacon
    calves liver   1 8-ounce can tomato sauce

Remove membranes from liver slices. Lay strips of bacon on top of liver. Roll into pin wheel. Secure with toothpick through middle. Place in 6 x 8-inch baking dish side by side with pin wheel facing up. Pour tomato sauce over all. Bake 45 minutes.

Phyllo Filet of Beef
With Madeira sauce

Preheat oven 400°   Serves 6

3 pounds filet mignon, trimmed   2 shallots, minced
Salt   1 package phyllo pastry
2 tablespoons sweet butter   ½ cup butter, melted
½ pound mushrooms, minced

Rub filet with salt. Melt butter in heavy skillet and sear meat over high heat on all sides. Set aside. In same pan, sauté mushrooms and shallots until soft, 2 to 3 minutes. Set aside. Layer 12 pieces phyllo pastry together, brushing each layer with melted butter. Spread ½ mushroom mixture on pastry and place beef on top. Place remaining mushrooms on top of filet and fold phyllo dough around beef. Prepare additional 5 to 6 layers phyllo pastry, each brushed with butter. Seal all edges by overlapping with additional pastry. Brush with butter. Place beef in buttered 9 x 13-inch baking pan and bake 40 to 45 minutes until pastry is browned and flaky. Remove beef to serving dish and serve with Madeira sauce.

Madeira Sauce

                                       Yields 1½ cups

3 tablespoons butter   1 teaspoon Kitchen Bouquet or Bovril
1½ tablespoons flour   ¼ cup Madeira
¾ cup beef stock

Melt butter, stir in flour and cook 5 minutes. Add beef stock, Kitchen Bouquet and Madeira. Cook until thickened.

Tip: **May be made ahead and sliced to serve cold for buffet or elegant picnic.**

Soak bacon in cold water for a few minutes before placing in skillet. This will lessen the tendency to shrink and curl.

Picadillo
Hearty Cuban dish

Serves 4

2 tablespoons olive oil
1 teaspoon garlic powder
1 cup onion, chopped
1 cup green pepper, chopped
1 pound ground beef
1 15½-ounce can tomatoes,
    chopped and undrained

2 small potatoes, peeled and cubed
1 tablespoon salt
1 teaspoon pepper
1 egg, hard-boiled and chopped
¼ cup Spanish olives, chopped
¼ cup raisins (optional)
¼ cup white wine (optional)
2 cups cooked white rice

Heat oil in 10-inch iron skillet. Add garlic powder, onion and green pepper. Sauté 10 minutes. Add ground beef. Cook 5 minutes, stirring often. Add remaining ingredients except rice. Cook 5 minutes on high. Reduce heat to medium. Cook until thick enough to hold its shape on spoon. Serve with rice.

Oriental Liver
For liver haters

Serves 4 to 6

¼ cup flour
1½ teaspoons salt
¼ teaspoon pepper
1½ pounds beef liver
2 tablespoons oil
2 medium onions, thinly sliced

1 green pepper, cut lengthwise into
    strips
1 tomato, cut into wedges
1½ cups water
1 teaspoon instant beef broth

Mix flour, salt and pepper. Cut liver into serving-size pieces. Coat with flour mixture. Sauté liver in hot oil in large skillet 4 minutes on each side. Remove from pan. Sauté onions and pepper strips in same skillet, adding more oil if needed. Stir in tomato and sauté 2 minutes longer. Remove from pan. Add water and instant beef broth to skillet. Bring to boil, stirring and scraping pan. Return liver and vegetables to pan with broth and heat through. Serve over rice or Chinese noodles.

Beef

Fillet in Shirtsleeves
Impressive

Preheat oven 425°   Serves 6

1 beef tenderloin
Salt
Freshly ground black pepper
Dried thyme
Butter, softened
1 large onion, finely chopped
2 tablespoons butter, melted

2 tablespoons olive oil
½ pound mushrooms, finely chopped
2 slices ham, cooked and finely
    chopped
½ cup walnuts, chopped
1 pound commercial puff pastry
1 egg yolk, beaten

Season beef generously with salt, pepper and thyme. Brush with softened butter and roast for 20 minutes or until beef is half cooked. Baste with pan juices after 10 minutes. Cool and remove cords. Sauté onion in 2 tablespoons butter and oil, stirring constantly until onion is transparent. Add mushrooms and continue to cook, stirring until liquid has almost evaporated, about 5 minutes. Add ham and walnuts. Season with salt and pepper. Cook 1 minute more. Cool. Spread cooled beef generously with onion-ham mixture. Brush with softened butter. Roll puff pastry into sheet large enough to encase meat. If desired, puff pastry may be rolled out to encase individual fillet slices. Wrap beef in pastry, cutting away excess. Secure neatly. Roll remaining pastry thinly. Cut "leaves" and "flowers" from pastry and adhere to wrapped meat with egg yolk. Place beef on baking sheet. Brush pastry with water; cover leaves and flowers with aluminum foil to keep from becoming too brown. Bake 10 minutes. Brush pastry slightly with egg yolk. Reduce heat to 375° and continue baking until crust is browned, 10 to 15 minutes.

Tip: **Ask butcher to trim off outside membrane and excess fat from beef tenderloin. The piece should be about 12 inches long, 3 inches in diameter and weigh 3 pounds. Have meat tied with cord at 3-inch intervals around circumference.**

Sauerbraten
Marinate 2 days

Preheat oven 400°   Serves 8 to 10

5 to 6 pounds sirloin tip roast   2 tablespoons butter
1½ tablespoons sea salt   1 tablespoon olive oil
1 onion, sliced   2½ tablespoons whole wheat flour
10 peppercorns   2 tablespoons honey
3 bay leaves   ¾ cup natural ginger and honey snaps,
2 cups water   crushed
1 cup raw unpasteurized apple   ½ cup red wine
 · cider vinegar   ½ cup sour cream

Wipe meat. Rub with sea salt and place in crock or glass bowl. Reserve unused salt. Mix onion, peppercorns, bay leaves, water and vinegar. Pour over meat. Add more water if necessary in order to cover meat. Marinate in refrigerator 36 to 48 hours. Turn meat twice a day. Remove meat from liquid. Set liquid aside. Heat butter and olive oil in skillet and brown meat on all sides. Remove meat from skillet and place in roasting pan. Brown flour in skillet with drippings. Add honey, ginger snaps, remaining sea salt and reserved marinade. Cook until smooth and creamy. Remove bay leaves from sauce. Roast meat allowing 20 to 30 minutes per pound. Do not pour sauce over meat all at once but baste frequently. Add wine to meat ½ hour before end of roasting time. Remove meat to platter. Add sour cream to sauce. Slice and serve with sauce poured over meat or serve sauce on side.

Tip: **Raw unpasteurized vinegar and natural snaps are found in health food stores.**

Pork

Grilled Pork Chops
Florida style

Grill   Serves 6

1¼ cups beef broth   6 tablespoons soy sauce
1¼ cups water   ½ teaspoon ginger
2 to 3 cloves garlic, minced   ½ teaspoon dry mustard
1 teaspoon onion, minced   2 large bay leaves
2 tablespoons Worcestershire sauce   6 lean pork chops

Combine all ingredients except chops and simmer 1 minute. Cool. Place chops in 13 x 9 x 2-inch glass baking dish. Pour marinade over chops. Refrigerate overnight, turning several times. Broil in oven 15 to 20 minutes or charcoal on grill 1 hour for well done. Baste often while cooking.

Peking Pork
Serve immediately

                                     Serves 6

6 pork chops   2 cups celery, sliced
2 tablespoons shortening   1 large green pepper, chopped
½ teaspoon salt   2 tablespoons cornstarch
¼ cup soy sauce   ¼ cup water
3 tablespoons honey   6 to 8 green onions, chopped
1 clove garlic, minced   1 6-ounce can water chestnuts,
½ teaspoon ginger   drained and sliced
½ cup boiling water   1 4-ounce jar pimientos, sliced
                                     1 6-ounce package Chinese pea pods

Brown chops in shortening in frying pan. Chop meat into bite-size pieces. Pour off drippings and salt meat. Reduce heat; cover and cook 30 minutes. Combine soy sauce, honey, garlic and ginger. Bring to boil. Pour over pork. Cover and cook slowly 15 to 30 minutes or until meat is tender. Pour boiling water over celery and green pepper in saucepan. Cover and cook 2 to 3 minutes. Drain vegetables. Remove pork to heated platter. Add enough water to liquid in frying pan to make 1 cup. Combine cornstarch and water. Stir into liquid in pan and cook, stirring until thickened. Stir in celery, green pepper, green onions, water chestnuts, pimiento and pea pods, separating the pods. Cook slowly until vegetables are heated through, 2 to 3 minutes. Mix with pork. Serve over rice.

Chinese Barbeque Ribs
Interesting change

Preheat oven 350°   Serves 4

1 10-ounce jar damson plum or   ⅓ cup soy sauce
  red plum jelly   2 cloves garlic, minced
⅓ cup dark Karo syrup   2 pounds spareribs, cut into
¼ cup onion, chopped   serving-size pieces
2 teaspoons ginger

Heat first 6 ingredients in 2–quart saucepan. Pour over ribs. Cover and
marinate overnight. Place on rack in foil-lined pan. Bake 1 hour, turning and
basting frequently.

Florida Lemon Chops Supreme
Easy family recipe

Preheat oven 350°   Serves 4

4 lean pork chops, ¾-inch thick   4 to 8 slices onion
1 cup water   8 tablespoons brown sugar
1 large lemon, sliced   4 to 8 tablespoons ketchup

Place pork chops in single layer in 9 x 13-inch glass baking dish. Do not
overlap. Pour in water. Place 1 slice lemon, 1 to 2 onion slices, 2 tablespoons
brown sugar and 1 to 2 tablespoons ketchup on each chop. Cover with
aluminum foil and bake 1 hour. Uncover and bake 30 minutes. Add more
water if needed. Remove lemon slices before serving.

Forty Thieves Ham Steak
Tangy and tasty

Grill   Serves 4

1 ham slice, ¾ to 1-inch thick   1 tablespoon prepared mustard
½ cup currant jelly   ½ cup apple juice

Grill ham steak over low flame of open fire until well heated. Place ham in pan
and cover with mixture of jelly, mustard and apple juice. Cook in pan on grill
15 minutes on each side.

Pork

Pork with Spicy Apples
The family will love it

Preheat oven 350°   Serves 6

6 pork chops, 1-inch thick   ¼ teaspoon nutmeg
¼ cup butter   ½ teaspoon cinnamon
2 tablespoons steak sauce   1½ tablespoons lemon juice
6 cups baking apples, sliced   ¾ cup brown sugar
½ teaspoon lemon rind, grated   ½ cup hot water

Brown chops in skillet in 2 tablespoons butter. Remove chops and place in 9 x 13-inch baking dish. Pour steak sauce over chops. Mix apples, lemon rind, spices, lemon juice and sugar. Place over chops. Dot with remaining butter. Add hot water. Cover and bake 30 minutes. Uncover and continue baking approximately 30 minutes longer or until chops are tender.

Sicilian Pork
Good way to use leftover pork

Serves 4 to 5

1 medium onion, chopped   1¼ teaspoons salt
1 clove garlic, minced   ¼ teaspoon pepper
1 tablespoon shortening, melted   Pinch thyme
1 16-ounce can tomatoes, cut up   1 10-ounce package frozen green
½ cup ketchup   beans, thawed or 1 16-ounce can,
2 tablespoons vinegar   drained
                                    2 cups pork, cooked and diced

Sauté onion and garlic 5 minutes in shortening. Add tomatoes, ketchup, vinegar, salt, pepper and thyme and simmer 15 minutes. Add beans and pork. Cover and simmer 15 minutes. Serve over noodles or hot macaroni ring.

Pork Loin Scaloppine
Preparation is last minute

Serves 4

1½ pounds pork loin scallops,
   thinly sliced
Salt and pepper
Flour
½ cup butter

½ teaspoon garlic, minced
½ pound fresh mushrooms, sliced
1 cup dry white wine
2 tablespoons parsley, minced

Pound scallops as thin as possible. Season with salt and pepper. Dust with flour. In large frying pan, heat 4 tablespoons butter until golden. Quickly brown scallops. Place on hot platter and keep warm. In same pan, sauté garlic and mushrooms in 2 tablespoons butter. Add wine and stir to dissolve brown bits. Over high heat, reduce liquid to about ½ cup. Swirl in remaining butter. Pour sauce over warm meat. Garnish with parsley and serve immediately.

Pork Roast with Cherry Glaze
Special enough for company

Preheat oven 350°

Serves 4

1 3- to 5-pound pork roast

Cherry Glaze

1 12-ounce jar cherry preserves
¼ cup red wine vinegar
¼ teaspoon cinnamon
¼ teaspoon ground cloves

2 tablespoons corn syrup
¼ teaspoon salt
¼ teaspoon nutmeg

Cook roast 2 hours. While roast is cooking, combine glaze ingredients in small saucepan. Bring to boil and simmer 5 minutes. Drain grease from roast. Pour glaze over roast and cook 30 minutes or until done.

Pork

Ham Rolls Continental
Great for a luncheon

Preheat oven 350°

Serves 6

6 slices boiled ham
6 slices Swiss cheese
1 10-ounce package frozen broccoli
  spears, thawed
1 cup onion, sliced
2 tablespoons butter

2 tablespoons flour
½ teaspoon salt
Dash pepper
¼ teaspoon basil
1 cup milk

Top ham slices with cheese. Place broccoli spear on each slice and roll. Secure with toothpick. Place in shallow baking dish. Cook onion slices in butter until tender; blend in flour and seasonings. Gradually add milk; stir until thickened. Pour over ham rolls. Cover and bake 25 to 30 minutes.

Tasty Ham Loaf with Glaze
Super way to use leftover ham

Preheat oven 350°

Serves 6

1 cup whole milk
2 cups corn flake cereal, crushed
1 small onion, grated
1½ pounds cooked ham, ground

½ pound lean pork, uncooked and
  ground
2 eggs, well beaten
2 teaspoons parsley, chopped
⅛ teaspoon black pepper

Pour milk over cereal and set aside. In bowl, mix onion with ham and pork. Add eggs, parsley and pepper. Combine with reserved cereal. Place in shallow 10 x 2-inch oval pan and mold into loaf. Bake 1½ hours. Baste with glaze frequently during first 15 minutes of baking and then periodically throughout remaining baking time.

Glaze

1 cup brown sugar
½ cup water

½ cup cider vinegar
1 tablespoon prepared mustard

Mix sugar, water, vinegar and mustard in saucepan. Cook over medium heat until well blended and sugar has dissolved.

Barbequed Leg of Lamb

Even lamb haters like this dish

Grill

Serves 8

1 leg of lamb, boned
2 tablespoons dry mustard
1 teaspoon soy sauce
2 teaspoons brown sugar

2 cups Miracle French dressing
1 teaspoon onion salt
1 teaspoon ginger

Flatten lamb as much as possible. Mix remaining ingredients. Marinate lamb in sauce 3 hours or more at room temperature. Grill ½ hour on each side, basting with sauce. Best cooked slightly pink or rare.

Charcoal Broiled Butterflied Leg of Lamb

A summertime "pleaser" for company

Grill

Serves 6

1 5- to 6-pound leg of lamb, boned
  and butterflied

1 onion, sliced

Marinade

1 cup olive oil
⅓ cup white wine
2 tablespoons lemon juice
1 tablespoon dried rosemary,
  crushed

1 teaspoon salt
2 cloves garlic, minced
Pepper to taste

Sauce

6 tablespons butter, melted
1 teaspoon dried rosemary, crushed

Salt and pepper to taste

Combine marinade ingredients in large, shallow glass or ceramic dish. Add lamb and onion. Cover and marinate overnight, turning once or twice. Drain meat. Combine sauce ingredients. Grill lamb over hot coals, turning and basting often with sauce, 25 to 30 minutes or until done to taste.

Tip: Leftovers can be ground and used for moussaka.

Lamb

Chutney Lamb Shanks
Cold weather dish

Preheat oven 300°   Serves 6 to 8

12 lamb shanks   ¼ cup brown sugar
1 cup ketchup   2 tablespoons Worcestershire sauce
1 cup water   2 tablespoons lemon juice
1 large onion, chopped   ¼ cup chutney
2 celery stalks, chopped   ½ teaspoon salt

Brown lamb shanks under broiler. Drain excess fat. Place lamb in large Dutch oven. Mix remaining ingredients and boil 10 minutes. Pour over meat. Cover and bake 4 hours. Turn and baste occasionally. Meat should be falling off bone; sauce will be dark when done. Serve on bed of rice.

Zippy Lamb Shanks
Barbeque flavor

Preheat oven 325°   Serves 4

4 lamb shanks   1 cup celery, chopped
Salt and pepper   1 12-ounce bottle chili sauce
¼ cup butter   1 cup water
1 medium onion, sliced   1 tablespoon Worcestershire sauce
1 clove garlic, minced

Trim excess fat from shanks. Season shanks with salt and pepper; brown in butter in roasting pan. In saucepan, combine onion, garlic, celery, chili sauce, water and Worcestershire sauce. Cover sauce and simmer 10 minutes, stirring often. Cover lamb shanks with sauce and bake approximately 2 hours, or until tender.

Cheesy Veal Bake
Delicious company meal

Preheat oven 350°   Serves 6

1½ cups fine dry bread crumbs
1 cup Parmesan cheese, grated
½ cup parsley, finely chopped
4 small cloves garlic, minced
6 veal chops, ¾-inch thick
⅓ cup salad oil
2 cups tomato or V-8 juice

1 6-ounce can tomato paste
1 tablespoon sugar
1 teaspoon salt
¼ teaspoon pepper
1 teaspoon oregano
1 envelope onion soup mix
6 slices Swiss cheese (optional)

Mix bread crumbs, Parmesan cheese, parsley and 2 cloves garlic. Dip veal chops in salad oil, then in crumb mixture. Set oil aside. Place chops in greased, shallow 13 x 9 x 2-inch baking dish. Mix reserved salad oil and crumb mixture; set aside. Combine tomato or V-8 juice, tomato paste, sugar, salt, pepper, oregano and 2 cloves garlic. Bring to boil. Add onion soup mix. Pour over chops. Top with reserved crumb mixture. Bake uncovered 45 to 60 minutes. Remove from oven and place Swiss cheese on top. Bake until cheese melts.

Crab Veal Oscar
Easy and elegant for company

Preheat oven 300°   Serves 4

1½ pounds veal tenderloin, trimmed
¼ cup flour
¾ teaspoon salt
Dash pepper
12 ounces crabmeat

1 egg, well beaten
½ cup bread crumbs
4 tablespoons butter, melted
½ cup sauterne
1 cup Bernaise sauce

Cut tenderloin into 8 pieces. Flatten with mallet. Combine flour, salt and pepper. Coat veal in flour mixture. Set aside. Dip crabmeat in same flour mixture, then in egg. Roll in bread crumbs. Set aside. Sauté veal in 2 tablespoons butter until golden brown. Remove to warm platter. Add sauterne to veal juices. Simmer 1 minute. Pour over veal. Place uncovered in oven. In another skillet, fry crab in 2 tablespoons butter until brown. Remove and also place in oven to keep warm. Prepare Bernaise sauce. Pour 1 tablespoon sauce over veal. Top with crab. Pass remaining sauce.

Veal

Veal Medallions Pierre
Guests will ask for "seconds"

Preheat oven 550°

Serves 4 to 6

12 2- to 3-ounce veal medallions
Salt to taste
¼ teaspoon white pepper
Flour
2 tablespoons butter
3 shallots or ½ onion, chopped

1 cup dry white wine
1½ cups whipping cream
1 tablespoon fresh or dry tarragon, chopped
3 to 4 ounces imported Swiss cheese, sliced

Flatten veal very thin. Salt and pepper veal; dredge in flour. Place butter in preheated saucepan and sauté medallions on both sides until golden brown. Place on 12 to 14-inch serving platter and keep hot. Remove excess fat from skillet; add shallots or onion and cook 10 minutes. Add wine and cook over high heat until liquid is ¼ original volume. Add cream and cook until reduced to ½ original volume or until sauce coats spoon. Taste for seasoning. Add tarragon and cook 2 minutes. If sauce is too thin, thicken with 1 teaspoon cornstarch diluted with wine. Pour sauce over veal and arrange cheese on top, covering meat. Place platter under broiler and let cheese melt about 2 minutes or until very soft. Serve at once.

Canadian Bacon Divan
Super quick and tasty

Preheat oven 375°

Serves 4 to 5

1 10¾-ounce can Cheddar cheese soup, undiluted
1 4-ounce can mushrooms, drained and sliced

2 10-ounce packages frozen broccoli spears, cooked
10 slices Canadian bacon, ¼-inch thick
1 3-ounce can onion rings

Combine soup and mushrooms. Cook over low heat until boiling. Place broccoli in bottom of 7 x 10-inch baking dish. Arrange bacon slices on top. Pour cheese sauce over bacon and broccoli. Bake 25 minutes. Cover with onion rings; bake 5 minutes.

Apricot-Chicken Kiev
From Russia with love

Serves 8

8 dried apricots
⅔ cup orange juice
4 whole chicken breasts, skinned,
  boned and halved

⅓ cup almonds, toasted and chopped
5 tablespoons butter, softened

Marinate apricots in orange juice 10 minutes. Place chicken between waxed paper and flatten. Remove apricots from orange juice; reserve juice. Chop apricots; combine with almonds and butter. Divide apricot mixture into 8 portions; roll into balls and place in freezer.

Glaze

⅓ cup wine vinegar
1 tablespoon orange rind, grated
⅔ cup apricot preserves
1 teaspoon dry mustard

1 teaspoon ginger
½ teaspoon salt
1 tablespoon soy sauce
⅔ cup reserved orange juice

Combine all ingredients. Simmer in saucepan 30 minutes. Set aside.

Batter

⅓ cup flour
1½ teaspoons salt
1 teaspoon water

2 eggs, slightly beaten
1 cup bread crumbs
2 cups oil

Remove apricot balls from freezer. Place on wide side of each chicken breast. Roll up, folding in ends to enclose filling completely. Fasten with toothpicks. Mix flour and 1 teaspoon salt. Set aside. Mix water, ½ teaspoon salt and eggs. Dip rolled breasts in flour mixture, then in egg mixture. Coat well with bread crumbs. Fry in oil until brown, 10 to 15 minutes, turning often.

Garnish

3 ounces cream cheese
1 tablespoon apricot juice

3 tablespoons almonds, toasted
12 canned apricot halves

Arrange chicken on platter; cover with glaze. Mix cream cheese, apricot juice and almonds. Stuff apricot halves. Place on platter with chicken kiev.

Asparagus Chicken
Asparagus makes chicken special

Preheat oven 350°   Serves 6

3 whole chicken breasts, halved   2 cups chicken broth
¼ cup oil   ½ cup heavy cream
4 tablespoons butter, melted   ½ teaspoon Tabasco
¼ cup flour   1 16-ounce can asparagus
½ teaspoon salt   ½ cup Parmesan cheese, grated

Brown chicken in oil. In saucepan, add flour and salt to butter. Stir in chicken broth and cook until thick. Remove from heat; add cream and Tabasco. Place asparagus in bottom of 9 x 13-inch casserole. Arrange chicken on top of asparagus. Pour sauce over chicken and asparagus. Sprinkle with cheese. Bake 40 minutes.

Breast of Chicken Queen Elizabeth
Make for any royalty

                                     Serves 6

3 whole chicken breasts   1 teaspoon shallots, chopped
6 thin slices ham   ⅓ cup dry white wine
6 thin slices Swiss cheese   4 to 5 firm tomatoes
1 egg, beaten   1 cup sweet cream
½ cup flour   Parsley, chopped
3 tablespoons butter, melted   Rice, cooked
½ pound small mushrooms   Truffles, sliced
                                    Watercress

Separate top and bottom fillet of chicken breast. Flatten smaller fillet, which is thicker, to same size as upper one. Put ham and cheese slices on top of fillets. Fold in half. Moisten edges with egg to hold together securely. Roll in flour and shake off excess. In shallow pan, sauté fillets in butter 10 to 12 minutes, or until golden brown on 1 side. Turn and continue to sauté until meat is cooked through. Transfer chicken to serving platter and keep warm. To remaining butter add mushrooms, shallots and wine and cook until liquid is reduced to half. Peel tomatoes, cut in half and squeeze gently to remove seeds and juice. Discard seeds and juice. Chop tomatoes and add to mushroom mixture. Cook for few minutes. Add cream and cook until cream is reduced to half. Pour cream sauce over chicken and sprinkle with parsley. Around chicken arrange 6 small molds of rice topped with slice of truffle and garnish with watercress.

Breast of Chicken with Wild Rice
Luscious

Serves 6

6 whole chicken breasts, skinned
   and boned
Salt to taste
Freshly ground pepper
3 tablespoons butter
2 medium onions, chopped
4 carrots, cut in thirds

1 clove garlic
2 celery stalks
3 large mushrooms, chopped
4 ounces sherry
4 ounces cognac
2 cups whipping cream
3 cups cooked wild rice

Season breasts with salt and pepper. Place all ingredients except wild rice in buttered, heavy frying pan. Cover and simmer slowly until breasts are done, about 1 hour. Remove celery stalks and garlic. Serve over rice.

Brunswick Stew
Great for Florida winter nights

Serves 8 to 10

1 2½- to 3-pound chicken
6 slices bacon, cooked and
   crumbled
2 onions, chopped
1 10-ounce package lima beans
1 cup whole kernel corn
4 potatoes, diced

1 1-pound can tomatoes, chopped
¼ cup butter
1½ tablespoons salt
½ teaspoon pepper
1 tablespoon sugar
1¼ teaspoons Tabasco

Cook chicken in large kettle 45 minutes. Remove chicken; cool and remove meat from bone. Return meat to broth. Add remaining ingredients. Cook over low heat 2 hours or longer, stirring occasionally.

One-half chicken breast is 160 calories and a single drumstick is only 88 calories. If there is reason to count calories, remove skin.

Chicken Accent
Surprise your unexpected guests

Preheat oven 350°   Serves 8 to 10

2 14½-ounce cans asparagus   8 ounces Cheddar cheese, shredded
  spears, drained   ¼ teaspoon Tabasco
6 whole chicken breasts, cooked   2 tablespoons soy sauce
  and cut up   ½ teaspoon pepper
1 medium onion, chopped   1 teaspoon Accent
1 4-ounce can mushrooms, drained   2 tablespoons pimiento
½ cup butter, melted   ½ cup pecans, chopped
¾ cup evaporated milk   Hot cooked rice

Place asparagus in greased 9 x 13-inch pan. Cover with chicken pieces. Sauté onion and mushrooms in butter. Add remaining ingredients except pecans and rice. Simmer until cheese melts. Pour sauce over chicken. Sprinkle pecans on top. Bake 35 to 45 minutes. Serve over hot rice.

Chicken and Green Noodles
Colorful

Preheat oven 375°   Serves 8

1 12-ounce package green noodles   1 8-ounce can mushroom pieces and
  or regular egg noodles   stems, undrained
3 pounds chicken   Dash mace
½ cup white wine   Salt and pepper to taste
1 cup milk   Parmesan cheese, grated
⅓ cup butter, melted   Paprika
½ cup flour

Cook noodles in boiling water until tender; drain. Boil chicken in water 30 minutes; reserve broth. Remove chicken from bone and cut into bite-size pieces. Set aside. Combine wine, milk and enough broth to make 3 cups liquid. Set aside. Combine butter and flour. Add to reserved liquid and cook, stirring, until mixture boils and thickens. Add mushrooms with liquid, mace, salt and pepper. Spread noodles in greased 12 x 8-inch baking dish. Place chicken on noodles; pour sauce over chicken. Sprinkle with cheese and paprika. Bake 25 minutes.

Chicken and Mushrooms
Excellent for leftover chicken

Serves 6

2 tablespoons vegetable oil
½ to ¾ pound fresh mushrooms,
  sliced
1 cup onion, chopped
1 cup celery, sliced
2 cups strong chicken broth or
  bouillon

1 16-ounce can tomatoes, crushed
½ to ⅔ cup rice, uncooked
3 bay leaves
3 cups chicken, cooked and cubed
Salt and ground pepper to taste

Heat oil in large iron skillet or pot. Add mushrooms, onion and celery; cook until tender. Add remaining ingredients. Bring to boil. Reduce heat; cover and simmer until rice is cooked, about 45 minutes. Remove bay leaves and serve.

Chicken Breasts Piquant
Oriental flair

Preheat oven 375°

Serves 4

1½ cups dry red wine
½ cup soy sauce
½ cup salad oil
4 tablespoons water
2 cloves garlic, sliced

2 teaspoons ground ginger
½ teaspoon oregano
2 tablespoons brown sugar
2 whole chicken breasts, halved

Combine all ingredients except chicken breasts. Arrange chicken breasts in 2½-quart baking dish. Pour mixture over top. Cover and bake 1 hour.

Poultry is high in nutrition and low in calories and cost. One-half chicken breast will give 61% of the protein needed daily. Two drumsticks supply 56% of daily protein requirements.

Chicken in White Wine
Elegant and easy

Serves 6

3 whole chicken breasts, halved
8 tablespoons butter
½ tablespoon peanut oil
3 tablespoons flour

Salt and white pepper to taste
½ cup chicken broth
½ cup white wine
½ cup whipping cream

Clean and remove skin and fat from chicken breasts. Heat 5 tablespoons butter and peanut oil in heavy skillet. Add chicken breasts and cook 8 to 10 minutes on each side. Chicken should be white and lightly golden. Remove chicken and keep warm in serving dish. In medium saucepan, melt remaining butter and blend flour, salt and white pepper to taste. Stir in chicken broth and heat until smooth and thickened. Add white wine and stir until smooth; simmer 2 minutes. Add cream and heat. Pour over chicken. Serve with white rice or boiled spring potatoes.

Chicken Stew with Parsley Dumplings
Your family will want this again and again

Serves 4 to 6

2½ to 3 pounds chicken pieces
4½ cups water
1 cup onion, chopped
5 teaspoons chicken flavor instant
  bouillon or 5 chicken flavor
  bouillon cubes
¼ teaspoon pepper

2 cups carrots, sliced
⅓ cup flour
1½ cups celery, sliced
2 cups Bisquick baking mix
⅔ cup milk
1 tablespoon parsley, chopped

Bring chicken, 4 cups water, onion, bouillon and pepper to boil in 4-quart Dutch oven. Reduce heat. Simmer uncovered 30 minutes. Remove skin from chicken if desired. Add carrots; simmer 10 minutes. Mix flour and ½ cup water. Stir flour mixture and celery into chicken mixture. Cook, stirring constantly, until thickened. Mix Bisquick, milk and parsley until soft dough forms. Drop by spoonfuls onto boiling stew. Cook uncovered over low heat 10 minutes. Cover and cook 10 minutes.

Chicken Julienne Paprika
A delicious entrée

Serves 4

2 whole chicken breasts, boned
   and skinned
¾ teaspoon salt
¼ to ½ teaspoon ground pepper
4 teaspoons cornstarch
4 teaspoons olive oil
1 egg white, unbeaten
1 cup sour cream
¼ teaspoon salt

½ cup butter, melted
½ cup green onion with tops, minced
½ pound mushrooms, thinly sliced
½ cup dry white wine
2 to 4 teaspoons paprika
2 large cloves garlic, pressed
½ cup watercress, chopped
Watercress sprigs

Pound chicken breasts between waxed paper until ½-inch thick. Cut breasts into ½-inch slivers. Place chicken in shallow pan and sprinkle with salt, pepper, cornstarch, olive oil and egg white. Turn pieces to cover evenly. Let stand 20 minutes. Combine ½ cup sour cream and ¼ teaspoon salt in serving bowl. In large skillet over medium high heat, sauté chicken in butter until slightly golden, about 5 minutes. Remove with slotted spoon. Add onion and mushrooms to pan. Over high heat, sauté until mushrooms are tender. Add wine, paprika and garlic and stir until liquid is reduced to about 2 tablespoons. Remove from heat and cool slightly. Return to low heat. Stir in chicken, remaining ½ cup sour cream, salt and pepper to season. Stir to mix; heat through. Remove from heat and sprinkle with chopped watercress. Garnish with watercress sprigs and serve at once. Pass salted sour cream.

Diet Chicken
Low calorie entrée

Preheat oven 350°

Serves 4 to 6

⅔ cup powdered milk
½ teaspoon pepper
2 teaspoons dry chicken bouillon
½ teaspoon dry mustard

1 teaspoon salt
2 teaspoons paprika
1 teaspoon poultry seasoning
1 2½- to 3-pound frying chicken, cut
   in pieces

Shake dry ingredients in bag to mix thoroughly. Add chicken and shake to coat. Arrange in 9 x 13-inch baking dish. Bake uncovered 1 hour.

Chicken Narragansett

Preheat oven 350°   Serves 6 to 8

4 whole chicken breasts, boned,   Creamy Italian salad dressing
  skinned and halved   Seasoned stuffing mix, finely ground

Place chicken breasts in shallow 2-quart casserole. Cover with salad dressing. Cover and marinate 5 hours or overnight. Roll breasts in stuffing mix. Bake uncovered 45 minutes to 1 hour.

Rice and Gravy

1 12-ounce jar chicken gravy   2 cups cooked rice
1 10¾-ounce can cream of
  mushroom soup

Mix chicken gravy with cream of mushroom soup. Heat and serve over rice and chicken.

Chicken Parmesan
With gravy

Preheat oven 350°   Serves 8 to 10

¾ cup bread crumbs   8 whole chicken breasts, boned and
¼ teaspoon garlic powder   halved
1½ teaspoons salt   ½ cup butter, melted
White pepper to taste   1⅓ cups chicken broth, heated
¾ cup Parmesan cheese, grated   1½ tablespoons cornstarch
                                     Water

Mix bread crumbs, garlic powder, salt, pepper and Parmesan cheese. Dip chicken breasts in butter, then in crumb mixture. Coat thoroughly. Place in lightly buttered baking dish and drizzle remaining butter over breasts. Bake 1 hour. Pour chicken broth into pan after removing cooked chicken. Stir to loosen all crusty particles. Continue heating on top of stove and thicken with thin cornstarch paste. Cook about 5 minutes until clear. Pour gravy over chicken.

Chicken Polynesian
Prepare 1 day ahead

Preheat oven 350°

Serves 4

1 3-pound frying chicken
½ cup flour
1 teaspoon salt
½ teaspoon celery salt
½ teaspoon garlic salt

½ teaspoon nutmeg
¼ cup butter, melted
2½ cups pineapple, sliced or chunk,
   drain and reserve syrup
½ cup soy sauce
2 tablespoons sugar

Cut chicken into pieces and shake in bag with flour, salt, celery salt, garlic salt and nutmeg. Place chicken in 2½-quart casserole. Pour 2 tablespoons butter over chicken. Reserve 2 tablespoons in skillet. Combine reserved pineapple syrup with soy sauce and sugar and pour over chicken. Cover and bake 45 minutes, basting several times. Sauté pineapple in reserved butter until golden. Pour over chicken and bake 15 minutes. Cool and refrigerate overnight. Before serving, bake 30 minutes.

Chicken Spaghetti
Nice change

Serves 10

1 4½- to 5-pound chicken
5 cloves garlic
1 16-ounce box spaghetti
2 large onions, chopped
2 tablespoons bacon grease
2 tablespoons chili powder
2 teaspoons cumin seed

1 16-ounce can tomatoes
1 cup water
2 8-ounce cans mushrooms,
   drained and sliced
1 tablespoon salt
¾ teaspoon pepper
Dash red pepper or Tabasco (optional)

Boil chicken with 4 cloves garlic 1½ hours. Remove garlic; reserve broth. Dice chicken. Cook spaghetti in reserved chicken broth; drain. Cook onions and 1 clove minced garlic in bacon grease until onions are clear. Do not brown. Add chili powder and cumin seed (tied in cheesecloth bag). Add tomatoes and water. Boil 5 minutes. Add spaghetti, chicken, mushrooms, salt and pepper. Stir well; simmer 30 minutes. Add red pepper or Tabasco, if desired.

Poultry

Cranberry Chicken
Sweet and sour taste

Serves 4 to 6

1 clove garlic, minced
2 tablespoons salad oil
3 pounds chicken, cut up
1 teaspoon salt
¼ teaspoon pepper
1 16-ounce can whole cranberry
   sauce
¼ cup vinegar

1 tablespoon orange peel, grated
½ cup orange juice
2 tablespoons cornstarch
¾ cup water
1½ tablespoons soy sauce
1 green pepper, sliced
½ cup onion, sliced
Hot fluffy rice

Sauté garlic in oil. Sprinkle chicken with salt and pepper and brown in oil with garlic. Combine cranberry sauce, vinegar, orange peel and juice. Pour over chicken. Cover and simmer until chicken is tender, about 30 minutes. Remove chicken to warm platter. Blend cornstarch, water and soy sauce; stir into skillet drippings. Add green pepper and onion. Cook and stir until thick and clear and until vegetables are crisp-tender. Serve over chicken, with rice.

Tropical Chicken
Peachy

Serves 6

3 whole chicken breasts, halved
½ cup flour
1 teaspoon salt
1 teaspoon pepper
1 teaspoon paprika
½ cup shortening

1 cup orange juice
2 tablespoons brown sugar
2 tablespoons vinegar
1 teaspoon nutmeg
1 teaspoon dried basil
12 small potatoes, peeled
1 29-ounce can peaches, drained

Lightly coat chicken with combined flour, salt, pepper and paprika. Sauté chicken in shortening until golden brown on all sides. Drain shortening. Combine orange juice, brown sugar, vinegar, nutmeg and basil. Pour over chicken. Place potatoes around chicken pieces. Cover and cook over medium heat 25 to 30 minutes or until chicken and potatoes are tender. Five minutes before serving, add peaches and heat.

Chicken with Cashews
Oriental chicken

Preheat deep fryer 360°　　　　Serves 4

1½ cups unsalted cashews
Oil
2 teaspoons ginger, mashed
4 tablespoons soy sauce
1 tablespoon wine
1 pound boneless chicken, cubed
1 egg white
1 tablespoon cornstarch
1 cup bamboo shoots, cubed
1 cup green pepper, cut in 1-inch
　squares

½ cup dried black forest mushrooms,
　quartered, soaked in water and
　drained
1 clove garlic, mashed
¼ teaspoon salt
1 tablespoon sugar
Hot pepper to taste, diced (optional)
½ cup water or chicken broth
2 teaspoons cornstarch

Fry nuts in oil until golden. Remove nuts and set aside. Combine ginger, 3 tablespoons soy sauce and wine. Pour over chicken and marinate 1 hour or longer. Beat egg white; add cornstarch to form batter. Drop chicken in batter to coat. Fry chicken in ½ cup oil, until slightly brown. Remove. In ¼ cup oil, stir-fry bamboo shoots, green pepper, mushrooms, garlic, salt, 1 tablespoon soy sauce, sugar and hot pepper. Add chicken mixture and nuts. Stir. Combine water and 2 teaspoons cornstarch and pour over vegetable-chicken-nut mixture. Stir until well coated and serve.

Tip: Dried black forest mushrooms may be found in Oriental food store. Fresh or canned mushrooms may be substituted for dried.

Oven Barbequed Chicken
For people on the go

Preheat oven 350°　　　　Serves 6

½ cup soy sauce
1 cup butter, melted

1¼ cups orange juice
6 to 10 chicken pieces

Mix soy sauce, butter and orange juice in large casserole. Add chicken. Bake 1 to 1½ hours. Baste and turn periodically.

Poultry

Marinated Chicken
Great for grilling

Preheat oven 350°   Serves 6

2 2½- to 3-pound chickens   1½ teaspoons thyme leaves
1 cup dry sherry   1½ teaspoons basil leaves
¼ cup salad oil   1 teaspoon tarragon leaves
2 tablespoons parsley flakes   ½ teaspoon curry powder
2½ teaspoons salt   ½ teaspoon garlic powder
2 teaspoons paprika   ⅛ teaspoon ground black pepper

Cut chicken into serving pieces. Place chicken in tight-fitting container or
plastic bag; set aside. Combine remaining ingredients; pour over chicken.
Cover and refrigerate 12 hours or longer. Remove chicken from marinade.
Place on grill over hot charcoal. Broil 45 to 60 minutes, turning and basting
frequently. If desired, place skin side up on rack in roasting pan and bake 1
hour or until chicken is tender, basting frequently with marinade.

Company Elegant Chicken Delight
Can be made days ahead

Preheat oven 350°   Serves 6

1 9-ounce package frozen artichoke   ¾ cup chicken broth
  hearts, thawed   ¼ cup sherry
12 small new potatoes, pared   ½ teaspoon salt
3 whole chicken breasts, halved   Dash pepper
¼ cup flour   2 tomatoes, cut in wedges
½ cup butter, melted   1 green pepper, cut in thin rings
2 tablespoons green onion, chopped   ½ cup sour cream
1 6-ounce can mushroom crowns   1 tablespoon flour
  broiled in butter, undrained

Place artichokes and potatoes in 2½-quart casserole. Coat chicken breasts
with ¼ cup flour; brown in butter. Place on top of vegetables in casserole. In
same skillet, cook green onion until tender. Stir in mushroom crowns, broth
and sherry; pour over chicken. Sprinkle with salt and pepper. Cover and bake
1 hour. Add tomatoes and pepper rings and bake ½ hour. Remove contents to
serving platter. Blend sour cream and flour. Add to juices in casserole. Heat
and stir. Do not boil. Serve with vegetables and chicken.

Crab Stuffed Chicken Breasts
Florida treat

Preheat oven 375°   Serves 6

6 whole chicken breasts, skinned   1 7½-ounce can crabmeat,
  and boned   drained and flaked
Salt and pepper   ½ cup herb seasoned stuffing mix
½ cup onion, chopped   2 tablespoons flour
½ cup celery, chopped   ½ teaspoon paprika
5 tablespoons butter, melted   1 envelope Hollandaise sauce mix
5 tablespoons dry white wine   ¾ cup milk
                                     4 ounces Swiss cheese, shredded

Pound chicken to flatten. Sprinkle with salt and pepper. Cook onion and celery in 3 tablespoons butter until tender. Remove from heat. Add 3 tablespoons wine, crab and stuffing mix; toss. Divide mixture among breasts. Roll up and secure with toothpicks. Combine flour and paprika; coat chicken. Place in 12 x 8-inch baking dish. Drizzle with 2 tablespoons butter. Bake uncovered 1 hour. Transfer to platter. Blend Hollandaise sauce mix and milk; cook and stir until thickened. Add 2 tablespoons wine and cheese; stir until cheese melts. Pour ½ sauce on chicken. Pass remaining sauce.

Oven Pecan Chicken
Yummy

Preheat oven 350°   Serves 4 to 6

1 cup buttermilk   1 teaspoon salt
1 egg, lightly beaten   ⅛ teaspoon pepper
1 cup flour   1 teaspoon paprika
1 cup pecan meal   1 cup butter-flavored popcorn oil
¼ cup sesame seeds   2½ pounds frying chicken pieces

Mix buttermilk and egg in shallow dish. Mix flour, pecan meal, sesame seeds, salt, pepper and paprika in separate dish. Put oil in bowl. Dip chicken in egg mixture, then flour mixture, then oil. Place skin side up in 9 x 12-inch baking dish. Bake 45 minutes to 1 hour. Serve with wild pecan rice or wild rice.

Poultry

Grilled Chicken
Made for Florida sunshine

Grill   Serves 4

2 pounds chicken pieces

Marinade

1 cup fresh orange juice   1 teaspoon brown sugar
½ cup fresh grapefruit juice   1 teaspoon dried tarragon
¼ cup peanut oil   1 teaspoon ground pepper
1 clove garlic, crushed

Combine all marinade ingredients. Pour over chicken and marinate 3 hours, turning occasionally. Charcoal grill 45 to 60 minutes, turning and basting frequently. Serve with maltaise sauce.

Maltaise Sauce

4 egg yolks, whipped   2 tablespoons lemon juice
Pinch salt   3 tablespoons fresh orange juice
¾ cup unsalted butter, melted   1 teaspoon orange rind, grated

Combine egg yolks and salt. Gradually drizzle butter into egg yolks. When sauce has absorbed butter, add lemon juice. Before serving, add orange juice and rind.

Sour Cream Chicken
Melts in your mouth

Preheat oven 350°   Serves 6

2 cups sour cream   ½ teaspoon garlic, chopped (optional)
1 tablespoon Worcestershire sauce   1¼ teaspoons paprika
2 teaspoons salt   6 whole chicken breasts, boned
½ teaspoon Tabasco (optional)   Fine bread crumbs

Mix first 6 ingredients. Dip chicken in mixture and place in shallow 8 or 9-inch glass dish. Pour remaining mixture over chicken. Cover and place in refrigerator overnight. Roll chicken in bread crumbs to cover both sides. Shape breasts into round balls and place in baking dish. Cover and refrigerate at least 1½ hours. Bake 1¼ to 1½ hours.

Italian Chicken
With tomato sauce

Serves 6

6 whole chicken breasts, skinned
  and boned
2 eggs, beaten
1 cup Italian-style bread crumbs

¼ cup oil or 2 tablespoons oil plus
  2 tablespoons butter
6 slices Mozzarella cheese

Pound chicken breasts between waxed paper until thin. Dip chicken in egg and coat with bread crumbs. In large frying pan, sauté chicken in oil until browned. Top each chicken breast with slice of Mozzarella; cover and melt slightly. Serve with tomato sauce.

Tomato Sauce

1 large onion, finely chopped
2 cloves garlic, finely chopped
1 tablespoon butter
2 tablespoons oil
1 6-ounce can tomato paste
1 1-pound 13-ounce can Italian
  peeled tomatoes, mashed

2 bay leaves
4 tablespoons parsley, finely chopped
¼ teaspoon oregano
1 small strip lemon peel, chopped
⅓ cup dry white wine
¾ cup water
Salt and pepper to taste
1 tablespoon Worcestershire sauce

Sauté onion and garlic in butter and oil in frying pan until soft and transparent. Stir in tomato paste and cook 1 minute, stirring constantly. Add tomatoes, bay leaves, parsley, oregano, lemon peel, wine, water, salt and pepper. Simmer 1 hour, stirring occasionally. Stir in Worcestershire.

Chicken is cooked when:

Juices are no longer pink but not clear.

Fork tender. (Fork inserted with ease.)

Leg moves readily when lifted or twisted.

Thick muscle of drumstick feels soft to finger touch.

Meat thermometer inserted into thickest part of thigh muscle registers 190°, or inserted in stuffing registers 165°.

India Chicken Curry
Guests choose condiments for topping

Serves 8 to 10

½ cup onion, finely chopped
½ cup celery, finely chopped
¼ cup oil
⅓ cup flour
2 cups chicken stock
½ teaspoon Worcestershire sauce

Salt and pepper
1 teaspoon curry powder
4 cups chicken, cooked and cubed
1 cup tomato juice
4 cups cooked rice

Sauté onion and celery in oil in 3-quart saucepan. Add flour and blend. Slowly add chicken stock and stir until thickened. Add remaining ingredients except rice and warm thoroughly. Serve over hot rice or make ring mold of rice and fill center with curry.

Tip: Have these condiments available for guests to top curry: chopped peanuts, chopped onion, chopped celery, chopped carrots, chopped hard-cooked egg, crisp bacon pieces, toasted coconut and chutney.

Chicken D' Elegant
Everyone wants more of this

Preheat oven 350°

Serves 4 to 6

2 10-ounce packages frozen
  broccoli spears
2 cups chicken or turkey, cooked
  and diced
2 10½-ounce cans of cream of
  chicken soup, undiluted
1 cup mayonnaise

1 tablespoon lemon juice
½ teaspoon oregano
½ cup bread crumbs
1 tablespoon butter, melted
½ cup sharp Cheddar cheese,
  grated

Cook broccoli according to package directions until tender. Arrange broccoli in buttered 11½ x 7-inch baking dish. Place cooked chicken or turkey on top of broccoli. Combine soup, mayonnaise, lemon juice and oregano. Blend thoroughly and spread over chicken or turkey. Mix bread crumbs, butter and cheese. Sprinkle over casserole right before baking. Bake 35 to 50 minutes, uncovered.

Hot Brown Turkey
Cheesy

Preheat oven 425°   Serves 6

4 tablespoons butter, melted   1 pound turkey, thinly sliced
4 tablespoons flour   8 slices ham (optional)
2 cups milk   6 to 7 slices toast, trimmed
¾ cup Cheddar cheese, shredded   3 tomatoes, sliced
¼ teaspoon salt   10 strips bacon, partially cooked
½ teaspoon Worcestershire sauce   2 ounces Parmesan cheese, grated

Add flour to butter. Whisk in milk and cook until thickened. Add cheese, salt
and Worcestershire, stirring until smooth. Arrange turkey and ham on toast in
9 x 13-inch baking dish. Top with sauce, tomato slices and bacon. Sprinkle
with Parmesan cheese and bake 20 minutes or until bubbly.

Petto di Tacchino alla Napoletana
Turkey breast with Mozzarella and tomatoes

Preheat oven 375°   Serves 3 to 6

6 tablespoons butter   6 slices Mozzarella cheese
6 slices raw turkey breast (2 pounds)   3 large tomatoes, peeled and chopped
Salt and pepper to taste   Parsley, finely chopped
                                                            Basil

Melt 4 tablespoons butter in frying pan. Add turkey and fry until golden brown
on both sides. Sprinkle lightly with salt and pepper. Put turkey in 1 layer in 9 x
13-inch baking dish. Cover each slice of turkey with slice of cheese and
tomatoes. Dot with slivers of butter and bake 20 minutes, or until tomatoes are
cooked and cheese has melted. Sprinkle with parsley and basil.

**Save stock when poaching or stewing poultry. It makes great
soup bases and fondue.**

Stir-Fry Turkey
Get out your chopsticks

Serves 6

¼ cup oil
1½ cups turkey, cooked and cubed
1 medium onion, sliced
4 ounces fresh mushrooms, sliced
1 4-ounce can water chestnuts, cut in half, drain and reserve liquid
½ cup sherry

¼ cup soy sauce
1 tablespoon cornstarch
¼ to ½ teaspoon ground ginger
2 6-ounce packages frozen pea pods
2 cups hot fluffy rice or chow mein noodles

Heat oil in wok, electric frying pan or skillet at medium high heat. Add turkey, onion, mushrooms and water chestnuts. Stir-fry a few minutes until onion is tender and mushrooms are browned. In small bowl, mix liquid from water chestnuts, sherry, soy sauce, cornstarch and ginger. Blend well. Pour into turkey-vegetable mixture. Add pea pods. Mix well. Cover and simmer 5 to 7 minutes. Serve over rice or noodles.

Turkey Chili
Low cholesterol dish

Serves 6 to 8

1 pound ground turkey
1 large onion, chopped
2 tablespoons butter, melted
1 10¾-ounce can tomato soup, undiluted

1 16-ounce can kidney beans, undrained
½ teaspoon salt
1 to 1½ tablespoons chili powder
½ teaspoon Worcestershire sauce
1 beef bouillon cube

Brown meat and onion in butter. Cook until meat is done, about 10 minutes. Add remaining ingredients. Cover and simmer 20 minutes.

Turkey Rolls
Italian flair

Preheat oven 325°   Serves 6

3 slices ham, cooked
3 slices part-skim Mozzarella cheese
6 turkey breast slices (1 pound)
½ teaspoon Italian seasoning
⅓ cup dry seasoned bread crumbs

2 tablespoons Parmesan cheese, grated
2 tablespoons parsley, snipped
4 tablespoons Italian salad dressing
1 medium ripe tomato, sliced

Place ½ slice ham and Mozzarella on each turkey slice. Top with Italian seasoning. Roll and secure with toothpicks. Combine bread crumbs, Parmesan cheese and parsley. Dip turkey rolls in salad dressing and roll in crumb mixture. Place tomato slice on each roll. Place in shallow baking dish. Cover and bake 1 hour.

Ground Turkey Italian Sauce
For lasagne

Serves 10

1 pound ground turkey
1 cup onion, chopped
1 clove garlic, minced
2 tablespoons olive oil
2 tablespoons Italian seasoning

1 6-ounce can tomato paste
1 16-ounce can tomato sauce
1 beef bouillon cube
1 tablespoon red wine
½ cup carrot, shredded
½ cup water (optional)

Brown turkey, onion and garlic in olive oil in 10-inch skillet. Add remaining ingredients. Cover and simmer on low heat 30 minutes. Add water if sauce is too thick.

Tip: Use as you would a ground beef sauce.

Wild Duck Casserole
Use any wild fowl

Preheat oven 350°   Serves 4

2 wild ducks
1 onion, chopped
2 celery stalks, chopped
1 16-ounce box fast cooking
   long grain and wild rice
½ cup butter
½ cup onion, chopped

¼ cup flour
1 6-ounce can mushrooms, sliced and
   undrained
1½ cups light cream
1 tablespoon parsley, chopped
1½ teaspoons salt
¼ teaspoon pepper
1 package slivered almonds

Clean ducks and put into roaster pan. Cover with water and add onion and celery. Cover and simmer approximately 2 hours on top of stove. Cook rice according to directions on package. In deep skillet, melt butter and sauté onion. Stir in flour, mushrooms and juice. Add cream, parsley, salt, pepper and cooked rice. Bone ducks and add meat to rice mixture. Put into 2-quart casserole and sprinkle with almonds. Bake 25 minutes.

Duck a l'Orange
A favorite

Preheat oven 375°   Serves 4 to 6

2 ducks
Salt and pepper
2 oranges
1 lemon
¼ cup sugar
¼ cup wine vinegar

2 cups chicken broth
1 heaping tablespoon arrowroot
¼ cup Curacao liqueur
2 tablespoons Kummel liqueur
1 heaping tablespoon currant jelly
¼ cup Madeira

Season ducks inside and out with salt and pepper. Prick all over with fork; bake uncovered on rack 1½ hours. Peel zest from oranges and lemon; cut into julienne strips. Blanch strips 5 minutes in boiling water; drain and set aside. Squeeze juice from oranges and lemon, reserving ⅓ cup; set aside. Stir sugar in saucepan over medium heat until melted and golden in color. Add vinegar and juices. Cook over medium heat until reduced by ½. Add broth; simmer gently about 5 minutes. Stir arrowroot into Curacao. Add Kummel and jelly; stir into sauce. Cook until thickened. When ducks are done, drain fat from pan. Add Madeira to pan and simmer 2 minutes. Strain into sauce. Add julienne peel to sauce. Cut ducks in serving-size pieces. Pour a little sauce over duck; pass remaining sauce.

Cedar Key Shrimp
Peel as you eat

Preheat oven broil

Serves 4

½ cup olive oil
⅓ cup white wine
⅓ cup lemon juice

1 teaspoon garlic salt
1 pound shrimp, unpeeled
1 tablespoon butter
1 teaspoon paprika

Mix oil, wine, lemon juice and garlic salt. Place shrimp in buttered pan. Pour sauce over shrimp; sprinkle with paprika. Place under broiler 15 minutes. Peel and devein.

Luncheon Shrimp
Extraordinary

Chill 24 hours

Serves 8 to 10

5 quarts water
1 cup celery leaves
2 tablespoons salt
½ cup pickling spice
Juice and rind of 2 lemons
5 pounds medium shrimp
2 small onions, sliced
14 bay leaves

1 tablespoon plus 2 teaspoons
  celery seed
2½ cups vegetable oil
1½ cups white vinegar
1 teaspoon salt
¼ cup capers, drained
Dash hot sauce (optional)
Watercress
Lemons, sliced

Combine first 5 ingredients; bring to boil. Add shrimp; cook 3 to 5 minutes. Drain shrimp and rinse in cold water. Peel and devein. Combine shrimp, onions and bay leaves in shallow 9 x 13-inch dish. Combine next 6 ingredients; mix well. Pour over shrimp. Cover and chill 24 hours. Remove shrimp with slotted spoon and serve over bed of watercress with lemon slices.

 To boil shrimp: Bring enough water to cover shrimp to boil. Add 1 bay leaf. Add shrimp. Return to boil 30 seconds for medium shrimp. Remove from heat and drain in colander. Shrimp are overcooked when tightly curled. Adjust cooking time according to size of shrimp.

Dill Shrimp Casserole
A favorite

Preheat oven 325°   Serves 5 to 6

6 large mushrooms, sliced   Juice of ½ lemon
1 tablespoon onion, chopped   Salt and pepper to taste
½ pound butter   ¼ to ½ cup sherry
1 tablespoon flour   2 pounds shrimp, cooked, peeled and
1 tablespoon dill, chopped   deveined
½ cup chicken broth   2 cups cooked rice
½ cup light cream   Buttered bread crumbs (optional)

Cook mushrooms and onion in butter until yellow. Add flour and dill; mix well.
Add broth and cream; bring to boil. Add lemon juice, salt, pepper and sherry.
Simmer until thickened. Add shrimp. Put rice in 2-quart casserole. Add shrimp
mixture. Sprinkle with bread crumbs. Bake 15 minutes. Serve immediately.

Curried Shrimp
Simply superb

                                     Serves 4

¼ cup flour   1½ cups milk
½ to 1 teaspoon curry powder   3 tablespoons ketchup
Dash paprika   ½ cup sherry
½ teaspoon salt   1½ pounds shrimp, cooked, peeled
¼ cup butter, melted   and deveined

Combine flour, curry, paprika and salt; stir into butter. Add milk. Cook over low
heat, stirring until thickened. Add ketchup and sherry. Add shrimp; mix well.
Serve over cooked rice.

Barbequed shrimp: For a different and easy barbeque and
marinade, toss raw, unpeeled shrimp in bowl and marinate in 1
cup Italian dressing 6 to 8 hours. Skewer and cook on hinged
grill until shrimp turns pink.

Shrimp ala VIP
Special

Preheat oven 375°   Serves 4

4½ tablespoons butter   1 pound shrimp, cooked, peeled and
4½ tablespoons flour   deveined
¾ cup milk   1 10-ounce package frozen artichokes
¾ cup heavy cream   or broccoli, cooked
Salt and pepper to taste   ¼ pound fresh mushrooms, sliced
¼ cup dry sherry   4 tablespoons butter, melted
1 tablespoon Worcestershire sauce   Parmesan cheese, grated
                                         Paprika

Combine first 4 ingredients in saucepan. Cook over low heat, stirring until thickened. Season with salt and pepper. Add sherry and Worcestershire sauce. Arrange shrimp and artichokes, or broccoli, in 8 x 8-inch buttered baking dish. Sauté mushrooms in butter and spread over artichokes. Pour cream sauce over ingredients in baking dish. Sprinkle liberally with Parmesan cheese and lightly with paprika. Bake 20 to 30 minutes. Serve immediately.

Shrimp and Avocado Boats
For a special luncheon

Preheat oven 350°   Serves 6

3 large avocados, halved and peeled   1½ cups milk
3 tablespoons lime juice   ⅔ cup Cheddar cheese, grated
Salt and pepper to taste   ½ cup celery, sliced and cooked
6 tablespoons flour   ½ cup pimiento, minced
4 tablespoons butter, melted   1 cup shrimp, cooked, peeled and
                                            deveined

Sprinkle avocados with lime juice, salt and pepper. Add flour to butter. Add milk. Cook over low heat, stirring constantly, until thickened. Add ⅓ cup cheese, celery, pimiento and shrimp. Stir until cheese melts. Place mixture in avocados. Sprinkle with remaining cheese. Bake 15 minutes.

Seafood

Shrimp and Pea Pods Stir-Fried
Chinese style

Serves 4

3 tablespoons corn oil
½ teaspoon ground ginger
1 clove garlic, minced
1 pound shrimp, uncooked, peeled
  and deveined
1 6-ounce package frozen pea pods

1 4-ounce can water chestnuts,
  drained and sliced
⅓ cup chicken stock
1 tablespoon soy sauce
1 teaspoon sugar
1 tablespoon sherry

Heat oil in wok or frying pan with ginger and garlic. Add shrimp and stir-fry 1½ minutes. Add pea pods and water chestnuts; stir-fry 2 minutes. Add remaining ingredients and stir-fry 2 minutes. Serve over rice.

Shrimp Creole
Bayside treat

Serves 4

6 cups water
¾ to 1 pound shrimp
½ lemon, sliced (optional)
2 tablespoons bacon drippings
2 tablespoons flour
½ cup celery plus leaves, chopped
1 cup onion, chopped
½ cup green pepper, chopped

1 15-ounce can tomatoes, cut in pieces
1 cup water
2 tablespoons dried parsley
1 teaspoon marjoram
1 teaspoon basil
½ teaspoon pepper
1½ teaspoons salt

Bring water to boil in 3-quart pan. Add shrimp and lemon. When water returns to boil, remove from heat. Drain and rinse shrimp in cold water. Make roux by heating bacon drippings in large skillet and adding flour, stirring until light brown. Add celery, onion and green pepper and sauté briefly. Add tomatoes, water and seasonings. Stir mixture. Cook 30 minutes on low heat. Peel and devein shrimp and add to creole. Cook 15 minutes. A small amount of additional water may be added. Creole should be medium thick. Serve on bed of fluffy white rice.

Crab Cakes
Family favorite

Preheat oven 450°   Serves 4

1 pound crabmeat   Salt and pepper to taste
1 egg, beaten   6 tablespoons butter, melted
2 teaspoons prepared mustard   Cracker meal
2 tablespoons mayonnaise

Combine first 6 ingredients. Add just enough cracker meal to hold mixture together. Shape into patties. Place on lightly greased cookie sheet. Bake 20 minutes or until golden brown. Serve immediately.

Crabmeat au Gratin
Cheese delight

Preheat oven 375°   Serves 6

4 tablespoons butter, melted   1½ tablespoons lemon juice
4 tablespoons flour   1½ teaspoons onion, grated
1 teaspoon salt   8 ounces Cheddar cheese, grated
¼ teaspoon pepper   Dash Worcestershire sauce
2 cups milk   Paprika
2 cups crabmeat

Combine butter, flour, salt and pepper over low heat. Stir until well blended. Remove from heat. Gradually stir in milk. Cook, stirring constantly, until thick and smooth. Combine crabmeat and white sauce. Add lemon juice, onion, cheese and Worcestershire sauce. Place in 2-quart buttered casserole. Sprinkle with paprika. Bake 20 to 25 minutes.

Cooking shrimp in the shell gives richer pink color and more natural curve.

Two pounds of shrimp in the shell will yield 1 pound cooked, peeled and deveined shrimp.

Fried shrimp: Coat shrimp in medium-ground cracker meal.

Crabmeat Florida
Simple elegance

Preheat oven 400°   Serves 1

6 ounces fresh lump crabmeat   Lemon wedges
3 tablespoons butter   Fresh parsley
1½ tablespoons lemon juice,
   freshly squeezed

Place crabmeat in shallow, oven-proof ramekin. Dot with butter and sprinkle with lemon juice. Bake 8 minutes or until golden brown. Serve with lemon wedges and parsley.

Crab and Shrimp Pavarotti
Encore

Preheat oven 350°   Serves 6

1 cup Italian bread crumbs   Pepper to taste
1 16-ounce can evaporated milk   1 8-ounce can mushrooms, drained
1 small onion, chopped   and sliced
1 tablespoon dried parsley   2 teaspoons lemon juice
10 hard-boiled eggs, chopped   4 teaspoons Worcestershire sauce
1 cup mayonnaise   1 pound lump crabmeat
1 teaspoon garlic powder   1 pound shrimp, cooked, peeled,
2 teaspoons salt   deveined and chopped
                                    Parsley or paprika

Combine first 12 ingredients. Fold in crab and shrimp. Pour into greased, shallow casserole. Bake 20 minutes. Garnish with parsley or paprika.

Rock shrimp: Place open shrimp tails on cookie sheet. Brush with melted butter; sprinkle with paprika. Broil 6 inches from heat. Meat will turn from opaque to white when done. The texture of meat is similar to lobster. Serve with melted butter and lemon.

Creamed Crabmeat and Shrimp
Easy to prepare

Serves 4

1 medium onion, minced
3 tablespoons butter, melted
1 tablespoon flour
1 teaspoon salt
¼ teaspoon pepper
¼ teaspoon Worcestershire sauce

½ teaspoon lemon rind, grated
1½ cups milk
½ cup light cream
2 4½-ounce cans shrimp, drained
2 7½-ounce cans crabmeat, flaked

In saucepan, sauté onion in butter until golden. Blend in flour and seasonings. Add lemon rind. Combine milk and cream and add to onion mixture. Cook about 8 minutes, stirring until slightly thickened. Add shrimp and crabmeat. Reheat about 10 minutes. Serve over hot biscuits or rice.

Scallops Divine
Impress your guests

Preheat oven broil

Serves 4

Juice of 1 lime
2 pounds bay or sea scallops
¼ cup butter, melted
½ teaspoon salt
Freshly ground pepper

1½ cups bread crumbs
8 slices bacon, cooked crisp and
   crumbled
Lime or lemon slices
Tartar sauce

Squeeze lime juice over scallops. Dip scallops into butter. Combine salt, pepper and bread crumbs. Dip scallops into bread crumbs. Place scallops on 8 metal skewers and broil. Turn to brown all sides. Top with bacon. Serve with lime or lemon slices and tartar sauce.

Thaw frozen shrimp under cold running water or place in refrigerator 18 to 24 hours.

When purchasing frozen shrimp, make certain they are solidly frozen.

Seafood

Scalloped Spinach
As good as it is colorful

Preheat oven 325°   Serves 6

1 10-ounce package spinach,   4 whole scallions, finely chopped
  thawed and chopped   1 pound scallops
1 egg, slightly beaten   ¼ cup sherry or white wine
2 tomatoes, peeled and sliced in   (optional)
  wedges   ¼ cup bread crumbs
6 tablespoons butter   ¼ cup Parmesan cheese, grated
2 cloves garlic, finely chopped

In greased 9-inch pie plate, spread spinach which has been combined with egg. Arrange tomato wedges around edge of pie plate. Melt 3 tablespoons butter. Sauté garlic and scallions 1 minute. Add scallops; simmer 1 minute. Add sherry or wine; simmer 1 minute. Place scallop mixture over spinach. Sprinkle bread crumbs and cheese over scallops and tomatoes. Drizzle remaining melted butter over all. Cover and bake 15 minutes. Remove cover and bake 5 minutes.

Oysters and Wild Rice
For the oyster lover

Preheat oven 350°   Serves 4 to 6

2 cups fresh mushrooms, sliced   1 cup dry white wine
½ cup green pepper, chopped   1 cup wild or brown rice, cooked
½ cup butter, melted   2 cups fresh oysters
Salt and pepper to taste

Sauté mushrooms and green pepper in ¼ cup butter. Sprinkle with salt and pepper. Add wine and simmer 10 minutes. Combine with cooked rice and spread in lightly greased shallow casserole. Sauté oysters briefly in ¼ cup butter. Place oysters over rice. Cover and bake 20 minutes. Remove cover and bake 10 minutes.

Oysters are at their best when served very cold.
Oysters should be served on bed of crushed ice.

Scallops en Coquille
For a beginning or a meal

Preheat oven 450°   Serves 4

3 tablespoons butter, softened   ½ teaspoon dried tarragon
1 teaspoon shallots, chopped   1 teaspoon lemon juice
1 clove garlic, minced   ¾ pound bay scallops
1 teaspoon chives, chopped   ½ cup fresh bread crumbs
1 tablespoon fresh parsley, chopped

Blend butter with shallots, garlic, chives, parsley, tarragon and lemon juice.
Butter 4 scallop shells. Spoon equal portions of scallops into each shell. Top
with equal portions of butter mixture. Sprinkle with bread crumbs. Arrange
shells on tray and bake 5 minutes. Serve immediately.

Scallops in Rice Pie Shell
Light summer supper

Preheat oven 325°   Serves 6

1 pound scallops   2 tablespoons sherry
3 scallions, finely chopped   3 tablespoons flour
1 bay leaf   3 tablespoons butter, melted
⅛ teaspoon white pepper   ½ cup heavy cream
Salt to taste   ½ cup mushrooms, sliced
¾ cup white wine   Paprika
                                     Fresh parsley

Place first 7 ingredients in saucepan and stir constantly on low heat 5 minutes.
Remove scallops; rapidly boil liquid 3 minutes. In skillet add flour to butter. Stir
1 minute. Add cream gradually. Cook and stir until thickened. Combine
scallops, wine liquid, cream sauce and mushrooms. Pour into rice pie shell.
Bake 30 to 40 minutes. Sprinkle with paprika. Garnish with parsley.

Rice Pie Shell

2½ cups cooked long grain rice,   ¼ cup butter, melted
  cooled   Salt to taste
2 eggs, beaten

Mix rice and eggs. Add butter and salt. Press into 9-inch pie plate.

Tip: Pie shell is also good with turkey in cream sauce.

Seafood

Baked Fish Florida
À la Sunshine State

Preheat oven 350°   Serves 4

2 pounds snapper, trout or flounder   1 teaspoon salt
   fillets   Dash pepper
1 onion, thinly sliced   4 tablespoons orange juice concentrate
¼ cup butter, melted   2 tablespoons soy sauce

Place fish in greased baking pan. Slash fish in several places and insert onion slices. Mix butter, salt, pepper, orange concentrate and soy sauce. Spread over fish and baste during cooking. Bake 20 minutes or until fish flakes easily when tested with fork.

Creamed Filet of Sole
Universal appeal

Preheat oven 400°   Serves 6

8 flounder or sole fillets   ¼ cup dry white wine
Salt   ¼ cup heavy cream
Freshly ground pepper   ¼ cup fresh bread crumbs
3 tablespoons butter   1 tablespoon parsley, chopped
4 tablespoons green onions, finely
   chopped

Salt and pepper fillets; roll each compactly. Grease 11 x 15-inch baking dish with 1 tablespoon butter. Sprinkle bottom of dish with salt, pepper and 3 tablespoons onions. Put fish in dish, seam side down. Pour wine and cream over fish. Sprinkle with bread crumbs, parsley and remaining onions. Melt 2 tablespoons butter; pour over fish. Bake 20 minutes or until fish rolls are cooked and crumbs browned.

The spiny lobster found in Florida waters (sometimes called crawfish) can be steamed, boiled or broiled. Fast cooking is recommended for tenderness.

Fish à la Normandy
Fit for a king

Preheat oven 400°   Serves 6

3 pounds filet of sole or flounder   ½ cup mayonnaise
Salt and pepper to taste   ½ cup milk
½ cup onion, chopped   ½ cup dry white wine
1 tablespoon vegetable oil   ½ cup mushrooms, sliced
1 teaspoon salt   2 tablespoons pimiento
¼ teaspoon pepper   3 cups cooked rice

Salt and pepper fish fillets. Arrange in shallow 9 x 13-inch casserole. Sauté onion in oil. Add remaining ingredients except rice and cook until thickened. Pour over fish. Bake 20 to 25 minutes. Serve fish and sauce over rice.

Fish Batter
Florida style

Preheat electric skillet 375°   Serves 4

2 eggs, beaten   1 teaspoon salt
½ cup milk   1 teaspoon butter or salad oil
1 cup flour   1½ pounds fresh fish
1 teaspoon baking powder   Oil

Combine eggs and milk. Sift in flour, baking powder and salt. Beat in melted butter or oil. Coat fish well. Fry fish in oil until brown.

To boil lobsters: Bring enough water to boil to cover lobsters. Drop head first into boiling water. Cover and return to boil 5 to 7 minutes.
To broil lobsters: Slice or cut down center of shell with sharp scissors to fantail. Lift uncooked meat through slit and place on shell. Brush with melted butter; place 6 to 8 inches from broiler.

Flounder Delight
Name says it all

Preheat oven 350°

Serves 4

1 egg, slightly beaten
1 10-ounce package spinach,
   thawed and chopped
1 pound flounder fillet
2 tablespoons onion, minced

1 clove garlic, minced
½ teaspoon salt
2 tomatoes, peeled and sliced
Parmesan cheese, grated
Butter

Mix egg with spinach. In greased 9 x 13-inch baking dish, layer fish, spinach, onion, garlic and salt. (Ingredients can also be combined and placed over fish.) Top with slices of tomato. Top each tomato with 1 teaspoon cheese and dot of butter. Bake 20 minutes or until fish flakes easily.

Rick's Bahama Fried Fish

Preheat electric skillet 350°

Serves 4

3 pounds fish
Lemon pepper
Garlic salt
1 cup pancake mix

1 cup Italian bread crumbs
¼ cup water
1 egg, beaten
Peanut oil

Cut fish in bite-sized pieces. Lightly sprinkle with lemon pepper and salt. Combine pancake mix and bread crumbs in paper bag. Dip fish in water and egg mixture. Shake fish in bag to coat with crumbs. Fry in oil 7 minutes, or until golden brown, turning once. Serve immediately.

Tip: To keep fish warm until serving, wrap in paper towels and place in brown bag.

To boil stone crab claws: Drop claws into cold water. Bring to a boil. Boil for 10 to 15 minutes depending on the size of the claws.

Spanish Fish Dinner
Spicy

Serves 4 to 6

1 onion, grated
1 green pepper, chopped
Olive oil
2 tomatoes, peeled and chopped
1 4-ounce jar pimiento, chopped
¼ cup parsley, chopped
1 teaspoon garlic powder
1 teaspoon paprika
1 teaspoon oregano

1 teaspoon basil
1½ teaspoons Italian seasoning
1 5-ounce can tomato sauce
1 cup dry sherry
1½ pounds flounder, cut in chunks
3 to 4 tablespoons flour
Salt, paprika, onion powder to taste
Oil

Sauté onion and pepper in olive oil 3 to 5 minutes. Add tomatoes; sauté 3 minutes. Add next 9 ingredients. Reduce heat; simmer 30 minutes. Shake fish in paper bag with flour, salt, paprika and onion powder. Fry in oil until light brown. Add to sauce and simmer 10 minutes. Serve over yellow rice.

Seafood Medley
A Sarasota favorite

Preheat oven 325°

Serves 16 to 18

¾ cup flour
¾ cup butter, melted
3 cups half and half
1½ teaspoons salt
½ teaspoon red pepper
2 cups sharp Cheddar cheese, grated
3 teaspoons onion juice
½ cup sherry
⅔ cup water or milk

1 pound crabmeat
1 pound shrimp, cooked, peeled and deveined
1 pound scallops, steamed 2 to 3 minutes
2 8½-ounce cans water chestnuts, drained
2 14-ounce cans artichoke hearts, halved
1 cup almonds, slivered
Parmesan cheese, grated

Add flour to butter. Stir over low heat 3 minutes. Add half and half, salt and red pepper. Stir constantly; continue cooking until thickened. Add Cheddar cheese; stir until cheese melts. Add onion juice, sherry and water or milk. Mix well. Line two 6 x 12-inch buttered baking dishes with crabmeat, shrimp, scallops, water chestnuts and artichoke hearts. Add cream sauce. Sprinkle with almonds and Parmesan cheese. Bake 30 minutes.

Seafood

Seafood Newburg
Elegant

Preheat oven 350°   Serves 4 to 6

1 cup scallions, chopped
½ pound mushrooms, sliced
6 tablespoons butter, melted
⅓ cup flour
1 cup dry white wine
1 cup light cream
½ teaspoon curry powder

⅓ cup Parmesan cheese, grated
1 pound shrimp, cooked, peeled and
  deveined
1 pound flounder fillets, cut into 1-inch
  strips
Salt and pepper to taste
½ cup corn flake crumbs

In saucepan, sauté scallions and mushrooms in 4 tablespoons butter. Stir in flour. Gradually stir in wine and cream. Add curry powder and cheese. Stir over low heat until sauce bubbles and thickens. Add shrimp and flounder. Season to taste with salt and pepper. Pour mixture into 2½ quart casserole. Mix crumbs and 2 tablespoons butter. Sprinkle evenly over seafood. Bake 40 to 60 minutes or until top is golden brown.

Seafood Paella
Festival feast

Preheat oven 350°   Serves 8 to 10

6 tablespoons olive oil
1 clove garlic, mashed
2 medium onions, finely chopped
1 6-ounce package long grain and
  wild rice
1 10-ounce package Paella rice
Chicken broth
¼ teaspoon thyme
¼ teaspoon rosemary

¼ teaspoon saffron, dissolved in
  1 tablespoon chicken broth
Salt and pepper to taste
1½ cups petit pois peas
1½ cups artichoke hearts
1½ cups chicken, cooked and diced
1½ cups shrimp, cooked, peeled
  and deveined
¼ cup pimiento strips
¼ cup butter, melted

Heat olive oil in skillet; sauté garlic and onions 5 to 6 minutes. Prepare wild and Paella rice according to package directions, using chicken broth in place of water. Add rice, thyme, rosemary, saffron, salt and pepper to onion mixture. Gently stir in peas, artichoke hearts, chicken and shrimp. Place in 16-inch casserole; bake 30 minutes. Remove; garnish with pimiento strips and butter. Bake 15 minutes.

Lobster Stew
A special beginning

Serves 4

1½ pounds lobster meat, cooked
½ cup sweet butter, melted
2 cups coffee cream

2 cups milk
Salt and pepper to taste

Sauté lobster meat in butter until firm. Add cream, milk, salt and pepper. Heat; do not boil.

Tip: Oysters may be substituted for lobster. Use oyster liquid with cream and milk.

Salmon Cheese Bake
Adds flavor to salmon

Preheat oven 450°

Serves 6

1 16-ounce can salmon, drained
  and flaked
½ cup onion, finely chopped
2 cups packaged biscuit mix
½ cup water
2 slices Mozzarella cheese
  (3 ounces)

2 tablespoons Parmesan cheese,
  grated
1 10¾-ounce can condensed cream
  of celery soup
¼ cup milk
¼ teaspoon dried dill weed

Combine salmon and onion; set aside. Combine biscuit mix and water; divide in half. Roll ½ dough into 8-inch square. Fit into bottom of greased 8 x 8 x 2-inch baking pan. Top with salmon mixture, then Mozzarella cheese. Roll remaining dough into 8-inch square, place over cheese layer. Sprinkle with Parmesan cheese. Bake 15 to 18 minutes. In small saucepan combine soup, milk and dill weed. Heat mixture. Pour part of dill sauce over squares in casserole. Pass remaining sauce.

To freeze fish, place in a container of water so fish will be encased in ice.

Bayfront

Flying over Sarasota by night, airborne observers are often struck by the coastline's unmistakable resemblance to a diamond bracelet, glittering between the inky velvet blacknesses of Gulf and inland. The visible and vivid concentration of population along the coastline is not a new phenomena. Though the early settlers were unable to fly by night or set the bayfront aglitter, they too were drawn to the coast. Sarasota's bayfront has traditionally demonstrated a magnetic attraction.

The custom of coastal living is an old one. Centuries before exploitive Europeans were attracted to "their" *la Florida*, the Indians of the Gulf coast made their homes along coastal rivers and bays. At Sarasota Bay, Indian villages stretched along the mainland shores. As time moved on, the little villages took on the shape of a cluster of low hills, or what came to be called "Indian mounds" or "middens." Middens (utilitarian areas) and mounds (sacred or ceremonial by design) comprised the village complexes, which in turn were encompassed by fields stretching out into the surrounding natural flatland.

Indian villages stretching along Sarasota Bay rose up along the islands as well as the mainland. They are sometimes visible in today's subdivisions where ancient oaks can be seen growing out of unlikely contours and "bumps" in landscaped lawns on Casey and Siesta Keys. Some downtown bayfront condominiums perch atop the sites of destroyed Indian middens, while U.S. 41 runs from the bay easterly over the right-of-way of a platted city route descriptively named "Mound Street."

From the beginning, the bayfront has attracted man for purposes basic to each successive culture. The mound builders sought the water's edge because of its proximity to a source of food, a medium for travel, and the communicative view across the water from village to village. Seafood comprised a mainstay of their diet, while they used shells for ornamentation as well as tools. The sea routes were their highways along with inland trails connecting them to other tribes.

With the passage of time, the pattern repeated itself. The earliest European and American settlers relied upon the bayfront for identical purposes and often built their homes atop the ancient mounds and middens of Indian villages. Despite technological advances and the upward spiralling of the twentieth century's coastal population, man continues his rush to the bayfront — for seafood, for launching his modern-day dugouts — and for the delightful view.

DO AHEAD ENTERTAINING

* Shrimp Ball with Crackers

* Marinated London Broil

* Incredible Hash Brown Potatoes

* Peas Pizzicato

* Patio Freeze

* Onion Herb Bread

* Allegretti Chiffon Cake

* Sangria

Condiments

Barbeque Sauce
For meats, chicken or fish

Yields 1 quart

1 cup butter
½ cup ketchup
½ cup lemon juice
Juice of ½ lemon
1 tablespoon salt
1 cup cider vinegar

1 teaspoon black pepper
1 teaspoon red pepper
1½ cups Worcestershire sauce
1½ teaspoons sugar
1 large onion, grated

Combine all ingredients in 2-quart pot and simmer 15 to 20 minutes.

Grandma's Raisin Sauce
For ham

Yields 2 cups

¼ cup sugar
1 tablespoon flour
1 cup boiling water

½ cup raisins
1 tablespoon butter, melted
Juice and grated rind of 1 orange

Mix sugar and flour. Add water and raisins. Simmer 5 minutes. Add butter, orange juice and rind.

Green Mayonnaise
For cold Stone Crab Claws or poached fish

Chill

Yields 1 cup

⅓ cup fresh greens
 (parsley, basil, scallion tops,
 spinach, watercress or chives)
1 egg

2 to 3 teaspoons fresh lemon juice
¼ teaspoon salt
1 teaspoon Dijon mustard
¾ cup safflower oil

Blanch fresh greens 1 minute. Squeeze dry and finely chop in food processor with steel blade. Remove greens. Mix egg, lemon juice, salt and mustard in food processor. With processor on very slowly, dribble in oil. Add mixture to greens and chill 1 hour. Sauce will keep 1 week in refrigerator.

Condiments

Hollandaise Sauce
For fresh green vegetables

Yields 1 cup

2 large egg yolks
2 teaspoons tarragon vinegar
2 tablespoons light cream

Salt and cayenne pepper to taste
½ cup sweet butter, cut in 8 pieces
1 teaspoon fresh lemon juice

Put egg yolks in top of double boiler; beat in vinegar and cream. Season with salt and cayenne pepper. Place over low heat and beat with small wire whisk until mixture is as thick as heavy cream. It is important that the water does not boil. Beat in butter, piece by piece, only after each piece has completely melted. Add lemon juice. Mix well.

Roast Beef Sauce
Makes prime rib special

Chill

Yields 1 cup

1 cup sour cream
3 tablespoons moist horseradish

1 teaspoon tarragon vinegar
1 teaspoon sugar
3 drops Worcestershire sauce

Mix sour cream, horseradish, vinegar, sugar and Worcestershire sauce. Cover and refrigerate. Serve cold with roast beef.

Vegetable Success Sauce
Makes any vegetable special

Preheat oven 350°

Yields 2 cups

½ cup mayonnaise
½ cup sour cream
½ teaspoon Worcestershire sauce
¼ teaspoon salt

White pepper to taste
½ cup Cheddar or Parmesan cheese, grated
½ cup scallions, finely chopped

In small bowl, combine mayonnaise, sour cream, Worcestershire sauce, salt and pepper. In separate bowl, combine cheese and scallions. Add cream mixture to cheese and scallions and toss well. Pour over warm vegetables and bake 3 minutes.

Lat's Gourmet Sauce for Beef
Crowning glory

Yields 2 cups

3 tablespoons butter, melted
3 tablespoons flour
2 teaspoons prepared mustard or
 ½ teaspoon dry mustard
2 teaspoons Worcestershire sauce

1¼ cups beef broth
1 cup Burgundy
4 scallions, thinly sliced
1 3-ounce can mushrooms, drained
 and sliced
Arrowroot

Over low heat, blend butter with flour. Stir in mustard and Worcestershire sauce. Add beef broth, a small amount at a time, blending well after each addition. Stir in Burgundy. Cook, stirring constantly until thickened. Add scallions and mushrooms. If more thickening is desired, add small amount of arrowroot. If too thick, add small amount of Burgundy. Serve over beef tenderloin slices.

Hot Pepper Jelly
Hot favorite

Yields 3 pints

2 cups green peppers, cored,
 seeded and chopped
½ cup jalapeno peppers, seeded
 and chopped
1½ cups cider vinegar

5 cups sugar
1 6-ounce container fruit pectin
Green food coloring (optional)
1 paraffin cake, melted

Combine ½ green peppers and ½ jalapeno peppers in blender or food processor. Add ½ cup vinegar; blend until smooth. Pour into large kettle. Repeat process with remaining peppers and ½ cup vinegar. Add remaining ½ cup vinegar to rinse container; pour into kettle. Add sugar. Bring mixture to boil. Cook 5 minutes, stirring constantly. Remove from heat. Strain and cool 5 minutes; skim foam from top and add pectin. Stir well. Ladle into 6 sterilized 8-ounce glasses or jars. Seal with paraffin.

Tip: For extra hot jelly increase jalapeno peppers to ¾ cup.

Pepper Relish
Excellent for making Thousand Island salad dressing

Yields 7 pints

12 red peppers
12 green peppers
12 jalapeno peppers
12 onions
1 large bunch celery

6 cups vinegar
3 cups sugar
3 tablespoons salt
2 tablespoons mustard seed
2 tablespoons celery seed

Using meat grinder, grind all peppers, onions and celery into large oven roaster. Scald in 3 cups vinegar 10 minutes. Drain well. Add sugar, remaining 3 cups vinegar, salt, mustard seed and celery seed. Boil gently 5 minutes. Place in sterilized jars and seal.

Pickled Dill Beans
Great for backyard barbeque

Chill

Yields 4 pints

½ cup sugar
3 cups cider vinegar
1 cup water
1 cup light corn syrup
3 teaspoons salt

3 tablespoons dill seed or weed
½ teaspoon ground turmeric
½ teaspoon red pepper, crushed
6 small white onions, sliced
3 pounds fresh, unblemished green
beans

Combine sugar, vinegar, water, corn syrup, salt, dill, turmeric, red pepper and onions in large saucepan. Bring to boil and cook 3 minutes. Trim tips of beans, leave whole. Cook in salted boiling water in large kettle 3 minutes. Pack beans upright in 4 pint jars. Reheat syrup to boiling and pour over beans, leaving ½ inch space at top of jar. Process jars 10 minutes in boiling water bath. Remove jars and cool to room temperature. Store in cool place. Chill before serving.

Pickles should only be made in enamel pots and stirred only with wooden spoons.

Three Day Pickles
Simply the best pickles ever

Stand 3 days   Yields 8 quarts

2 gallons cucumbers, sliced   2½ quarts vinegar
1½ gallons boiling water   16 cups sugar
2 cups coarse salt   3 tablespoons celery seed
2 tablespoons powdered alum   3 tablespoons pickling spice
1 gallon water   1½ tablespoons turmeric

Stir cucumbers in water with salt until salt is dissolved. Cover and let stand 2 days. Drain and rinse cucumbers well. Mix alum in 1 gallon water. Pour over cucumbers and let stand 24 hours. Rinse well. Pack cucumbers in jars. Mix vinegar, sugar, celery seed, pickling spice and turmeric. Simmer 30 minutes. Pour into each jar of cucumbers. Seal.

New Orleans Tartar Sauce
For Sarasota seafood

Chill   Yields 1½ cups

1¼ cups mayonnaise   2 tablespoons green onion, finely
1 tablespoon Creole mustard   chopped
½ teaspoon hot pepper sauce   2 tablespoons parsley, finely chopped
2 tablespoons sweet pickle relish   1 tablespoon capers, drained

In large bowl, blend mayonnaise, mustard and hot pepper sauce. Add pickle relish, onion, parsley and capers. Mix thoroughly. Refrigerate sauce 1 to 2 hours to allow flavors to blend.

Sauce Cardinale
Serve over fruit or ice cream

Chill   Serves 4 to 6

1 10-ounce package frozen   Water
  raspberries, thaw, drain   1 tablespoon cornstarch
  and reserve liquid   ¼ cup currant jelly

In saucepan, combine reserved raspberry juice with enough water to make 1 cup liquid. Add cornstarch. Boil 1 minute. Stir in jelly and berries. Chill at least 1 hour.

Condiments _____

Sweet and Sour Mustard Sauce
Super with ham and chicken

Chill   Yields 2 cups

4 ounces dry mustard   ½ cup white sugar
1 cup malt vinegar   Pinch salt
½ cup brown sugar, packed   3 large eggs, beaten

Soak mustard and vinegar together overnight. Add sugars and salt. Stir until smooth. Place in top of double boiler. Add eggs. Cook over simmering water, beating with whisk until mixture is custard-like in consistency. Pour into jars and refrigerate. Will keep 3 weeks.

Mango Chutney
Tropical specialty

Age 4 weeks   Yields 4 pints

3½ cups brown sugar   1 large onion, chopped
2 cups white vinegar   1½ cups white raisins
1 quart mangoes, chopped   6 to 8 pieces fresh ginger, chopped

Boil sugar and vinegar. Add remaining ingredients, cooking slowly and stirring occasionally until desired consistency. Do not overcook. Pour in containers and seal. Age 4 weeks before serving.

Spiced Orange Slices
Lovely served with your favorite entrée

Stand overnight   Serves 6

3 medium Florida oranges,   2 cups sugar
   unpeeled   ½ cup cider vinegar
6 whole cloves   ½ cinnamon stick

Cut each orange in 5 or 6 slices. Cover with water; simmer in covered pan 90 minutes or until tender. Drain. Combine remaining ingredients and boil 5 minutes. Add drained orange slices. Cook uncovered 20 to 30 minutes. Let stand in syrup overnight. May be made a week before serving.

Sea Grape Jelly
Florida special

Yields 3 cups

2 pounds sea grapes
4 cups cold water

2 cups sugar

Combine sea grapes and water. Boil rapidly 20 minutes. Mash grapes; strain juice through jelly bag. Combine 2 cups juice and sugar in saucepan. Stir over low heat until sugar dissolves and juice boils. Boil rapidly to 223° on jelly thermometer. Pour into jelly glasses.

Mustard Pickle
Marinated vegetables

Chill

Yields 16 pints

1¾ pounds sugar
4 tablespoons dry mustard
⅔ cup flour
½ tablespoon turmeric
8 cups vinegar
Celery seed to taste (optional)
Mustard seed to taste (optional)
4 cups green tomatoes, cut up and cooked
4 cups carrots, sliced and cooked

4 cups lima beans, cooked
4 cups celery, chopped and cooked
4 cups cauliflower, broken in flowerets and cooked
6 red peppers, chopped and cooked
6 green peppers, chopped and cooked
1 16-ounce jar boiled whole onions, drained
1 16-ounce jar sweet pickles, drained and chopped

Combine first 7 ingredients. Cook over low heat until creamy. Add remaining ingredients. Cook until hot, 15 to 20 minutes. Pour into pint jars while hot and seal. Chill before serving.

Condiments

Corn Relish
Colorful mixture

Yields 2 cups

½ cup sugar
½ teaspoon salt
½ teaspoon celery seed
½ teaspoon dry mustard
½ cup vinegar
¼ teaspoon Tobasco

1 12-ounce can whole kernel corn, undrained
1 tablespoon onion, minced
2 tablespoons green peppers, chopped
1 tablespoon pimiento, chopped

In saucepan, bring sugar, salt, celery seed, mustard, vinegar and Tabasco to boil; boil 2 minutes. Remove from heat and stir in remaining ingredients. Cool. Cover; refrigerate several days before serving.

Orange Marmalade
Best made with Florida oranges

Yields 8 pints

3 large navel oranges
2 large lemons

8 cups sugar
11 cups water

Cut fruit in halves. Remove seeds and slice into paper thin pieces, using all of rind and pulp. Cover with water; let stand overnight. Boil until tender; add sugar. Let stand overnight again. Boil until mixture thickens. Pour into hot sterile jars and seal.

Pumpkin Butter
A terrific use for Halloween pumpkin, just in time for Christmas gifts

Preheat oven 350°   Yields 4 pints

1 medium pumpkin, about 8 pounds   1 teaspoon allspice
3 to 4 cups honey   2 teaspoons cinnamon

Halve pumpkin and remove seeds. Bake 1 hour. Remove cooked pumpkin and mash in blender, leave slightly lumpy. Place pumpkin in pan; add honey to taste, allspice, and cinnamon. Cook 2 to 3 hours over medium-low heat, reducing heat as butter thickens. Leave lid slightly aside so steam can escape. Place small quantity of butter on plate; when no rim of liquid separates around the edges, butter is done. Place in sterile jars and seal tightly. Refrigerate after opening. Should keep up to 6 months.

Tips: May use sugar in place of honey. May add finely chopped nuts, if desired.

Strawberry Butter
Excellent served on pancakes

                                     Yields 2½ cups

1 pint fresh strawberries   1 cup powdered sugar
16 tablespoons unsalted butter

Put all ingredients in blender. Blend until smooth and creamy.

Beaches

The beach is a modern-day mecca. It beckons to all — young people, retirees, fitness fans, and lovers of the lazy life. Stretching out as a strip of reflective sand between the land and the Gulf, Sarasota's beaches are of prime importance in today's scope of things.

Originally, the beaches were seasonal places. The Indians relied on them only periodically. Archaeologists surmise the Indians may have been drawn in summer rainy seasons to beaches and the soothing Gulf breezes to escape the torment of mosquitoes. They also came in the season when the great turtles lumbered up from the sea to deposit their eggs in the sand. From the time of Indians to settlers, the then plentiful turtles and their beach-lain eggs provided a periodic food source.

As the population changed from one of settlement to commercial development, the beaches took on increasing attractiveness. While the early period had seen the islands utilized only for isolated homesteads, fish camps, and gardens, the developers envisioned something quite different.

The beaches, which attracted mainlanders on what amounted to all-day boat excursions, promptly took on new possibilities as developers conceived linking mainland and island. John Ringling first linked Sarasota's downtown with Bird Key and St. Armands with his personally-built causeway. For St. Armands and Lido, Ringling and Owen Burns entered upon a grand plan for homes, yacht basins, a shopping district, and a gambling casino on the beach.

The utilization of Sarasota's beaches was dramatically altered by a second technological advancement — air conditioning. With the advent of temperature and climate control, man found he might live in comfort, relatively unaffected by seasonal winds off the Gulf, moisture, and destructive salt spray. The population of barrier islands soared following the routine implementation of governmental mosquito control, bay bridges, air conditioning, and a Florida Supreme Court's expanded view of homestead exemption application. The situation further increased as decades of historic forgetfulness insulated investors from the memory of hurricane forces which for days have covered all the islands to navigable depths and re-routed passes in an evening.

As the surf rolls in on a spring evening, seagulls cry, joggers trot along, and boats troll offshore. The beach represents a kind of freedom, the freedom of modern men to revel in the pleasures of a place historically inaccessible and uncomfortable, freedom to reach the beach at will and wiggle toes in the Sarasota's acclaimed powder-soft sand, or to walk bent forward in endless search for shell treasures.

As tourism has become Florida's number one industry, as natural resources are increasingly cherished, and as Sarasota's cultural dominance continues to define itself, the beaches have become the cement that glues it all together.

PICNIC ON THE GO

* Suncoast Pita Pocket Salad
* Oeufs Cressoniere
  Seasonal Fruit
* Three Day Pickles
* Toffee Strips
  Lemonade

SUNSET SAILING

* Gazpacho
* Avocado and Crabmeat Quiche
* Chicken Liver Paté
  French Bread
  Assorted Cheeses
* Hermits
  Wine: Vouvray

Breads

Apricot Bread
With honey-whipped cream cheese spread

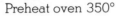

Preheat oven 350°

Yields 1 loaf

1 cup dried apricots
1 cup sugar
2 tablespoons butter
1 egg
¼ cup pineapple juice
½ cup orange juice

2 cups flour, sifted
2 teaspoons baking powder
¼ teaspoon baking soda
1 teaspoon salt
½ cup walnuts or pecans, chopped
¼ cup cream sherry
¼ cup brandy

Cover apricots with warm water and soak 30 minutes to soften. Drain and finely chop. In large mixing bowl, cream sugar, butter and egg. Stir in fruit juices. Combine flour, baking powder, baking soda and salt. Stir into butter mixture. Add apricots and nuts. Pour batter into greased 9½-inch loaf pan and bake 55 to 65 minutes. Cool 10 minutes. Remove from pan and cool completely on wire rack. Combine sherry and brandy and pour over bread.

Spread

8 ounces cream cheese, whipped
¼ cup honey

1 teaspoon vanilla

Blend all ingredients until creamy and serve with bread.

Apple Puffed Pancake
For special breakfasts

Preheat oven 425°

Serves 6 to 8

6 eggs
1½ cups milk
1 cup flour
3 tablespoons sugar
1 teaspoon vanilla

½ teaspoon salt
¼ teaspoon cinnamon
½ cup butter
2 apples, peeled and thinly sliced
2 to 3 tablespoons brown sugar

In large bowl, mix eggs, milk, flour, sugar, vanilla, salt and cinnamon until well blended. Batter will be slightly lumpy. Melt butter in 12-inch fluted porcelain quiche dish or 13 x 9-inch baking dish in oven. Add apple slices to baking dish. Return to oven until butter sizzles. Do not brown. Remove dish from oven and immediately pour batter over apples. Sprinkle with brown sugar. Bake in middle of oven 20 minutes. Serve immediately.

Breads

Beer Bread
Easy

Preheat oven 350°   Yields 1 loaf

Glaze

1 egg   ½ teaspoon salt

Place rack in lower 1/3 of oven. Grease 8 x 4-inch loaf pan. Make glaze by mixing egg and salt in food processor using steel blade. Remove glaze and set aside. Do not clean work bowl.

Bread

3 cups unbleached flour   1½ teaspoons salt
1 tablespoon plus 1 teaspoon   ½ teaspoon baking soda
  baking powder   1 12-ounce can beer, at room
3 tablespoons light brown sugar   temperature

Combine flour, baking powder, sugar, salt and baking soda in work bowl, and mix 2 seconds. Add ½ of beer. Blend, using 4 off-on turns. Add remaining beer and mix just until batter is blended. Do not overmix. Transfer to prepared pan and brush lightly with glaze. Bake until golden brown, about 45 minutes. Remove from pan and cool on rack about 10 minutes. Serve warm.

Blueberry Bread
For fresh or frozen berries

Preheat oven 350°   Yields 1 loaf

1 egg, beaten   ½ teaspoon baking soda
1 cup sugar   ½ teaspoon salt
2 tablespoons oil   1½ teaspoons baking powder
⅔ cup fresh orange juice   1 cup blueberries
2 cups flour   ½ cup pecans, chopped

Combine egg, sugar, oil and juice. Sift dry ingredients together and carefully combine with egg mixture, mixing well. Gently add blueberries and pecans. Pour into well-greased 9 x 5-inch loaf pan and bake 1 hour. Cool on rack. Store bread in refrigerator.

Banana Streusel Coffee Cake
For family breakfasts

Preheat oven 375°   Serves 8

½ cup butter   ½ teaspoon baking soda
¾ cup sugar   ⅛ teaspoon salt
1¾ cups flour   ½ teaspoon cinnamon
1 teaspoon vanilla   ⅔ cup banana, mashed
2 large eggs   ⅓ cup buttermilk or sour milk
1½ teaspoons baking powder

Cream butter and ½ cup sugar. Cut ¾ cup flour into creamed mixture with pastry blender to form crumb mixture. Remove ½ cup crumb mixture and set aside. To remaining crumb mixture, add remaining ¼ cup sugar, vanilla and eggs. Beat until smooth. Combine remaining 1 cup flour with baking powder, soda, salt and cinnamon. Stir to blend. Combine banana with buttermilk. Add these 2 mixtures to egg mixture, alternately, beginning and ending with dry ingredients. Blend well and pour into buttered 10-inch pie or cake pan. Sprinkle remaining crumb mixture over batter and bake 35 to 40 minutes or until cake tests done.

Tip: For variety, add ½ cup chopped walnuts to crumb topping mixture.

Corn Bread
Southern style

Preheat oven 400°   Serves 6 to 8

6 to 8 tablespoons bacon grease   1 teaspoon salt
  or butter   1 tablespoon baking powder
1½ cups cornmeal   2 eggs, lightly beaten
1 cup flour   1½ cups milk
⅓ cup sugar

Melt bacon grease or butter in 9-inch iron skillet. Sift cornmeal, flour, sugar, salt and baking powder into mixing bowl. Add 4 tablespoons bacon grease or butter to eggs and milk. Pour into dry ingredients and beat. Do not overbeat. Pour batter into iron skillet containing remaining grease or butter. Bake 25 to 30 minutes. Serve hot.

Christmas Stollen

For Christmas morning

Preheat oven 350°   Serves 20, yields 2 rings

1 cup milk   2 eggs, beaten
1 cup butter, melted   ½ teaspoon lemon rind, grated
½ cup water   ½ teaspoon orange rind, grated
5¼ cups flour   ½ cup seedless raisins
¼ cup sugar   ½ cup candied fruit, chopped
1 teaspoon salt   ½ cup walnuts or pecans, chopped
2 packages dry yeast

Combine milk, butter and water in saucepan. Heat until lukewarm. Combine flour, sugar, salt and yeast in large mixing bowl. Stir in warm milk mixture and eggs, mixing well. Add lemon and orange rind, raisins, fruit and nuts. Mix well. Cover dough and refrigerate overnight.

Filling

6 tablespoons unsalted butter,   1 cup sugar
  softened   2 tablespoons cinnamon

Divide dough in half. Place half on floured surface and roll into 12 x 18-inch rectangle. Spread with 3 tablespoons soft butter. Combine ½ cup sugar and 1 tablespoon cinnamon and sprinkle over butter. Set remaining butter, sugar and cinnamon aside for other half of dough.
Beginning with long edge, roll up like jelly roll, pinching edges to seal. Place roll on large greased cookie sheet and shape into ring, joining ends. Brush ends with water and pinch together to seal. Using kitchen shears, cut dough every inch around ring, cutting ⅔ way into roll at each cut. Turn each inch wedge to side, slightly overlapping previous piece. Repeat with other half dough. Let rise in warm place, uncovered, 1 hour. Bake 25 to 30 minutes or until brown.

Topping

1 cup powdered sugar   ¼ teaspoon vanilla
2 to 3 tablespoons water or milk   Candied cherrry halves

Combine powdered sugar, water and vanilla and drizzle over hot rings. Decorate with candied cherries.

Tip: Substitute ½ cup dried apricots and finely chopped dates for candied fruit. Omit candied cherries and decorate with pecans.

Carrot Muffins
Delicious

Preheat oven 350°

Yields 2½ dozen muffins

2 cups sugar
1¼ cups oil
4 eggs, lightly beaten
3 cups flour
2 teaspoons baking powder

1 teaspoon baking soda
½ teaspoon salt
2 cups carrot, grated
½ cup walnuts or pecans, chopped
½ cup raisins

Grease muffin tin or prepare with paper liners. Beat sugar and oil in medium bowl. Blend in eggs. Sift flour, baking powder, baking soda and salt into another bowl. Gradually stir dry ingredients into oil mixture. blending well. Fold in carrot, nuts and raisins. Fill muffin cups 2/3 full. Bake 35 to 40 minutes, or until tester inserted comes out clean. Serve warm.

Fresh Apple-Nut Bread
For fall mornings

Preheat oven 350°

Yields 1 loaf

¼ cup unsalted butter
1 cup light brown sugar
2 eggs
3 cups flour
2 cups apple, peeled and grated
 (about 2 large)
¾ cup walnuts or pecans, chopped

1½ teaspoons baking soda
1 teaspoon baking powder
1 teaspoon lemon peel, grated
1 teaspoon salt
2 teaspoons cinnamon
¼ teaspoon nutmeg
¾ cup buttermilk

Grease and flour 9 x 5-inch loaf pan. Cream butter and sugar in medium bowl. Beat in eggs. Combine flour, apple, nuts, soda, baking powder, lemon peel, salt, cinnamon and nutmeg in separate bowl. Blend into butter mixture alternately with buttermilk. Turn into pan and bake until toothpick inserted in center comes out clean, about 1 hour. Cool in pan 10 minutes. Remove from pan and cool completely on wire rack.

When using glass loaf pans, reduce oven temperature by 25 degrees. Glass retains heat longer than the average metal baking pan and consequently food may stick to it at a higher temperature. Increase cooking time to compensate for lower oven temperature.

Breads

Irish Soda Bread
Serve warm with butter

Preheat oven 375°   Serves 6 to 8

2 cups flour   1 tablespoon sugar
½ teaspoon baking soda   4 tablespoons shortening
1½ teaspoons baking powder   ½ cup raisins
½ teaspoon salt   ¾ cup buttermilk or sour milk

Sift first 5 ingredients together. Cut in shortening with pastry blender. Add raisins and milk. Knead 1 minute. Shape into round loaf and place in greased 9-inch glass pie plate. Bake 30 minutes. Serve immediately.

Tip: To make sour milk, add 1 tablespoon vinegar to sweet milk and let stand 5 minutes. If desired, add 1 tablespoon cinnamon to batter for extra flavor.

Lavash
Sesame cracker bread

Preheat oven 375°   Serves 14

5 cups unbleached flour   4 tablespoons butter, melted
1 package dry yeast   1¼ to 1½ cups warm water
2¼ teaspoons salt   (120° to 130°)
¾ teaspoon sugar   ¾ cup sesame seeds

Combine flour, yeast, salt and sugar in large mixing bowl. Add butter and water slowly to dry ingredients, beating continuously. A small amount of additional water may be added if dough seems very dry. Knead until dough is smooth and elastic. Place in large greased bowl, turning to coat surface. Cover with plastic wrap and hot, damp towel and let rise in warm place until doubled, 1 to 2 hours. Divide into 14 balls and refrigerate. One at a time, roll as thinly as possible. Sprinkle with sesame seeds and push seeds into dough with rolling pin. Place on cookie sheet and bake 10 to 13 minutes on lowest oven rack. When Lavash is light golden brown, remove to cooling rack. Repeat. When all are completely cool, place in airtight container.

When making muffins or quick breads, handle batter as little as possible, and work quickly to guarantee the maximum rising action for baking powder. As soon as muffins or quick breads are baked, remove from tins or pans and cool on rack.

Monkey Bread
With variations

Preheat oven 375°

Serves 8

1 cup milk
1 cup butter
4 tablespoons sugar

1 teaspoon salt
1 package dry yeast
3½ cups flour

Combine milk, ½ cup butter, sugar and salt in saucepan. Heat until butter is melted. Cool to 110° and stir in yeast until dissolved. Place flour in large bowl and stir in liquid until well blended. Cover and let rise until doubled. Turn dough out on floured surface. Roll ¼-inch thick. Cut into 3 inch squares. Dip in ½ cup melted butter and layer squares in 10-inch tube pan or bundt pan. Cover. Let rise until doubled. Bake 30 to 40 minutes. Rich and buttery.

Tip: **Add cinnamon, nuts and raisins, garlic or herbs to melted butter in which squares of dough are dipped.**

Orange Bread
For Florida breakfasts

Preheat oven 350°

Yields 1 loaf

1 orange, juice and rind
5 ounces dates
½ cup pecans
3 tablespoons unsalted butter
½ cup sugar
1 egg, lightly beaten

1 teaspoon vanilla
1 cup unbleached flour
1 cup whole wheat flour
1 teaspoon baking soda
1 teaspoon baking powder
1 teaspoon salt

Squeeze orange juice into measuring cup and add enough boiling water to make 1 cup. In food processor using steel blade, finely chop orange rind. Add dates and chop; add pecans and chop. Combine juice, butter, sugar, egg and vanilla in large bowl. Add chopped date mixture and mix well. Add remaining dry ingredients and stir only to moisten. Pour into well-greased 9 x 5-inch loaf pan. Bake 50 minutes. Cool on rack. If desired, serve with cream cheese.

At any point in the process of making yeast bread, the uncooked dough can be stored in the refrigerator up to 24 hours, wrapped loosely in plastic. Allow dough to reach room temperature before working with it again.

Oatmeal Bread
Make in food processor

Preheat oven 350°   Yields 2 loaves

1 cup oatmeal (not instant)   ½ cup water
1¼ cups boiling water   2 tablespoons dry yeast
⅓ cup butter   2 eggs
½ cup honey   6 cups flour
1 tablespoon salt

Combine first 5 ingredients. Cool to lukewarm. Add next 3 ingredients and mix well. Using steel blade in food processor, mix 2 cups flour with 1 cup liquid until dough forms a ball. Do 3 batches. Let rise in large bowl. Punch down. Put into 2 buttered 9 x 5-inch bread pans. Let rise. Bake 45 minutes.

Tip: If desired, use 3 cups whole wheat and 3 cups unbleached flour.

Onion Herb Bread
Absolutely delicious

Preheat oven 350°   Yields 1 loaf

1 package dry yeast   1 tablespoon butter, softened
¼ cup warm water   ¼ teaspoon baking soda
1 cup cottage cheese, heated to   1 teaspoon salt
   lukewarm   1 egg
2 tablespoons sugar   2¼ to 2½ cups flour, sifted
1 tablespoon dry onion   ½ cup butter, melted
2 teaspoons dill seed   1½ teaspoons celery seed

Dissolve yeast in warm water. In large bowl, combine cottage cheese, sugar, onion, dill seed, butter, soda, salt and egg. Add yeast. Gradually add flour, enough to make a stiff dough. Mix well. Cover and let rise until double. Punch down. Turn dough into greased 9 x 5-inch loaf pan. Let rise until double. Bake 40 to 50 minutes. When bread is removed from oven, pour mixture of melted butter and celery seed over top.

To test loaf of yeast bread for doneness, tap on top with your finger; if it sounds hollow, it is done.

Popovers
And variations thereof

Preheat oven 375° to 400°   Yields 8 popovers

3 eggs   3 tablespoons butter, melted
1 cup flour   ½ teaspoon salt
1 cup milk

In small, deep mixing bowl, beat eggs slightly. Add flour, milk, butter and salt. Beat just until well blended; do not overbeat! Pour batter into 8 well-greased 5-ounce custard cups or muffin cups. Place custard cups on baking sheet. For custard cups, bake at 400° for 45 minutes. For muffin cups, bake at 375° for 50 minutes.

Variations for Popovers

Whole Grain Popovers:
Substitute ⅔ cup fine whole grain flour, plus ⅓ cup all purpose flour for flour in recipe.

Cheese Popovers:
Prepare popovers. Grate into separate bowl, ½ cup fresh Parmesan or Gruyere cheese. Add dash cayenne pepper. Pour 1 scant tablespoon batter into each cup and cover with a few teaspoons cheese and another tablespoon batter. Bake.

Strawberry Bread
Or strawberry muffins

Preheat oven 350°   Yields 1 loaf

3 cups flour   3 eggs, beaten
1 teaspoon baking soda   1 cup vegetable oil
½ teaspoon salt   2 10-ounce packages frozen
1 tablespoon cinnamon   strawberries, thawed and sliced
2 cups sugar

Combine first 5 ingredients. Mix well. Combine eggs, oil and strawberries. Add to dry ingredients, mixing well. Pour batter into greased and floured 9 x 5-inch loaf pan. Bake 1 hour or until cake tester inserted in center comes out clean. Bread is particularly good toasted.

Tip: If making muffins, fill buttered muffin tins 2/3 full. Bake about 35 minutes.

Breads

Sally Lunn Bread
An old fashioned favorite

Preheat oven 350°   Serves 12

1 cup milk   ⅓ cup sugar
½ cup unsalted butter   2 teaspoons salt
¼ cup water   2 packages dry yeast
4 cups unbleached flour, sifted   3 eggs

Grease 10-inch tube cake pan or bundt pan. Heat milk, butter and water until very warm (about 120°). Blend 1⅓ cups flour, sugar, salt and dry yeast in large mixing bowl. Blend warm liquid into flour mixture. Beat with electric mixer at medium speed 2 minutes. Gradually add ⅔ cup remaining flour and eggs and beat at high speed 2 minutes. Add remaining flour and mix well. Cover and let rise about 1 hour 15 minutes. Beat dough down with wooden spoon and turn into prepared pan. Let rise again 30 minutes. Bake 40 to 50 minutes. Run knife around center.

Stone Ground Wheat Bread
Batter bread

Preheat oven 375°   Yields 1 loaf

1¼ cups warm water (105°-115°)   2 tablespoons unsalted butter, at room
1 package dry yeast   temperature
2 cups stone ground wheat flour   2 tablespoons brown sugar
1 cup plus 2 tablespoons   2 teaspoons salt
   unbleached flour

Combine water and yeast in large mixing bowl. Stir in 1 cup wheat flour, ½ cup unbleached flour, butter, brown sugar and salt. Beat at medium speed with electric mixer 2 minutes. Add remaining flour and beat 1½ minutes longer. Cover bowl with plastic wrap and let rise in warm area 1 hour. Punch down. Turn into well-buttered 8 x 4-inch loaf pan and let rise 45 minutes. Bake until bread is browned and loaf sounds hollow when tapped, 45 to 50 minutes. Remove from pan and cool on rack before slicing.

Walnut Gems
A family tradition

Preheat oven 375°

Yields 1½ dozen muffins

1¾ cups flour
2½ teaspoons baking powder
½ teaspoon salt
¾ cup wheat germ
¾ cup unsalted butter

½ cup sugar
2 eggs
1¼ cups milk
1 cup walnuts, chopped

Thoroughly sift flour, baking powder and salt. Stir in wheat germ. In medium size mixing bowl, cream butter and sugar. Beat in eggs with electric mixer. Add flour mixture alternately with milk. Stir in walnuts. Fill well-greased muffin cups 2/3 full. Bake 20 to 25 minutes. Serve warm.

Wind Puffs
Lovely for a morning treat

Preheat deep fryer 375°

Yields 40 puffs

Oil for frying
1 cup sour cream
1¼ teaspoons baking soda
¼ teaspoon salt
1 teaspoon vanilla
2 cups flour

⅛ teaspoon cinnamon
⅛ teaspoon nutmeg
½ cup sugar
1 egg, beaten
½ cup powdered sugar

Add oil to deep fryer. Mix all ingredients except powdered sugar. Drop from teaspoon into deep fryer. Lightly brown each side about 1 minute. Drain on paper towel. Sift powdered sugar on puffs. Serve immediately.

Tip: Batter will keep in refrigerator several days.

Breads

Zucchini Date Nut Bread
A delicious gift

Preheat oven 350°

Yields 1 loaf

1¾ cups unbleached flour
¾ teaspoon baking powder
¾ teaspoon cinnamon
½ teaspoon baking soda
½ teaspoon cardamom
¼ teaspoon allspice
¼ teaspoon salt
1 cup dates, cut into small pieces

1 tablespoon flour
2 eggs
½ cup light brown sugar, firmly packed
½ cup safflower oil
¼ cup buttermilk
1 cup zucchini squash, unpeeled and grated
¾ cup walnuts, chopped

Grease 9 x 5-inch loaf pan; line bottom and sides with waxed paper. Sift flour, baking powder, cinnamon, baking soda, cardamom, allspice and salt together in medium bowl. Spread dates on waxed paper; sprinkle lightly with flour. Combine eggs and sugar; beat 1 minute. Add oil and buttermilk. Add flour mixture and zucchini alternately to egg mixture. Fold in nuts and dates. Bake 60 minutes. Cool in pan 10 minutes. Remove from pan and cool completely on wire rack.

Substitutions

1. 1 teaspoon baking powder = ¼ teaspoon baking soda plus ½ teaspoon cream of tartar
2. 1 cup butter (margarine) = 1 cup shortening plus ½ teaspoon salt
3. 1 tablespoon cornstarch (for thickening) = 2 tablespoons flour or 1 tablespoon arrowroot starch or 2 tablespoons granulated tapioca
4. 1 cup cake flour = 1 cup minus 2 tablespoons all purpose flour

Ginger Muffins
Old fashioned flavor

Preheat oven 350°   Yields 2½ dozen

½ cup shortening   1 teaspoon ginger
1 cup brown sugar   ¼ teaspoon cinnamon
2 eggs   ¼ teaspoon nutmeg
½ cup molasses   ¼ teaspoon allspice
2 1/3 cups flour   1 cup hot water
½ teaspoon salt   1 cup raisins
1 teaspoon baking soda   1 cup walnuts, chopped

Cream shortening and sugar together. Add eggs and molasses; beat well. Sift dry ingredients together. Add to mixture, alternating with water. Add raisins and walnuts. Fill lined muffin cups 2/3 full. Bake 20 to 25 minutes.

Southern Biscuits
A Southern tradition

Preheat oven 450°   Serves 12

2 cups flour   ¼ teaspoon baking soda
3 teaspoons baking powder   6 tablespoons shortening
½ teaspoon salt   1 cup buttermilk

Sift dry ingredients together. Cut in shortening. Add milk and stir until dough is smooth. Turn onto lightly floured waxed paper. Knead lightly; roll out and cut. Place on greased pan; bake 10 to 12 minutes. Serve hot.

Spanish Point at the Oaks

A unique historic site became one of the region's newest civic assets in 1980. On New Year's Eve of that year, a deed transferred ownership to a non-profit charitable organization to continue the preservation of a site long prized for its singular qualities.

It all started with a Junior League effort underway in, 1973 and 1974. When an informal survey indicated the need for an interpretative historic complex in Sarasota County, the League established a community steering committee, which formally became a charitable organization in 1974. In the course of consideration of public and private locations, one place in particular stood out.

In the little bay community of Osprey, nearly the geographic center of the county, lay a very protected historic and archaeological site. Long sheltered as part of the winter estate of the Chicago-based Palmer family, it was part of the 400-acre estate locally called "The Oaks." On the southwest corner of The Oaks lay prehistoric Indian village middens and mound, homestead houses, pioneer chapel ruins, and formal gardens constructed by the famous Mrs. Potter Palmer for her winter estate. Mrs. Palmer, a developer who ranked with John Ringling in the scope of her Sarasota projects, had carefully preserved the historic features as had successive generations of her family after her death in 1918.

The sector's first owners had been, Eliza and John Greene Webb. Eliza and John had named their homestead "Spanish Point" in 1867, but renamed it "Osprey" when they were granted a U.S. Post Office there in 1884 and a short, one-word name was required. The homestead was destined to become part of the internationally famed Mrs. Potter Palmer's estate after the turn of the century.

As the steering committee was considering sites, the Palmer family simultaneously entertained thoughts of developing or selling the old estate and setting aside the thirty-acre historic and archaeological sector. In 1975, a Sarasota historian researched the site's significance and, with Florida's Department of State agency, nominated it to the **National Register of Historic Places**. Within the year, it became the first in Sarasota County to be included.

At final sale of The Oaks in 1980, the Palmer family officially deeded the site to the organization, headed then by a former Junior League President. The group then finalized its name as "Gulf Coast Heritage Association, Inc." The Junior League and Gulf Coast Heritage have long planned to transfer the Junior League's Pioneer Program for fourth graders to the site from temporary housing in the old Osprey Elementary School. As Sarasota's oldest-yet-new historic/cultural civic asset to emerge, "Spanish Point at the Oaks" is a must for visitors and residents alike.

DINNER FOR TWO

* Won Ton Soup

* Green Salad with Chinese Noodles

* Shrimp and Pea Pods Stir-Fried

  Fluffy White Rice

* Walnut Gems

* Orange Torte

  Fortune Cookies

  Chinese Tea

Desserts

Apple Dumplings
Home style

Preheat oven 375°   Serves 6

1 cup sugar
1 cup water
⅛ teaspoon cinnamon
⅛ teaspoon nutmeg
2 tablespoons butter
2 cups flour

2 teaspoons baking powder
1 teaspoon salt
⅔ cup shortening
½ cup minus 1 tablespoon milk
3 to 4 large apples, sliced
1 tablespoon butter

Combine sugar, water, cinnamon and nutmeg. Bring to boil. Add butter and mix thoroughly. Set aside. Sift together dry ingredients; cut in shortening. Add milk and stir until just moistened. Roll dough ¼-inch thick on lightly floured surface. Cut with pastry wheel or knife into 6-inch squares. Place apple slices in center of each pastry square. Pour filling mixture generously over each apple dumpling. Dot with butter. Fold corners to center and pinch edges together. Place 1 inch apart in greased 11 x 7-inch baking dish. Bake 35 minutes.

Braised Pears à la Bressane
Tantalizingly different

Preheat oven 400°   Serves 6

6 pears, peeled, cored and halved
¼ cup honey
3 tablespoons unsalted butter

2 cups heavy cream
3 to 4 tablespoons cognac
2 tablespoons honey

Place pears, cut side down, in single layer in 9 x 13-inch baking dish. Dribble honey over pears; dot with butter. Bake 35 to 40 minutes or until tender. Remove from oven and reduce heat to 350°. Pour 1 cup cream over pears and return to oven 10 minutes, or until sauce is thick and caramel colored. Baste pears a few times. Cool. Whip remaining 1 cup cream with cognac and honey and serve over pears.

Desserts

Cranberry Pudding

Serve when fresh cranberries are in season

Serves 8

2 cups raw cranberries, halved
1/3 cup citrons, chopped
1/2 cup light molasses
1 1/2 cups flour

1/2 teaspoon salt
2 teaspoons baking soda, dissolved
   in 2 tablespoons water
1 cup pecans, chopped

Mix all ingredients and pour into oiled mold, filling mold not more than 2/3 full. Cover mold tightly and place on rack in deep kettle. Pour boiling water around mold to depth of 2 to 3 inches. Cover kettle and steam 2 hours, adding more boiling water if needed. Serve hot with creamy pudding sauce.

Creamy Pudding Sauce

1 cup sugar
3/4 cup half and half
1/2 cup butter

1 egg yolk, beaten
1 teaspoon vanilla

Cook sugar, cream and butter together 2 minutes. Stir in egg yolk and cook gently, stirring 2 minutes longer. Add vanilla. Serve warm over pudding.

Flan de Leche

Spanish flair

Preheat oven 350°

Serves 6

3 cups sugar
1/2 cup water
6 eggs, beaten
1 teaspoon vanilla

1/4 teaspoon anisette (optional)
Pinch salt
2 cups boiling milk

Boil 1 cup sugar and water until brown. Pour caramel into 6 greased custard cups. Combine eggs, 2 cups sugar, vanilla, anisette and salt; beat. Slowly add milk. Strain if necessary. Pour mixture into custard cups. Place cups in water-filled pan and bake 30 minutes. Cool in refrigerator. When ready to serve, press edges of custard away from mold; turn upside down. The caramel tops the custard. May be served cold or at room temperature.

Lemon Curd Filling
Serve on toast or as pie filling

Yields 1 quart

¾ cup lemon juice
2 tablespoons lemon rind, grated
1 cup sugar

½ cup butter
6 egg yolks
2 whole eggs

Combine lemon juice, rind, sugar and butter in heavy saucepan. Bring to boil over low heat. Beat egg yolks and whole eggs until combined. Gradually add lemon mixture, beating continuously. Heat and stir until mixture thickens. Remove from heat and continue to stir 3 to 4 minutes. Pour into quart jar and refrigerate when cool.

French Silk
Delicious crunch under silky chocolate

Preheat oven 400°

Serves 12 to 16

Crust

½ cup dark brown sugar
½ cup butter, softened

1 cup flour
½ cup pecans, broken

Mix sugar, butter, flour and pecans. Pat in 9 x 13-inch baking dish. Bake 15 minutes. Break up with fork and pat down again. Chill.

Filling

1 cup butter
1½ cups sugar
3 ounces unsweetened chocolate, melted
½ teaspoon almond extract

2 teaspoons vanilla
Pinch salt
4 eggs
12 to 16 maraschino cherries with stems (optional)
Whipped cream (optional)

Cream butter and sugar. Add chocolate, flavorings and salt. Add eggs, 1 at a time, beating well after each. Spread mixture over chilled crumbs and refrigerate 3 hours. Cut in squares to serve. Garnish with cherries on top of whipped cream rosettes.

Desserts

Hot Fudge Pudding
Chocolate delight

Preheat oven 350°   Serves 8 to 10

1 cup flour, sifted   ½ cup milk
2 teaspoons baking powder   2 tablespoons shortening, melted
¼ teaspoon salt   1 cup pecans, chopped
¾ cup sugar   1 cup brown sugar
6 tablespoons cocoa   1¾ cups hot water
                                     Whipped cream

Sift together flour, baking powder, salt, sugar and 2 tablespoons cocoa. Stir in milk, shortening and nuts. Spread in 9-inch square pan. Sprinkle with brown sugar and 4 tablespoons cocoa. Pour water over batter. Bake 45 minutes. Invert square of pudding on dessert plate, dip sauce from pan over each serving. Serve warm or cold with whipped cream.

Sweet Potato Pudding
Perfect ending to a traditional meal

Preheat oven 300°   Serves 12

2½ cups half and half   ½ cup blanched almonds
3 medium sweet potatoes, peeled   2 tablespoons butter
3 eggs, beaten   ½ cup rum
1 cup honey
2 teaspoons cinnamon

Butter shallow 2-quart baking dish. Add half and half. Grate sweet potatoes into cream. Combine eggs, honey, cinnamon and almonds. Add to potatoes and mix well. Dot with butter. Bake until pudding is set, about 1½ hours. Just before serving, pour rum over top.

 A pinch of salt added to a very sour fruit while cooking will greatly reduce the quantity of sugar needed to sweeten them.

Bananas Caribbean
Easy, inexpensive and romantic

Serves 4

½ cup brown sugar
1 tablespoon butter, melted
3 tablespoons banana liqueur

2 bananas, sliced lengthwise
Brandy
Vanilla ice cream

Add brown sugar to butter in skillet. Add banana liqueur and bananas. Warm brandy in small saucepan. Pour over bananas and ignite. Serve over vanilla ice cream.

Benz à la Orange
Serve after a heavy meal

Freeze

Serves 16

½ gallon vanilla ice cream, softened
½ cup brandy or orange liqueur

1 12-ounce can frozen orange juice
  concentrate, thawed

Stir all ingredients until well mixed. Place in 2-to 3-quart container. Cover tightly and freeze. Serve in hollow orange shells.

Tip: Substitute ice milk for ice cream to reduce calories.

Champagne Sorbet
Serve after heavy meal

Freeze

Yields 1¼ quarts

1 cup heavy cream
¾ cup sugar
1½ cups champagne
1 10-ounce package frozen
  strawberries, thawed

2 egg whites
¼ teaspoon cream of tartar
2 drops red food coloring (optional)

Combine cream and ½ cup sugar. Cook and stir over medium heat until sugar dissolves. Cool. Stir in champagne and undrained berries. Pour into 8 x 8 x 2-inch pan. Cover and freeze. Beat egg whites and cream of tartar to soft peaks. Slowly add remaining sugar, beating to stiff peaks. Break up frozen mixture. Place in chilled bowl. Beat smooth with electric mixer. Fold in egg whites. Tint with food coloring. Return to pan. Cover and freeze.

Desserts

Bombe Josephine
Only the brave serve this

Freeze

Serves 10 to 12

2 cups sugar
⅔ cup water
¼ teaspoon cream of tartar
8 egg yolks, beaten
2 cups heavy cream, whipped
1 cup pistachio nuts, chopped

½ cup kirsch
½ gallon coffee ice cream, softened
1 cup heavy cream
2 teaspoons sugar
2 cups peaches, sliced
1 10-ounce bottle Sauce Melba

Combine sugar, water and cream of tartar. Bring to boil and cook rapidly until syrup spins a light thread (232° on candy thermometer). Gradually add 1 cup syrup to egg yolks, beating constantly. Cook over boiling water, stirring constantly, until thick and smooth. Strain into bowl set in larger bowl of crushed ice; beat until cool. Fold in whipped cream, pistachio nuts and ¼ cup kirsch. Chill. Coat 2-quart round mold with coffee ice cream; fill center with pistachio nut cream. Freeze until set, at least 3 hours. To serve, remove bombe from mold and place on chilled, round platter. Decorate with 1 cup heavy cream whipped with sugar. Spoon peaches over sliced bombe. Pour Sauce Melba diluted with remaining ¼ cup kirsch over bombe.

Choco-Mint Dessert
For chocolate lovers

Freeze

Serves 8 to 16

4 tablespoons butter, melted
1¼ cups vanilla wafers, finely
    crushed (approximately 28)
1 quart peppermint or mint ice
    cream, softened
½ cup butter

2 ounces unsweetened chocolate
3 egg yolks, well beaten
1½ cups powdered sugar, sifted
½ cup pecans, chopped (optional)
1 teaspoon vanilla
3 egg whites

Combine 4 tablespoons butter and wafer crumbs. Press on bottom of 9 x 9-inch pan. Spread ice cream over crumbs and freeze. Melt ½ cup butter and chocolate over low heat. Stir into egg yolks. Add powdered sugar, nuts and vanilla. Cool thoroughly; do not allow mixture to harden. Beat egg whites into stiff peaks. In separate bowl, beat chocolate mixture until smooth; fold in egg whites. Spread over ice cream. Cover and freeze.

Cold Lime Soufflé
Light treat

Chill

Serves 6 to 8

1 envelope unflavored gelatin
¼ cup cold water
4 egg yolks
1 cup sugar
½ cup lime juice
½ teaspoon salt

1 tablespoon lime rind, grated
2 drops green food coloring (optional)
6 egg whites
1 cup heavy cream, whipped
Coconut, grated (optional)
Lime slices (optional)

Wrap waxed paper around top of 1½-quart soufflé dish, extending 4 inches above rim. Brush inside paper with oil. Sprinkle gelatin over water. In top of double boiler, mix egg yolks, ½ cup sugar, lime juice and salt. Cook over simmering water, stirring constantly until slightly thickened. Remove from heat. Add gelatin and stir until completely dissolved. Add lime rind and food coloring. Cool. Beat egg whites until stiff, gradually adding remaining sugar. Fold into lime mixture. Fold whipped cream into mixture. Spoon into prepared dish. Chill until firm. Remove paper to serve. Garnish with coconut and lime slices.

Orange Torte
Florida fruit at its best

Chill

Serves 8 to 10

16 ounces marshmallows
¾ cup orange juice
¼ cup lemon juice

1 cup graham cracker crumbs
½ cup butter, melted
¼ cup sugar
2 cups heavy cream, whipped

Melt marshmallows with orange juice and lemon juice in top of double boiler. Chill. Combine graham cracker crumbs, butter and sugar. Press into 9-inch spring-form pan. Fold whipped cream into marshmallow mixture. Pour into crust. Chill overnight.

Jade Cream Torte
Ice cream specialty

Freeze   Serves 12

2 cups chocolate wafer crumbs   5 tablespoons green crème de menthe
1/3 cup butter, softened   3 pints vanilla ice cream, softened

Combine chocolate wafer crumbs and butter. Press into 10-inch spring-form pan. Refrigerate until well chilled, about 1 hour. In separate bowl, swirl crème de menthe into ice cream. Pour into crust. Freeze.

Tip: Substitute peppermint, mint chocolate chip or coffee ice cream for vanilla ice cream.

Fudge Sauce

3 ounces unsweetened chocolate   1/4 teaspoon salt
1/2 cup water   4 1/2 tablespoons butter
3/4 cup sugar   3/4 teaspoon vanilla

Combine chocolate with water over low heat, stirring until chocolate is melted. Add sugar and salt. Cook, stirring constantly until sugar is melted and mixture is thickened, about 5 minutes. Remove from heat and stir in butter and vanilla. Cool thoroughly. Drizzle sauce over torte. Freeze. Serve extra sauce on side.

Patio Freeze
Make with or without sugar

Freeze   Serves 6 to 8

2 tablespoons lemon juice   1 cup sugar (optional)
2 cups orange juice   2 cups bananas, mashed
1 8-ounce can crushed pineapple

Mix all ingredients. Pour into 9 x 10-inch baking dish. Cover and freeze 2 hours. Cut into squares and serve.

Pots de Crème
Delightfully smooth

Chill

Serves 4

¾ cup milk
1 6-ounce package chocolate bits
2 tablespoons sugar
Dash salt

1 tablespoon dark rum or vanilla
   extract
1 egg
Whipped cream

Heat milk to boiling point. Place all ingredients except whipped cream in blender. Blend 1 minute on low speed. Pour into 4 pots de crème cups or ramekins. Chill 2 hours or until firm. Top with whipped cream.

Strawberries Café
Dim the lights

Serves 8 to 10

2 pints strawberries
2 tablespoons sugar
¾ cup dry red wine

¼ cup brandy
1 gallon coffee ice cream

Hull, wash and drain strawberries. Sprinkle with sugar and let stand 1 hour. Put strawberries in chafing dish with wine and heat. Pour brandy over berries and ignite. Stir. Spoon berries, while still flaming, over ice cream.

Strawberry Sherbet
Refresh your palate during or after a meal

Freeze

Yields 3½ cups

2 pints fresh strawberries
½ cup sugar

1 tablespoon fresh lemon juice

Wash and hull strawberries. Put in processor with steel blade. Add sugar and lemon juice. Process until fruit is finely puréed. Spread mixture in 8-inch aluminum cake pan and freeze until almost firm. Return to processor and process until smooth and fluffy. Place in airtight quart container. Freeze 2 hours.

Tip: If sherbet freezes solid, let soften in refrigerator 30 to 45 minutes before serving.

Desserts

Sarasota Snowball
Summertime dessert

Chill

Serves 6 to 10

1 envelope unflavored gelatin
¼ cup cold water
½ cup boiling water
1½ cups orange juice
Juice of 2 lemons

1 cup sugar
1 large angel food cake
2 cups heavy cream, whipped
2 cups coconut, grated

Soften gelatin in cold water 10 minutes. Add boiling water, orange juice, lemon juice and sugar. Cool until partially set. Remove brown crust from angel food cake. Break cake into small pieces. Line 3-quart mixing bowl or mold with waxed paper. Fold 1 cup whipped cream into gelatin mixture. Layer gelatin mixture and cake pieces in mold until all is used, ending with gelatin. Cover and refrigerate overnight. Unmold and spread 1 cup whipped cream over gelatin. Sprinkle generously with coconut.

Suwannee River Ice Cream
A taste of almond

Freeze

Serves 15

6 medium eggs, separated
2½ cups sugar
2 13-ounce cans evaporated milk
2½ tablespoons vanilla
½ teaspoon almond extract
½ teaspoon nutmeg

½ cup Amaretto
Dash salt
4 cups half and half
Whole milk
Amaretto

Beat egg whites until fluffy; set aside. Beat egg yolks until fluffy; add sugar gradually. Add canned milk slowly; beat until stiff. Add extracts, nutmeg, Amaretto, salt and half and half. Pour into 6-quart freezer can and fold in egg whites. Fill can with whole milk, if needed. Alternate ice and rock salt. Freeze 40 to 45 minutes in electric freezer. Remove dasher and pack in ice or deep freeze 3 to 5 hours. Pour 1 ounce Amaretto on each ice cream serving.

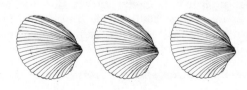

Strawberries Romanoff
From Russia with love

Chill   Serves 4 to 6

1 pint fresh strawberries   ½ pint vanilla ice cream, softened
½ cup sugar   3 tablespoons Cointreau
½ cup whipping cream, whipped   Juice of ½ lemon

Wash and remove stems from berries. Sprinkle sugar over berries and chill.
Chill whipped cream. When ready to serve, blend ice cream with whipped
cream. Add Cointreau and lemon juice. Pour over berries and lightly toss.
Serve immediately.

Cranberry Ice or Sherbet
Serve between courses or as a finale

Freeze   Serves 6 to 8

1 16-ounce package fresh   2 cups sugar
   cranberries   4 cups water

Cook cranberries with sugar in 2 cups water until berries pop. Add 2 more
cups water and liquefy in blender. Strain carefully and freeze.

Ice Cream
Especially made for the 4th of July

Freeze   Yields 4 quarts

2¼ cups sugar   4 to 6 teaspoons vanilla
4 eggs, beaten   4 cups heavy cream
5 cups milk   ½ teaspoon salt

In large mixing bowl, gradually add sugar to eggs; beat until thick and stiff.
Add remaining ingredients; mix well. Pour into 4-quart freezer can. Freeze
according to appliance directions.

Tip: If fruit is added, use 2 cups milk, 3 cups heavy cream and 4 cups
    crushed fruit. Other ingredients remain the same.

Desserts

Tortoni Alexis
Perfect ending to traditional meal

Freeze

Serves 10

1½ cups almond macaroons,
  crumbled
2 tablespoons kirsch liqueur
3 tablespoons Framboise liqueur
1 cup heavy cream, whipped

1 quart vanilla ice cream, softened
¾ cup blanched almonds, toasted and
  chopped
½ cup semi-sweet chocolate, shredded

Sprinkle macaroon crumbs with kirsch. Beat Framboise into whipped cream. Using chilled bowl, beat ice cream until light and mounding. Fold in whipped cream, almonds, chocolate and macaroon crumbs. Pour into 2-quart ice cream mold or bundt pan. Cover and freeze until firm. To serve, dip mold in hot water for few seconds and invert onto serving dish.

Tip: If Framboise is not available, use other red fruit liqueur.

Pink Lady Dessert
A beautiful luncheon dessert

Chill

Serves 12

30 lady fingers
1 3-ounce package raspberry
  gelatin
1 cup boiling water
48 miniature marshmallows
1 8½-ounce can sliced pineapple,
  drain, cut in wedges and
  reserve liquid

Water
2 cups fresh raspberries or
  strawberries, hulled and halved
½ cup blanched almonds, chopped
1 cup heavy cream, whipped
Whipped cream (optional)

Line bottom and sides of 10-inch ungreased, spring-form pan with lady fingers. Set aside. Dissolve gelatin in boiling water. Add marshmallows, stirring well. Refrigerate until partially set. Add enough cold water to pineapple juice to make ½ cup liquid. Add to gelatin mixture, stirring well. Add pineapple, raspberries or strawberries and almonds, blending well. Fold in whipped cream. Pour mixture into prepared pan and refrigerate until firm. Remove outer rim of pan and cut into wedges. Serve with whipped cream.

Chocolate Angel Torte
Melts in your mouth

Preheat oven 325°   Serves 16 to 18

¾ cup cake flour, sifted   1 6-ounce package chocolate bits
⅞ cup sugar   16 marshmallows
¼ cup cocoa   ¼ cup milk
1½ cups egg whites   1 cup heavy cream, whipped
1½ teaspoons cream of tartar   ½ cup pecans, broken in pieces
¼ teaspoon salt   2 cups heavy cream, whipped
1 teaspoon vanilla   2 teaspoons sugar
¾ cup sugar, sifted

Sift first 3 ingredients together 3 times. In large mixing bowl, combine next 4 ingredients. Beat until mixture stands in soft peaks. Gradually add ¾ cup sugar, 2 tablespoons at a time. Beat until stiff, but not dry. Sift flour mixture into egg whites, 4 tablespoons at a time. Fold 8 to 10 times after each addition. Pour into 10-inch tube cake pan. Bake 35 minutes. In top of double boiler, mix chocolate, marshmallows and milk. When melted and smooth, remove from heat and cool. Fold whipped cream into chocolate mixture; add pecans. Cut cake into 3 layers, spreading mixture between each layer. Ice completely with sweetened whipped cream. Chill.

Chocolate Delight
A rich treat

Chill   Serves 9

½ angel food cake   2 egg whites, stiffly beaten
12 ounces chocolate chips   2 cups heavy cream, whipped
2 egg yolks, slightly beaten   ½ cup walnuts, chopped

Break cake into walnut-size pieces. Place in 9-inch square pan. In top of double boiler, melt chocolate chips. Remove from heat and add egg yolks. Fold in egg whites. Cool. Add ½ the whipped cream and stir gently. Pour over cake. Refrigerate 2 to 3 hours. Cut into squares and serve topped with remaining whipped cream and nuts.

 1 cup heavy cream makes 2 cups whipped cream.

Desserts

Mocha Torte
An elegant presentation

Chill

Serves 10 to 14

3 tablespoons instant coffee crystals
1 cup boiling water
16 ounces marshmallows
⅛ teaspoon salt

2 cups heavy cream, whipped
1 cup pecans, coarsely chopped
2 dozen lady fingers, split

Combine coffee crystals, water, marshmallows and salt in top of double boiler. Stir constantly until marshmallows are melted. Chill until partially set, stirring 3 times. Fold in 1 cup whipped cream and ½ cup nuts. Line sides and bottom of 10-inch spring-form pan with ½ lady fingers. Pour ½ mixture into pan. Layer remaining lady fingers and mixture. Top with remaining whipped cream and nuts. Chill 2 hours.

Lemon Sherbet
Creamy

Freeze

Serves 6

1 cup sugar
8 tablespoons lemon juice

2 cups half and half

Mix sugar with lemon juice. Add half and half. Freeze in shallow 4 x 6-inch pan. Mix thoroughly. Cover and freeze.

Mango Ice Cream
Tropical fruit delight

Freeze

Yields 2½ quarts

4 eggs
2 cups sugar
¼ teaspoon salt

4 cups milk, scalded
1 cup heavy cream
1 tablespoon vanilla
4 cups mangoes, puréed

Blend eggs, sugar and salt. Add milk and cook over hot water until mixture coats spoon. Chill. Add cream, vanilla and mangoes. Freeze according to churn directions.

Allegretti Chiffon Cake
Chocolate cake with a taste of orange

Preheat oven 325°   Serves 8 to 10

1 cup plus 2 tablespoons cake flour,   1½ teaspoons baking powder
  sifted   ¼ cup plus 2 tablespoons cold water
½ teaspoon salt   1½ tablespoons orange rind, grated
¼ cup oil   4 egg whites
2 egg yolks, unbeaten   ¼ teaspoon cream of tartar
1 teaspoon vanilla   1½ squares chocolate (sweet or
¾ cup plus 2 tablespoons sugar   unsweetened), coarsely grated

Sift together flour and salt. Make a well in center and add oil, egg yolks, vanilla, sugar, baking powder, water and rind. Mix well. Set aside. In separate bowl, combine egg whites and cream of tartar. Beat into very stiff peaks. Do not underbeat. Pour egg yolk mixture gradually over egg whites, gently folding just until blended. Fold in chocolate. Pour into 10 x 5 x 3-inch ungreased loaf pan. Bake 50 minutes or until top springs back when lightly touched. Turn pan upside down resting edges on 2 other pans. Cool. Remove from pan. Ice with allegretti icing.

Allegretti Icing

4½ tablespoons butter   1½ teaspoons vanilla
1 egg yolk   1½ squares chocolate (sweet or
3 tablespoons cream   unsweetened)
3 cups powdered sugar, sifted   ¼ teaspoon oil

Cream butter. Blend in egg yolk. Stir in cream, sugar and vanilla. Beat well. Add additional cream, if needed, to reach spreading consistency. Frost cake. Melt chocolate with oil. Cool slightly. Dribble over top and sides of cake. Refrigerate.

Substitutions

1. For whole egg, for thickening or baking: 2 egg yolks.
2. For 1 square (1 ounce) chocolate: 4 tablespoons cocoa plus ½ tablespoon butter.

Apple Dapple Cake
Better than apple pie

Preheat oven 350°   Serves 12 to 15

1⅓ cups oil
2 cups sugar
3 eggs
2 teaspoons vanilla
3 cups flour

1 teaspoon baking soda
1 teaspoon salt
1½ cups pecans, chopped
3 cups apples, peeled and chopped

Mix first 4 ingredients. Sift flour, baking soda and salt together. Combine both mixtures. Fold in pecans and apples. Bake in greased 10-inch tube pan 1½ hours.

Topping

1 cup brown sugar, firmly packed   ½ cup butter
¼ cup milk

Combine all ingredients and cook 2 minutes. Pour hot topping over hot cake. Cool cake in pan 2 hours. Remove and turn right side up.

No milk? Try:

For 1 cup buttermilk or sour milk:
1. 1 cup yogurt (plain)
2. 1 cup sour cream
3. 1 cup sweet milk plus 1 tablespoon vinegar or 1 tablespoon lemon juice or 1¾ teaspoons cream of tartar and let stand 5 minutes at room temperature.

For 1 cup sweet milk:
1. 1 cup buttermilk plus ½ teaspoon baking soda
2. ¼ cup powdered skim milk plus 1 cup water and 2 tablespoons butter
3. ½ cup evaporated milk plus ½ cup water

For 1 cup light cream:
1. ⅞ cup milk plus 3 tablespoons butter

For 1 cup heavy cream:
1. ¾ cup milk plus ⅓ cup butter

Blueberry Lemon Cake
Two special flavors

Preheat oven 350°

Serves 10 to 12

1 18½-ounce package lemon
   cake mix
8 ounces lemon yogurt

4 eggs
9 ounces unsweetened blueberries

In large mixing bowl, combine cake mix, yogurt and eggs. Blend until moistened. Beat 2 minutes at medium speed. Fold in blueberries. Pour into greased and floured 10-inch tube pan. Bake 40 to 45 minutes or until cake tests done. Cool in pan 15 minutes.

Sauce

Yields 3 cups

1 cup sugar
3 tablespoons cornstarch
1 cup boiling water

9 ounces unsweetened blueberries
3 tablespoons lemon juice

Combine sugar and cornstarch. Gradually stir in water. Cook and stir until thickened. Cook 2 minutes longer. Remove from heat. Stir in blueberries and lemon juice. Cool. Serve over cake slices.

Calamondin Cake
Tropical treat

Preheat oven 325°

Serves 12

1 18½-ounce package lemon
   supreme cake mix
¾ cup oil
½ cup sugar

4 eggs
1¼ cups calamondins, seedless
   and puréed
1 cup powdered sugar

Mix lemon cake mix, oil, sugar, eggs and 1 cup calamondins at medium speed 2 minutes. Pour into greased and floured bundt pan. Bake 1 hour. Mix ¼ cup calamondins and powdered sugar. Remove cake from pan. Pour fruit glaze over warm cake.

Cakes

Carrot Cake with a Difference
Serve with glaze or spread

Preheat oven 350°   Serves 10 to 12

2 cups sugar   3 cups carrots, grated
1½ cups salad oil   1 cup black walnuts, chopped
2 cups self-rising flour   1 teaspoon vanilla
1 teaspoon cinnamon   ¼ teaspoon walnut extract
4 eggs, beaten

Mix sugar and oil. Blend in flour and cinnamon. Add eggs; mix well. Fold in carrots, nuts and extracts. For buttermilk glaze, pour into greased 10-inch spring-form pan. Bake 1½ hours. For cream cheese spread, pour into three 8-inch round, greased and floured cake pans. Bake 1 hour.

Buttermilk Glaze

1 cup sugar   ½ teaspoon baking soda
½ cup buttermilk   1 tablespoon corn syrup

Blend all ingredients well. Pour glaze over hot cake. Cool 1 hour. Remove cake from pan.

Cream Cheese Spread

1 1-pound box powdered sugar   2 3-ounce packages cream cheese,
½ cup butter, softened   softened
                                         2 teaspoons vanilla

Beat all ingredients until smooth. Spread over cooled cake.

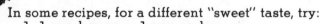

In some recipes, for a different "sweet" taste, try:
1. 1 cup honey or 1 cup molasses
   For 1¼ cups sugar and ¼ cup liquid (from recipe's ingredients)
2. 1 cup corn syrup
   For ¾ cup sugar and ¼ cup liquid (from recipe's ingredients)
3. 1 cup white sugar blended with 4 tablespoons unsulfured molasses
   For 1 cup dark brown sugar
4. 1 cup white sugar blended with 2 tablespoons unsulfured molasses
   For 1 cup light brown sugar

Checkerboard Chocolate Cupcakes
They dress themselves for your party

Preheat oven 350°   Serves 18

1½ cups flour   1 tablespoon vinegar
1 cup sugar   1 teaspoon vanilla
¼ cup cocoa   8 ounces cream cheese
1½ teaspoons baking soda   1 egg
1 cup water   ⅓ cup sugar
⅓ cup oil   ⅛ teaspoon salt
                                      6 ounces chocolate chips

Mix first 8 ingredients; beat well. Fill paper cups in muffin pans ⅓ full. In separate bowl, combine next 4 ingredients; beat well. Add chocolate chips. Dot each cupcake with heaping tablespoon of cheese mixture. Bake 30 minutes or until done.

Chocolate Cheesecake
Smooth, rich and creamy

Preheat oven 325°   Serves 10 to 12

Crust

1⅓ cups chocolate wafer crumbs   ¼ teaspoon ground cinnamon
2 tablespoons sugar   ¼ cup butter, softened

Combine all ingredients. Press on bottom of 10-inch spring-form pan.

Filling

1½ cups semi-sweet chocolate   8 ounces sour cream
   morsels   2 8-ounce packages cream cheese,
2 eggs   cubed and softened
½ cup sugar   2 tablespoons butter, melted
2 teaspoons rum   Whipped cream (optional)

Melt chocolate morsels over hot water in top of double boiler. Set aside. Combine eggs, sugar, rum and sour cream in blender or food processor. Process 15 seconds. Continue blending and gradually add chocolate and cream cheese. Add butter and blend well. Pour into crust. Bake 45 minutes or until cheesecake is set in center. Cool at room temperature 1 hour. Chill 6 hours. Garnish with whipped cream.

Cakes

Cranberry Cake
Autumn treat

Preheat oven 350°   Serves 10

1 cup sugar   ¼ teaspoon salt
2 cups flour   3 heaping tablespoons shortening
4 teaspoons baking powder   1 cup milk
                                     2 cups whole cranberries

Combine first 4 ingredients. Cut in shortening. Add milk and cranberries and stir just to mix ingredients. Place in greased 9 x 13-inch pan and bake 35 to 40 minutes.

Sauce

1⅓ cups sugar   1 cup butter, melted
2 tablespoons cornstarch   1½ teaspoons vanilla
2 cups half and half

Mix sugar and cornstarch. Add half and half and sugar mixture to butter. Cook until thickened. Add vanilla. Pour warm sauce over cake.

Coffee Angel Food Cake
Heavenly

Preheat oven 350°   Serves 12

1 tablespoon instant coffee   1 16-ounce package angel food cake
1⅓ cups cold water   mix

Dissolve coffee in cold water. Add cake mix and beat on low speed of mixer 30 seconds. Beat on medium speed 1 minute. Pour into ungreased 10-inch tube pan. Bake 40 to 50 minutes. Cool in pan.

Icing

¾ cup butter   4 to 6 tablespoons milk
¼ teaspoon salt   1½ teaspoons vanilla
3¾ cups powdered sugar   Almonds, toasted
2 to 3 tablespoons instant coffee

Cream butter. Gradually add salt and sugar, beating continuously. Dissolve coffee in milk. Add coffee mixture and vanilla to sugar mixture. Beat until light and fluffy. Ice cake; sprinkle with almonds.

Early Morning Coffee Cake
Mouth-watering

Preheat oven 350°   Serves 12 to 14

1 cup butter   ½ teaspoon vanilla
2 cups sugar   2 cups flour
2 eggs   1 teaspoon baking powder
1 cup sour cream   ¼ teaspoon salt

Topping

½ cup brown sugar   2 tablespoons flour
2 tablespoons butter   2 teaspoons cinnamon

Cream butter and sugar; add eggs. Fold in sour cream and vanilla. Add dry ingredients. Combine all topping ingredients. Spoon ½ batter into greased and floured 10-inch tube pan. Cover with ½ topping; repeat. Bake 1 hour. Cool completely before removing from pan.

Frozen Date-Nut Cake
Rich, creamy and intoxicating

Freeze   Serves 8

1 tablespoon sugar   8 lady fingers, broken in 1-inch
2 cups heavy cream   pieces
1 ounce bourbon or brandy   1 cup boiled custard
8 macaroons, broken in 1-inch   ½ cup dates, chopped
  pieces   ½ cup pecans, chopped
                                     Eggnog

Add sugar to cream and whip. Fold in bourbon, macaroons, lady fingers, custard, dates and pecans. Pour into 6-cup melon mold. Freeze. Before serving, unmold and pour eggnog over top.

Egg whites whip best when temperature is approximately 75°.

Cakes

Granny Cake
Brings back childhood memories

Preheat oven 350°   Serves 10

2 cups sugar
½ cup butter, melted
2 eggs
1 teaspoon baking soda
½ cup buttermilk

2 cups flour
3 heaping tablespoons cocoa
1 teaspoon vanilla
1 cup boiling water

Mix sugar, butter and eggs in bowl. Dissolve soda in buttermilk. Add to sugar and egg mixture. Sift flour and cocoa and stir into batter. Add vanilla and water. Pour into greased 9 x 13-inch pan and bake 15 to 20 minutes or until center springs back to touch. Cool.

Minute Fudge Frosting

¼ cup butter
3 tablespoons cocoa
¼ cup milk

1 cup sugar
⅛ teaspoon salt

Combine all ingredients. Cook slowly until sugar dissolves. Bring to full, rolling boil for 1 minute. Remove from heat. Beat until thickened and smooth enough to pour on top of cooled cake.

Hot Milk Cake
Good plain or frosted

Preheat oven 325°   Serves 12

½ cup butter
1 cup milk
4 eggs, beaten
2 cups sugar

2 cups flour
2 teaspoons baking powder
1 teaspoon vanilla

Melt butter in milk. Cool. Mix eggs, sugar, flour and baking powder. Add milk mixture and vanilla. Bake in 10-inch greased tube pan 1 hour.

Layered Butter-Cocoa Dessert
Creamy make-ahead treat

Chill   Serves 20

2 cups butter   2 1-pound boxes graham crackers
1 1-pound box powdered sugar   3 cups cold, strong black coffee
4 egg yolks   4 tablespoons cocoa
1½ teaspoons vanilla   ½ pound salted almonds, ground

Cream butter and sugar 15 minutes. Add eggs and vanilla; beat well. Dip graham crackers, 1 at a time, in coffee. Place on cookie sheet, edges touching, in 4 rows of 5 crackers, forming a rectangle. Spread butter mixture thinly over crackers. Repeat layers, using all crackers and ½ butter mixture. Add cocoa to remaining butter mixture and frost top and sides. Sprinkle with nuts. Cover and refrigerate. Remove 1 hour before serving.

Little Chocolate Cakes
Tastes elegant but so simple

Preheat oven 350°   Yields 18 to 20 cakes

1 cup butter   1 cup flour
4 ounces semi-sweet chocolate bits   1¾ cups sugar
4 eggs   ½ to 1 cup pecans, chopped
2 tablespoons vanilla

Melt butter with chocolate bits. Remove from heat. Add eggs 1 at a time, beating well after each. Add remaining ingredients. Pour mixture into well-greased muffin tins. Bake 20 minutes.

Chocolate Glaze
Basic

                                       Yields 1¼ cups

2 tablespoons cocoa   1 tablespoon oil
5 teaspoons hot water   1 cup powdered sugar

Dissolve cocoa in hot water. Add oil and sugar. Blend well. Spoon or drizzle glaze over cake.

Cakes

Louise's White Cake
Light and versatile

Preheat oven 350°   Serves 12

1 cup shortening   1 cup milk
2 cups sugar   1 teaspoon vanilla
3 cups flour   4 egg whites, at room temperature
2 teaspoons baking powder

Cream shortening and sugar well. Sift flour and baking powder together. Add to mixture, alternating with milk and vanilla, ending with dry ingredients. Beat well between additions. Beat egg whites until stiff but not dry; fold into mixture. Pour into two 8-inch greased and floured cake pans or 24 cupcake pans. Bake cake 30 minutes; cupcakes 15 to 20 minutes.

Merry Cheese Cakes
Indispensable when time is short

Preheat oven 350°   Serves 12

1 cup flour   ½ cup brown sugar, firmly packed
½ cup butter, softened   ½ cup pecans, chopped

Combine flour, butter and brown sugar. Beat with mixer until particles are fine. Stir in pecans. Reserve 1 cup mixture for topping. Pat remaining mixture in ungreased 8-inch square pan. Bake 8 to 10 minutes. Cool.

Filling

1 8-ounce package cream cheese,   2 tablespoons milk
   softened   2 tablespoons lemon juice
¼ cup sugar   ½ teaspoon vanilla
1 egg

Mix cream cheese, sugar, egg, milk, lemon juice and vanilla. Spread over pie crust. Sprinkle with reserved crumb mixture. Bake 25 to 30 minutes or until brown. Cool; cut into bars. Chill.

Mex-Tex Sheet Cake
Medley of ingredients likely to succeed

Preheat oven 350°   Serves 12

1 cup butter, melted
¼ cup unsweetened cocoa
1 tablespoon instant coffee
1 cup water
1½ cups light brown sugar, firmly
   packed
2 cups flour

1 teaspoon baking soda
1 teaspoon ground cinnamon
½ teaspoon salt
⅓ cup sweetened condensed milk
2 eggs
1 teaspoon vanilla

In saucepan, combine butter, cocoa, coffee and water. Bring to boil. Remove from heat. In large bowl, combine sugar, flour, soda, cinnamon and salt. Add butter mixture. Beat well. Mix in condensed milk, eggs and vanilla. Pour into lightly greased 9 x 13-inch pan. Bake 15 to 25 minutes or until cake springs back to touch. Cool 10 minutes. Spread with Mex-Tex frosting.

Mex-Tex Frosting

Yields 2 cups

¼ cup butter, melted
¼ cup cocoa
1 tablespoon instant coffee

1 cup sweetened condensed milk
1 cup powdered sugar
½ cup almonds, toasted and slivered

Over low heat, combine butter, cocoa and coffee. Remove from heat. Add condensed milk. Stir in sugar and nuts. Spread on warm cake.

Pineapple Refrigerator Cake
Refreshing

Chill   Serves 16

16 ounces vanilla wafers, crushed
4 eggs
1 cup butter

4 cups powdered sugar
2 cups heavy cream, whipped
2 cups crushed pineapple, drained

Spread 8 ounces vanilla wafer crumbs on bottom of 9 x 12-inch dish. Beat eggs, butter and powdered sugar until stiff. Pour over crumbs. Combine whipped cream and pineapple. Pour over sauce. Sprinkle remaining crumbs over top. Refrigerate 24 hours. Cut into squares.

Cakes

Mini Chip Cake Roll
Hit of the day

Preheat oven 375°   Serves 8

¼ cup butter
1½ cups coconut, flaked
1 cup semi-sweet chocolate mini
  chips
½ cup sweetened condensed milk
4 eggs
1 cup sugar

⅓ cup orange juice
1 tablespoon orange peel, grated
1 cup flour
1 teaspoon baking soda
¼ teaspoon salt
Powdered sugar

Line 15½ x 10½ x 1-inch pan with aluminum foil. Melt butter in pan. Sprinkle coconut and chocolate mini chips over butter. Drizzle with condensed milk. Beat eggs in mixing bowl at high speed 2 minutes. Gradually add sugar; continue beating 1 minute. Combine orange juice and orange peel. In separate bowl, mix flour, baking soda and salt. Add to sugar and egg mixture alternately with orange juice. Pour evenly into pan. Bake 20 to 25 minutes or until cake springs back when touched in center. Sprinkle powdered sugar over cake. Cover with towel. Place baking sheet over towel and invert; remove pan and aluminum foil. Starting at narrow end, roll cake. Cool completely. Dust with powdered sugar before serving.

Pumpkin Cheesecake
A different combination

Preheat oven 400°   Serves 10 to 12

Crust

⅓ cup butter
⅓ cup sugar

1 egg
1¼ cups flour

Cream butter and sugar. Blend in egg; add flour. Press dough on bottom and sides of 9-inch spring-form pan. Bake 5 minutes. Reduce oven to 350°.

Filling

2 8-ounce packages cream cheese
¾ cup sugar
1 16-ounce can pumpkin
1 teaspoon cinnamon

¼ teaspoon ginger
¼ teaspoon nutmeg
2 eggs, beaten

Beat cream cheese until smooth. Add remaining ingredients. Pour into crust. Bake 50 minutes. Cool completely before removing from pan. Chill.

Mississippi Mud Cake
Sinfully sweet

Preheat oven 350°   Serves 16

1 cup butter, melted   1 teaspoon vanilla
⅓ cup cocoa   1½ cups self-rising flour
2 cups sugar   1½ cups pecans, chopped
4 eggs   1 7-ounce jar marshmallow creme

Mix butter, cocoa, sugar, eggs and vanilla. Beat in flour. Stir in pecans. Pour in greased and floured 8 x 13-inch pan. Bake 45 minutes. Spread marshmallow creme on warm cake.

Tip: Place marshmallow creme jar in warm water to make spreading easier.

Icing

4 tablespoons butter, melted   1 teaspoon vanilla
⅓ cup cocoa   ⅓ cup milk
1 1-pound box powdered sugar

Combine butter and cocoa. Add sugar, vanilla and milk. Beat until smooth. Pour over cake.

My Nutty Fruit Cake
Good holiday cake

Preheat oven 275°   Serves 20

1½ pounds dates, pitted and   2 teaspoons baking powder
    chopped   ¼ teaspoon salt
1 pound pecans, chopped   10 eggs
½ pound candied fruit, chopped   2 cups sugar
1 cup flour   2 teaspoons vanilla

Mix dates, pecans, candied fruit, flour, baking powder and salt in paper bag. Beat eggs until thick. Add sugar and vanilla. Add date mixture to egg mixture. Pour into two 8½-inch cake pans lined with greased brown paper. Bake 30 minutes, pat cake down and bake 30 minutes longer. Remove from oven and pull off paper while still hot. Cool on rack.

Cakes

My Mother's Cheesecake
A crowd pleaser

Preheat oven 350°   Serves 12

Crust

1 box Zwieback   ¼ cup sugar
6 tablespoons butter, melted   Dash cinnamon
¼ teaspoon lemon rind, grated

Crush Zwieback in food processor or blender. Add butter, lemon rind, sugar and cinnamon. Pat firmly on bottom and sides of 9-inch spring-form pan.

Filling

3 8-ounce packages cream cheese   ⅓ cup lemon juice
6 eggs, separated   1 tablespoon vanilla
1 cup sugar   1 heaping tablespoon flour
1 cup coffee cream   Pinch salt
1 lemon rind, grated

Beat cream cheese, egg yolks and sugar in mixing bowl until creamy. Add cream, lemon rind, lemon juice, vanilla, flour and salt. Mix until well blended. Whip egg whites until peaks form and fold into mixture. Pour into crust. Bake 1 hour. Turn off heat and cool cheesecake completely in oven.

Oatmeal Banana Cupcakes
Nutritious snack

Preheat oven 375°   Yields 24 cupcakes

½ cup sugar   1½ cups flour
½ cup butter   1 teaspoon baking powder
2 eggs   1 teaspoon baking soda
3 to 4 bananas, mashed   ¾ teaspoon salt
¾ cup honey   1 cup quick cooking rolled oats

Cream sugar and butter. Beat in eggs, bananas and honey. Sift together flour, baking powder, soda and salt. Add to creamed mixture, beating just until blended. Stir in oats. Line muffin pan with paper cups. Fill ⅔ full with mixture. Bake 18 to 20 minutes. Remove from pan and cool on wire rack.

Oatmeal Cake
A change

Preheat oven 350°   Serves 12

1¼ cups boiling water   1 teaspoon vanilla
1 cup oatmeal   1 teaspoon cinnamon
½ cup butter   1⅓ cups flour
1 cup brown sugar   1 teaspoon baking soda
1 cup white sugar   1 teaspoon baking powder
2 eggs

Pour water over oatmeal. Let stand 20 minutes. Cream butter and sugars. Add eggs, vanilla and cinnamon. Mix thoroughly. Add oatmeal. Sift remaining ingredients together and add to oatmeal mixture. Bake in greased 9 x 13-inch cake pan 30 minutes or until done.

Broiled Topping

3 tablespoons butter, melted   1 cup pecans
⅔ cup brown sugar   Milk
⅔ cup coconut

Combine all ingredients except milk. Add milk until spreading consistency is reached. Spread on hot cake. Return cake to oven. Broil until topping bubbles.

Orange Slice Cake
Better than fruit cake

Preheat oven 300°   Serves 10 to 12

2 cups pecans, chopped   1 cup butter, melted
2 8-ounce packages dates,   4 eggs, beaten
  chopped   1½ cups sugar
16 ounces orange slice candy,   2 cups flour
  chopped   1 teaspoon baking soda
1 3½-ounce can coconut, flaked   ½ cup buttermilk

Combine nuts, dates, candy and coconut. Add butter. Mix remaining ingredients and add to nut mixture. Pour into greased 10-inch tube pan. Bake 2 hours. Cool in pan.

Cakes

Seven Minute Coconut Frosting
Coconut may be substituted

2 egg whites
1½ cups sugar
1½ teaspoons light corn syrup
⅓ cup cold water

Dash salt
1 teaspoon vanilla
2 cups moist coconut

Place all ingredients except vanilla and coconut in double boiler. Mix thoroughly. Cook, beating constantly with electric mixer, until mixture forms peaks, about 7 minutes. Remove from heat and add vanilla. Beat until spreading consistency. Add 1½ cups coconut. Mix well. Ice cake. Sprinkle with remaining coconut.

Sherry's Apple Cake
Destined to be the hit of the day

Preheat oven 325°

Serves 12

1¼ cups oil
2 cups sugar
2 eggs
3 cups flour, sifted
3 cups apples, peeled and sliced
1 tablespoon cinnamon
1 teaspoon baking soda

1½ teaspoons salt
2 teaspoons vanilla
½ cup pecans, chopped
1 cup powdered sugar
2 teaspoons cinnamon
3 to 6 tablespoons orange juice

Combine oil, sugar and eggs; beat well. Add flour, apples, 1 tablespoon cinnamon, soda, salt, vanilla and nuts. Mix until well blended. Pour into greased 13 x 9-inch pan. Bake 50 to 60 minutes. Combine powdered sugar and cinnamon; add orange juice to reach spreading consistency. Spread on hot cake.

Dip the spoon in hot water to measure butter; the fat will slip out more easily.

Sour Cream Pound Cake
Traditional

Preheat oven 325°   Serves 10 to 12

1 cup butter   3 cups flour
3 cups sugar   ¼ teaspoon baking soda
6 eggs   1½ teaspoons vanilla
1 cup sour cream

Cream butter; gradually add sugar, continuing to mix. Add eggs 1 at a time, mixing well after each. Add sour cream. Sift flour and soda together; gradually add to mixture. Stir in vanilla. Pour batter into greased 10-inch tube pan. Bake 1½ hours. Do not overcook. Cool 15 minutes before removing from pan.

Special Occasion Walnut Cake
Rich and tasty

Preheat oven 350°   Serves 15 to 20

½ cup butter   ½ teaspoon salt
½ cup shortening   1 cup buttermilk
2 cups sugar   1 teaspoon vanilla
5 eggs, separated   1 teaspoon coconut extract
2 cups flour, sifted twice   1 3½-ounce can coconut
1 teaspoon baking soda   1 cup walnuts, finely chopped

Blend butter, shortening and sugar. Add egg yolks, beating well after each. Sift together dry ingredients. Alternate adding flour mixture and buttermilk. Continue blending after each addition. Stir in extracts, coconut and walnuts. Beat egg whites until stiff; fold into batter. Pour into 3 greased and floured 9-inch cake pans. Bake 35 minutes.

Frosting

1 8-ounce package cream cheese,   1 teaspoon coconut extract
   softened   1 1-pound box powdered sugar
½ cup butter, softened

Combine all ingredients and beat until smooth and creamy. Remove cake from pans when cooled. Frost.

Cakes

Tipsy Cake
Plan ahead

Preheat oven 350°

Serves 15 to 20

6 eggs, separated
1½ cups sugar
1 teaspoon vanilla
1½ cups flour
1½ teaspoons baking powder

½ teaspoon salt
4½ tablespoons cold water
2 cups sherry
1 cup apricot preserves
1½ cups almonds, toasted and sliced

Custard

1½ cups sugar
¼ cup flour
⅛ teaspoon salt

6 eggs, beaten
4 cups milk
2 teaspoons vanilla

Beat egg yolks until light; gradually add ¾ cup sugar, beating until thick and lemon colored. Add vanilla. Combine flour, baking powder and salt; add to egg mixture alternately with water, mixing well. Beat egg whites until stiff peaks form; gradually add remaining ¾ cup sugar. Fold egg whites into cake batter until thoroughly mixed. Pour cake batter into an ungreased 10-inch tube pan; bake 30 minutes or until cake tests done. Invert and cool on cake rack. Remove from pan. Split cake into 2 layers. Drizzle 1 cup sherry over each layer; cover loosely with waxed paper or plastic wrap and let sit one day. Spread bottom layer of cake with ½ cup apricot preserves and sprinkle with ½ cup almonds. To prepare custard: combine sugar, flour and salt in top of double boiler. Add eggs and beat well. Gradually add milk, stirring constantly until well blended. Place over boiling water and cook, stirring constantly, until mixture thickens and coats spoon. Remove from heat and cool. Stir in vanilla. Top cake with layer of custard. Place second layer of cake on top and repeat layers of preserves, almonds and custard. Cover cake and refrigerate until ready to serve.

Whipped Cream Frosting

2 cups heavy cream
3 tablespoons sugar

2 teaspoons vanilla

Whip cream until it begins to thicken. Gradually add sugar and vanilla and continue beating until stiff peaks form. Frost cake with whipped cream frosting, and sprinkle with remaining almonds. Will keep one week in refrigerator.

Texas Cake
Serve with pride

Preheat oven 350°   Serves 24

2 cups flour   ½ cup sour cream
2 cups sugar   1 cup butter
1 teaspoon baking soda   4 tablespoons cocoa
2 eggs   1 cup cold water
½ teaspoon salt

Mix first 6 ingredients. Bring butter, cocoa and water to boil. Add to flour mixture and beat well. Pour into greased 10½ x 15½-inch cake pan. Bake 20 minutes.

Icing

½ cup butter   1 1-pound box powdered sugar
4 tablespoons cocoa   1 cup pecans, chopped
6 tablespoons milk   1 teaspoon vanilla

Bring butter, cocoa and milk to boil. Pour over powdered sugar, pecans and vanilla. Mix well. Spread on warm cake.

White Fruit Cake
Fruit cake for warmer weather

Preheat oven 250°   Serves 20

16 ounces white raisins   4 cups flour
8 ounces glazed pineapple,   2 cups butter
   chopped   2 cups sugar
8 ounces cherries, chopped   10 eggs
8 ounces citrons, chopped   1 teaspoon lemon extract
16 ounces walnuts or pecans,   1 teaspoon salt
   chopped

Dredge fruits and nuts with ½ cup flour; set aside. Cream butter and sugar. Add eggs, beating well after each addition. Beat in lemon extract. Gradually add salt and remaining flour; beat until smooth. Add fruits and nuts and mix thoroughly. Line 10-inch tube pan with 2 layers oiled heavy brown paper. Pour mixture into pan and bake 3½ hours. Place pan of hot water in oven while baking to keep cake from drying out.

Tip: Prepare cake 2 to 4 weeks before serving. Wrap in cheesecloth soaked in brandy, sherry or bourbon. Wrap in foil.

Cakes

Zucchini Cake
Mystery cake

Preheat oven 350°   Serves 12

2½ cups flour   3 eggs, beaten
2 teaspoons baking powder   ½ cup oil
1 teaspoon baking soda   1⅓ cups sugar
1 teaspoon salt   ½ cup orange juice
2 teaspoons cinnamon   1 teaspoon almond extract
½ teaspoon ground cloves   1½ cups zucchini squash, shredded
                                         (2 medium)

In large bowl, mix flour, baking powder, soda, salt, cinnamon and cloves; set aside. Combine eggs, oil, sugar, juice, extract and zucchini; mix well. Add to flour mixture, stirring just to moisten. Pour into greased 13 x 9 x 2-inch pan. Bake 35 to 40 minutes. Cool in pan.

Orange Icing

                                      Yields 1½ cups

2 tablespoons butter, softened   ¼ cup orange juice
3 cups powdered sugar   2 teaspoons lemon juice

In small bowl, mix all ingredients until well blended. If icing is too thick, thin with orange juice. Ice cake when cool.

Buttermilk Pie
A Southern tradition

Preheat oven 325°   Serves 8 to 12

4 eggs   ½ cup butter, softened
1¼ cups sugar   Pinch salt
1 cup buttermilk   1 teaspoon vanilla
                                      2 8-inch pie shells, unbaked

Beat eggs and sugar together. Add next 4 ingredients, blending well. Pour into pie shells. Bake until firm, about 60 minutes.

Calamondin Chiffon Pie
Adapted from Key Lime Pie

Chill

Serves 6

1 14-ounce can sweetened
   condensed milk
½ cup calamondin juice
2 tablespoons calamondin peel,
   grated

3 egg whites
¼ teaspoon cream of tartar
1 9-inch graham cracker crust

Beat condensed milk 10 minutes with electric mixer. Add juice and peel. Beat another 10 minutes. Beat egg whites slowly, adding cream of tartar, until stiff but not dry. Fold egg white mixture into milk mixture. Pour into crust. Chill at least 3 to 4 hours.

Chocolate Angel Pie
Unique crust

Preheat oven 275°

Serves 6 to 8

Meringue Crust

3 egg whites
⅛ teaspoon cream of tartar

½ cup sugar

Beat egg whites until foamy. Sift cream of tartar and sugar gradually into egg whites. Beat until smooth and glossy. Line well-buttered 9-inch pie pan with mixture. Bake 1 hour. Cool.

Filling

Chill

¾ cup semi-sweet chocolate chips
3 tablespoons hot water
2 tablespoons sugar

1 teaspoon vanilla
1 cup heavy cream, whipped

In top of double boiler, combine chocolate, water and sugar. Cook until thickened. Cool. Add vanilla. Fold in whipped cream. Pour into meringue shell and chill 3 hours or overnight.

Chocolate Chip Pie
A favorite

Preheat oven 350°   Serves 6

1 cup sugar
½ cup flour
2 eggs, beaten
½ cup butter, melted and cooled
1 cup pecans, chopped

1 cup chocolate chips
1 teaspoon vanilla
½ teaspoon bourbon (optional)
1 9-inch pie shell, unbaked
Whipped cream

Combine sugar and flour. Add eggs and blend well. Add butter, nuts, chocolate chips, vanilla and bourbon. Pour into pie shell and bake 30 minutes. Serve with whipped cream.

Chocolate Silk Pie
Like chocolate mousse

Preheat oven 400°   Serves 8

Crust

1¼ cups walnuts, finely chopped
2 tablespoons light brown sugar

2 tablespoons unsalted butter,
   softened

Combine walnuts, brown sugar and butter. Press into buttered 9-inch pie pan. Bake 15 minutes. Cool.

Filling

Chill

6 tablespoons unsalted butter
4½ ounces unsweetened chocolate
¾ cup sugar
3 eggs, lightly beaten

1 teaspoon vanilla
Pinch salt
2 tablespoons brandy
Whipped cream

In top of double boiler, heat butter, chocolate and sugar, stirring occasionally until chocolate is melted. Remove from heat. Stir in eggs, vanilla, salt and brandy. Pour into crust. Chill at least 4 hours. Serve with whipped cream.

Cranberry Pie
A Thanksgiving alternative

Preheat oven 325°   Serves 6

1 cup raw cranberries   ½ cup flour
¾ cup sugar   ⅓ cup butter, melted
¼ cup walnuts, chopped   Whipped cream
1 egg, beaten

Place cranberries in well-buttered 8-inch pie pan. Sprinkle with ¼ cup sugar and nuts. Combine egg and remaining sugar; beat well. Add flour and butter; mix thoroughly. Pour batter over cranberries. Bake 45 minutes or until golden brown. Serve with whipped cream.

Dutch Peach Pie
Family favorite

Preheat oven 400°   Serves 8

3 cups fresh peaches, sliced   Pinch salt
1 9-inch deep dish pie shell,   ⅔ cup heavy cream
  unbaked   ⅓ cup milk
1¼ cups sugar   Cinnamon
4 tablespoons flour

Place peaches in pie shell. Mix next 5 ingredients and pour over fruit. Sprinkle with cinnamon. Bake 40 to 50 minutes. Cool.

Perfect Crust
Wonderful texture

Preheat oven 350°   Yields 1 crust

1 cup flour   ¼ cup walnuts or pecans, chopped
¼ cup powdered sugar   ½ cup butter, softened

Combine flour, sugar and nuts in mixing bowl with butter. Press into 9-inch glass pie pan. Bake 15 minutes.

Frozen Raspberry Pie
Cool and delicious

Freeze

Serves 6 to 8

1 10-ounce package frozen
  raspberries, thawed
1 cup sugar
2 egg whites, at room temperature
1 tablespoon lemon juice

Dash salt
1 cup heavy cream, whipped
¼ cup blanched almonds, sliced and
  toasted
1 9-inch pie shell, baked and cooled

Reserve a few raspberries for garnish. Combine raspberries, sugar, egg whites, lemon juice and salt. Beat until stiff. Fold in whipped cream and almonds. Place in pie shell and freeze until firm. Garnish with reserved raspberries.

Fruit Cobbler
For fresh fruits

Preheat oven 350°

Serves 4

½ cup butter
¾ cup flour
2 teaspoons baking powder
1 cup sugar

¾ cup milk
2 cups fresh fruit, sliced and sweetened
  (peaches, guavas, blueberries)

Melt butter in 2-quart baking dish. Combine flour, baking powder, sugar and milk. Add to butter. Top with fresh fruit. Bake 40 minutes or until brown. Serve warm.

CITRUS

1 lemon = 3 tablespoons juice (approximately)

1 orange = 6 to 8 tablespoons juice

Grated rind/1 lemon = 1½ teaspoons

Grated rind/1 orange = 1 tablespoon

Fresh Strawberry Pie
To celebrate Florida's strawberry season

Preheat oven 450°   Serves 8

Crust

1½ cups flour   ½ cup shortening
½ teaspoon salt   1 egg
1 tablespoon sugar   1 tablespoon water (optional)

Place flour, salt and sugar in mixing bowl. Cut in shortening with pastry blender until mixture resembles crumbs. Stir in egg. Add water. Form a ball and roll on floured board into a thick crust. Ease into 9-inch pie pan without stretching dough. Prick evenly with fork. Bake 10 minutes or until light brown.

Filling

Chill

4 cups strawberries, hulled   3 tablespoons cornstarch
¾ cup water   Cream cheese (optional)
¾ cup sugar   Whipped cream
¼ teaspoon salt

Crush 1 cup strawberries. Add water and bring to boil. Simmer 3 minutes. Strain juice; add enough water to make 1 cup. Combine sugar, salt and cornstarch in saucepan. Slowly add juice, stirring until smooth. Bring to boil, stirring constantly. Cook 3 minutes or until thick and clear. Cool slightly. Place thin layer of cream cheese on crust. Add strawberries. Cover with glaze. Chill. Serve with whipped cream.

Tip: Substitute fresh peaches for strawberries.

Pies

Fresh Peach Pie
No bake

Chill   Serves 8

Crust

3 tablespoons butter, melted   1 cup vanilla wafer crumbs

Combine butter and crumbs. Press on bottom and sides of 9-inch pie pan.

Filling

½ cup butter   10 to 12 fresh peaches, sliced
1½ cups powdered sugar   1 cup heavy cream, whipped
2 eggs, beaten   ½ cup pecans, chopped

Cream butter and sugar. Add eggs. Spoon mixture into crust and chill 1 hour.
Place peaches over sugar mixture. Spread with whipped cream. Sprinkle with
nuts. Serve same day.

Zucchini Spice Pie
Different

Preheat oven 450°   Serves 8

¾ cup brown sugar   ½ teaspoon salt
1½ cups zucchini squash, unpeeled   1 teaspoon ground ginger
  and chopped   1½ teaspoons cinnamon
1½ cups evaporated milk   2 eggs
2 tablespoons molasses   ½ teaspoon ground cloves
¼ teaspoon ground nutmeg   1 tablespoon flour
                                      1 9-inch pie shell, unbaked

Combine all ingredients except pie shell. Blend at high speed with electric
mixer at least 1 minute. Pour into shell. Bake 10 minutes; reduce oven
temperature to 350° and bake 45 minutes.

Grasshopper Pie
Chocolate mint delight

Freeze   Serves 8

Crust

1¾ cups chocolate wafer crumbs   ⅓ cup butter, melted

Combine crumbs and butter. Press evenly on bottom and sides of 10-inch pie pan. Chill.

Filling

25 large marshmallows   3 to 4 tablespoons white crème de
⅔ cup half and half   cocoa
3 to 4 tablespoons green crème de   1 cup heavy cream, whipped
  menthe   Whipped cream
                                   Shaved chocolate curls

Combine marshmallows and cream in double boiler. Heat until melted. Cool. Fold in liqueur and whipped cream. Pour into chilled crust. Freeze. Before serving, spread whipped cream over pie and garnish with chocolate.

Key Lime Pie
Original

Preheat oven 350°   Serves 6

3 eggs, separated   ¼ teaspoon salt
¼ cup key lime juice   1 9-inch pie shell, baked
3 tablespoons hot water   Whipped cream
1 cup sugar

Beat egg yolks lightly. Add lime juice, water, ½ cup sugar and salt. Place in top of double boiler. Cook, stirring constantly until thickened. Beat egg whites until stiff, adding remaining sugar gradually. Fold into lime mixture. Pour into pie shell and bake until delicately brown, about 15 minutes. Serve with whipped cream.

Pies

Rainbow Fruit Pie
Light and refreshing

Preheat oven 400°   Serves 8

Crust

¼ cup butter, softened   1 egg yolk
¼ cup sugar   1 cup flour

Combine butter, sugar and egg yolk. Cut in flour with pastry blender until mixture forms crumbs. Press into 9-inch pie pan. Bake 8 minutes, or until edge is browned. Cool.

Filling

Chill

½ cup sugar   1 teaspoon lemon rind, grated
3 tablespoons cornstarch   5 cups fresh fruit, sliced
1½ cups orange juice   (combination of peaches, grapes,
¼ cup lemon juice   blueberries, strawberries)

Combine sugar and cornstarch in saucepan. Slowly add orange juice, stirring until smooth. Boil 1 minute over medium heat. Remove from heat. Stir in lemon juice and rind. Cool. Fold in fruit. Pour into crust and chill at least 4 hours.

French Coconut Pie
Southern specialty

Preheat oven 350°   Serves 6

¼ cup buttermilk   1½ cups sugar
1¼ cups coconut   1 tablespoon flour
2 eggs   ½ cup butter, melted
1 teaspoon vanilla   1 9-inch pie shell, unbaked

Combine first 7 ingredients. Pour into pie shell and bake 1 hour.

Luscious Key Lime Pie
Sarasota favorite

Preheat oven 350°   Serves 4 to 6

4 eggs, separated   ⅓ cup lime juice
½ teaspoon cream of tartar   2 lime rinds, grated
1 14-ounce can sweetened   1 9-inch graham cracker crust
  condensed milk

Beat egg whites until foamy. Add cream of tartar and beat until stiff. Set aside. Beat egg yolks with 1 cup beaten egg whites, mixing well. Add condensed milk, lime juice and grated rind. Fold in remaining egg whites. Pour into crust and bake until golden, about 15 minutes. Chill.

Tip: This pie will not be green.

No Name Pie
Adaptable and adoptable

Preheat oven 350°   Serves 6 to 8

Crust

4 egg whites   1 cup pecans, chopped
1 cup sugar   18 Ritz crackers, crushed

Beat egg whites until stiff. Gradually add sugar. Fold in pecans and cracker crumbs. Press into well-buttered 9-inch pie pan. Bake 20 minutes. Cool.

Filling

Chill

1 cup heavy cream, whipped   ½ teaspoon vanilla
2 tablespoons powdered sugar   1 cup shaved chocolate curls

Combine whipped cream, sugar and vanilla. Pour into crust. Sprinkle with chocolate curls. Chill at least 2 hours or overnight.

Pies

Lemon Cloud Pie
Heavenly

Preheat oven 400°   Serves 8

Crust

1 cup flour   1 egg, slightly beaten
½ teaspoon salt   1 teaspoon lemon rind, grated
⅓ cup shortening   1 teaspoon lemon juice

Combine flour and salt. Cut in shortening with pastry blender. Combine egg, rind and juice. Add to flour mixture. Press into 9-inch pie pan. Bake 12 to 15 minutes.

Filling

¾ cup sugar   2 egg yolks
¼ cup cornstarch   4 ounces cream cheese, softened
1 cup water   2 egg whites
1 lemon rind, grated   ¼ cup sugar
⅓ cup lemon juice   Whipped cream

Combine sugar and cornstarch. Add water, rind, lemon juice and egg yolks. Cook over medium heat until thickened. Add cream cheese. Cool. Beat egg whites until soft peaks form. Add sugar and continue beating until stiff. Fold into filling mixture. Pour into crust. Serve with whipped cream.

Pretzel Ice Cream Pie
Favorite of children

Preheat oven 350°   Serves 6 to 8

1 cup pretzels, crushed   ½ gallon ice cream (any flavor)
½ cup butter, melted   Topping (optional)
⅔ cup sugar   (fresh fruit, chocolate, etc.)

Combine pretzel crumbs, butter and sugar. Pat mixture into 8-inch pie pan. Bake 10 minutes. Cool 15 minutes. Fill with ice cream. Freeze. Serve with favorite topping.

Ribbon Alaska Pie
Baked Alaska

Preheat oven 375°   Serves 8

Crust

1⅓ cups chocolate wafer crumbs   3 tablespoons butter, softened

Combine ingredients and press over bottom and sides of 9-inch pie pan. Bake 8 minutes. Cool.

Pie

Preheat oven 525°

2 pints strawberry ice cream   ⅛ teaspoon cream of tartar
1 cup chocolate fudge sauce   ½ cup sugar
4 egg whites

Soften 1 pint ice cream. Spoon evenly over crust. Spread fudge sauce over ice cream. Freeze until firm, about 2 hours. Soften remaining ice cream; spread over fudge layer. Freeze until firm, about 2 hours. Beat egg whites until foamy. Add cream of tartar. Add sugar slowly and beat until soft peaks form. Spread meringue over pie, sealing edges. Sprinkle lightly with additional sugar. Place on wooden board and bake until lightly browned, about 1 minute.

Tip: For variation, try different flavors of ice cream.

Peanut Butter Fudge Pie
Very rich

Chill   Serves 6 to 8

1 cup peanut butter   1 cup heavy cream, whipped
8 ounces cream cheese   1 tablespoon vanilla
1 cup sugar   1 9-inch graham cracker crust
2 tablespoons butter, melted   ⅓ cup fudge sauce, heated

Cream peanut butter, cream cheese and sugar. Add butter, whipped cream and vanilla. Mix well. Pour into crust. Chill 4 to 5 hours, or until set. Top with fudge sauce. Chill 30 minutes.

Pies

Peanut Butter Chiffon Pie
When children entertain

Chill   Serves 6

⅓ cup peanut butter   1 cup heavy cream, whipped
3 ounces cream cheese   1 9-inch pie shell, baked
½ cup powdered sugar

Cream peanut butter, cream cheese and powdered sugar. Fold in whipped cream. Pour into pie shell. Chill 2 to 3 hours.

Topping

⅓ cup peanut butter   ⅔ cup powdered sugar

Mix peanut butter and powdered sugar with pastry blender until crumbly. Sprinkle crumbs over pie.

Praline Pumpkin Pie
Extra special Thanksgiving pie

Freeze   Serves 8

1 pint butter pecan ice cream,   1 teaspoon vanilla
  softened   1 cup heavy cream, whipped
1 cup cooked pumpkin   1 tablespoon heavy cream
¾ cup brown sugar   2 tablespoons brown sugar
Dash salt   2 tablespoons butter
½ teaspoon pumpkin pie spice   ½ cup pecans, chopped

Spoon ice cream into bottom and sides of 9-inch pie pan. Freeze. Combine pumpkin, ¾ cup brown sugar, salt, pumpkin pie spice and vanilla. Fold in whipped cream. Spoon into frozen ice cream shell. Freeze. Combine cream, brown sugar and butter in saucepan. Heat to boiling. Cook 1 minute. Stir in pecans. Cool to lukewarm. Spoon pecan mixture in a ring on top of pie. Freeze at least 3 hours.

Whole Wheat Pie Crust
Wholesome

Preheat oven 350°   Yields 2 crusts

½ cup unbleached flour   ½ teaspoon salt
1 cup whole wheat pastry flour   ½ cup plus 2 tablespoons cold butter
½ cup wheat germ   3 to 4 tablespoons ice cold water

Place flours, wheat germ and salt in food processor with steel blade. Turn on 4 times to combine ingredients. Cut butter into tablespoons and place in processor. Turn on and off 10 times. Add water and process. Mixture should take on pie dough consistency in about 20 seconds and roll onto blade. Remove dough and divide into 2 balls. Place 1 ball in center of buttered 9-inch pie pan. Working from the center out, spread dough over pan and up the sides. Repeat with second ball in another pie pan. Cover and refrigerate 2 hours. Prick bottom and sides with a fork. Bake 5 minutes.

Tip: If filling and crust are to be baked together, do not prick with fork. Bake according to pie directions.

Apple Cookies
Spicy

Preheat oven 350°   Yields 4 dozen

1¼ cups dark brown sugar   ½ teaspoon salt
1 cup butter   ½ teaspoon cloves
2 eggs, beaten   ½ teaspoon nutmeg
¼ cup milk   1½ cups apples, chopped
2 cups flour   1 6-ounce package butterscotch bits
1 teaspoon baking powder   1 cup raisins, chopped
1 teaspoon cinnamon   1 cup walnuts, chopped

Cream together brown sugar and butter. Add eggs and milk. Mix flour, baking powder, cinnamon, salt, cloves and nutmeg. Blend mixtures together. Fold apples, butterscotch bits, raisins and nuts into batter. Blend gently. Drop from teaspoon onto greased cookie sheets. Bake 10 minutes.

Cookies

Butterscotch Brownies
Not your basic brownies

Preheat oven 350°   Yields 2 dozen

¾ cup butter, melted   2 cups flour, sifted
1 1-pound box light brown sugar   2 teaspoons baking powder
2 eggs   1 teaspoon salt
2 teaspoons vanilla   1 cup pecans, chopped

Combine butter and sugar in saucepan over low heat. Stir until sugar is dissolved. Cool slightly. Beat in eggs, 1 at a time. Add vanilla. Resift flour with baking powder and salt. Stir into butter mixture. Add nuts. Pour into 9 x 13-inch greased pan. Bake 40 minutes or until toothpick comes out clean. Cool 20 minutes; cut into bars.

Buttery Bitters Bars
Finger dessert

Preheat oven 350°   Yields 18 bars

1 cup butter   1 teaspoon baking powder
½ cup sugar   1 cup coconut
3 cups graham cracker crumbs   1 cup walnuts, chopped
2 cups light brown sugar, firmly   1 tablespoon bitters
  packed   3 eggs, well beaten
1 tablespoon flour   Powdered sugar

Mix first 3 ingredients. Press firmly into two 9-inch square pans. Combine next 3 ingredients. Add coconut and nuts. Add bitters to eggs; beat into brown sugar mixture. Spread over crumb mixture. Bake 35 minutes or until set. Do not overcook. Sprinkle with powdered sugar. Cut into bars while warm.

Chocolate Cups
Let your imagination create finishing touches

Yields 8 shells

²/₃ cup semi-sweet chocolate
  morsels
2 cups coconut, flaked

½ cup walnuts, chopped
Ice cream or fruit

Melt chocolate morsels over low heat, stirring constantly. Remove from heat. Stir in coconut and nuts, mixing well. Line muffin tin with 8 paper baking cups. Spoon chocolate mixture evenly into paper cups. Press mixture firmly on bottom and sides of cups, forming a shell. Let stand at room temperature 2 hours or until hardened. To serve, gently peel paper cup from chocolate shells. Fill with ice cream or fruit.

Coconut Wheaties Crisps
Lunchbox cookie

Preheat oven 350°

Yields 6 to 7 dozen

1 cup butter
1 cup brown sugar
1 cup sugar
2 eggs
2 cups flour
1 teaspoon baking soda

1 teaspoon baking powder
½ teaspoon salt
2 cups coconut
2 cups Wheaties cereal
1 cup pecans, chopped

Beat butter, sugars and eggs until fluffy. Sift together flour, baking soda, baking powder and salt. Add to butter mixture. Gently mix in coconut, Wheaties and nuts. Drop from teaspoon onto ungreased cookie sheet. Bake 10 to 12 minutes.

Drop Sugar Cookies
These will disappear rapidly

Preheat oven 400°   Yields 5 dozen

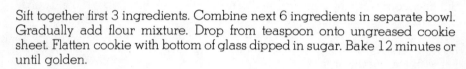

2½ cups flour
½ teaspoon baking soda
¾ teaspoon salt
½ cup butter, melted
1 cup sugar

1 teaspoon vanilla
1 egg
1 tablespoon milk
½ cup shortening
Sugar

Sift together first 3 ingredients. Combine next 6 ingredients in separate bowl. Gradually add flour mixture. Drop from teaspoon onto ungreased cookie sheet. Flatten cookie with bottom of glass dipped in sugar. Bake 12 minutes or until golden.

Forgotten Cookies
Fun to make with children

Preheat oven 350°   Yields 2 dozen

2 egg whites
¾ cup sugar
1 8-ounce package chocolate chips

1 teaspoon vanilla
1 cup Rice Krispies cereal
1 cup pecans, chopped

Beat egg whites until stiff. Add sugar, chocolate chips, vanilla, cereal and nuts. Drop mixture from teaspoon onto ungreased cookie sheet. Place in oven; turn off heat. Leave in oven overnight.

Mexican Wedding Cakes
Olé

Preheat oven 325°   Yields 2 dozen

1 cup butter
2 teaspoons vanilla
2 cups flour

4 tablespoons sugar
2 cups pecans, ground
1 cup powdered sugar

Mix first 5 ingredients until smooth. Knead into balls or fingers. Place on cookie sheet 2 inches apart. Bake 35 to 40 minutes. Roll in powdered sugar while hot. Cool, then roll again.

Frosted Jumbles
Cookies with a surprise ingredient

Preheat oven 375°   Yields 4 to 5 dozen

2¾ cups flour   ½ cup sugar
½ teaspoon baking soda   2 eggs
¼ teaspoon salt   1 teaspoon vanilla
1 cup butter, softened   ¼ cup ketchup
½ cup brown sugar, firmly packed

Sift together flour, baking soda and salt. Cream butter and sugars. Add eggs
and vanilla; mix thoroughly. Stir in flour mixture alternately with ketchup.
Drop from teaspoon onto greased baking sheet 2 inches apart. Bake 10 to 12
minutes. Frost while warm.

Frosting

1½ cups powdered sugar, sifted   2 tablespoons water

Combine powdered sugar and water. Frost immediately.

Ginger Snaps
Old fashioned cookies

Preheat oven 375°   Yields 3½ dozen

2 cups flour   ¼ teaspoon salt
2 teaspoons baking soda   ¾ cup shortening
1½ teaspoons cinnamon   1⅓ cups sugar
1½ teaspoons cloves   ¼ cup molasses
2 teaspoons ginger   1 egg, beaten

Sift together flour, baking soda, cinnamon, cloves, ginger and salt. Set aside.
Cream shortening; gradually add 1 cup sugar. Beat until light and fluffy. Blend
in molasses and egg. Beat in flour mixture just until well mixed. Shape dough
into 1¾-inch balls. Roll in remaining sugar. Place on greased cookie sheet 2½
inches apart. Bake 8 to 10 minutes.

Cookies

Frosted Fudge Nut Thins
Chocolate delight

Preheat oven 375°   Yields 35 bars

¾ cup flour   1 cup sugar
1 teaspoon baking powder   2 eggs, beaten
¼ teaspoon salt   ½ teaspoon vanilla
½ cup butter   ½ cup black walnuts, chopped
2 squares unsweetened chocolate

Sift together flour, baking powder and salt. Over low heat, melt butter and chocolate. Stir until blended. Blend in sugar, eggs and vanilla. Add flour mixture. Stir in nuts. Grease and line 15½ x 10½ x 1-inch jelly roll pan with waxed paper. Grease again. Spread dough evenly in pan. Bake 15 to 20 minutes. Cool and frost. Cut into bars.

Frosting for Fudge Nut Thins

1 tablespoon butter   ½ teaspoon almond extract
1 square unsweetened chocolate   1½ cups powdered sugar
¼ cup water   ½ cup black walnuts, finely chopped

Melt butter and chocolate. Add water. Stir in extract. Remove from heat and add sugar. Blend well. Spread over cookies. Sprinkle with nuts; press in slightly.

Heath Bars
Munchy, crunchy good

Preheat oven 350°   Yields 32 cookies

2 cups flour   1 cup pecans, chopped
1 cup butter   1 6-ounce package semi-sweet
1½ cups brown sugar   chocolate chips

Mix flour, ⅓ cup butter and 1 cup brown sugar until fine. Spread mixture into 9 x 13-inch pan. Cover with pecans. In small saucepan, combine ⅔ cup butter and ½ cup brown sugar. Cook over medium heat, stirring constantly until entire surface boils ½ to 1 minute. Spread over nuts. Bake 18 to 22 minutes. Remove from oven. Immediately sprinkle chocolate chips over top; spread evenly. Cool. Cut into bars.

Hermits
Good for picnic

Preheat oven 350°   Yields 16 bars

1²/₃ cups flour   ¼ teaspoon allspice
½ teaspoon baking powder   ½ cup butter
½ teaspoon baking soda   ½ cup sugar
1 teaspoon cinnamon   1 egg
¼ teaspoon cloves   ½ cup dark molasses
¼ teaspoon mace   ²/₃ cup raisins, chopped
¼ teaspoon salt   ²/₃ cup walnuts, chopped

Sift together flour, baking powder, baking soda, cinnamon, cloves, mace, salt and allspice. Cream butter until light; gradually add sugar. Add egg and beat well. Add molasses, flour mixture, raisins and nuts. Mix well. Spread evenly in greased 8 x 12-inch pan. Bake 20 to 25 minutes. Cool completely. Cut into 16 rectangles. Wrap tightly in plastic. Store 24 hours before serving.

Hungarian Bars
Holiday treat

Preheat oven 325°   Yields 16 bars

1 cup butter   2 cups flour
1 cup sugar   1 cup pecans, chopped
2 egg yolks   ¾ cup strawberry jam
                                     Powdered sugar

Cream butter and sugar. Add egg yolks; blend well. Add flour; mix well. Stir in pecans. Put ½ mixture in greased and floured 8-inch square pan. Spread with jam; top with remaining batter. Bake 1 hour or until lightly browned. Cool. Dust with powdered sugar. Cut into small bars.

Cookies

Peanut Butter Chocolate Kisses
Guaranteed success

Preheat oven 375°   Yields 5 to 6 dozen

2¾ cups flour   1½ cups brown sugar
2 teaspoons baking soda   2 eggs
1 teaspoon salt   2 teaspoons vanilla
1 cup butter   Brown sugar
⅔ cup peanut butter   5 to 6 dozen chocolate kisses

Sift together flour, baking soda and salt. In separate bowl, beat butter and peanut butter. Add sugar; beat well. Add eggs and vanilla; mix well. Add flour mixture. Chill dough 1 hour. Shape into balls. Roll in brown sugar. Place on ungreased cookie sheet. Bake 8 minutes. Remove and press kiss on top of each cookie. Return to oven 2 minutes. Cool on rack.

Potato Chip Cookies
Children's favorite

Preheat oven 350°   Yields 9 to 10 dozen

2 cups butter   3 cups flour
1 cup sugar   1½ cups potato chips, crushed
2 teaspoons vanilla   Powdered sugar

Cream butter until light and fluffy. Add sugar; beat well. Gradually add vanilla and flour. Add potato chips. Drop from teaspoon onto ungreased cookie sheet. Bake 6 to 7 minutes until slightly brown. Sprinkle with powdered sugar.

Linzer Tartlettes
Tasty

Preheat oven 350°   Yields 48 tartlettes

2 cups butter   4 teaspoons vanilla
1 cup sugar   3 cups walnuts, ground
4 cups flour   Raspberry jam

Cream butter and sugar. Measure flour and sift; measure again for 4 cups. Add flour to butter and sugar. Add vanilla and nuts. Mix well. Roll into 1-inch balls. Place on lightly greased cookie sheet. Flatten ball and impress with thumb. Beat raspberry jam with fork. Fill thumb impression with jam. Bake 15 minutes.

Mince Mixup Bars
Unusual fruit cookie

Preheat oven 350°

Yields 2 dozen

¼ cup shortening
¾ cup sugar
2 eggs
¾ cup mincemeat
½ cup crushed pineapple, drain
   and reserve juice

½ cup pecans, chopped
1½ cups flour
½ teaspoon salt
½ teaspoon cinnamon
¼ teaspoon baking soda

Cream shortening and sugar. Add eggs, mincemeat, pineapple and nuts. Sift together flour, salt, cinnamon and baking soda. Add dry ingredients to mixture. Place in greased and floured 15 x 10-inch pan. Bake 25 minutes. Cool slightly. Frost. Cut into bars.

Frosting

1½ cups powdered sugar

1½ tablespoons reserved pineapple
   juice, heated

Mix sugar and juice; spread on warm bars.

Molasses Cookies
Worth the effort

Preheat oven 375°

Yields 3 dozen

¾ cup shortening
1 cup sugar
1 egg
¼ cup sorghum or molasses
2 cups flour

2 teaspoons baking soda
1 teaspoon cinnamon
½ teaspoon cloves
½ teaspoon ginger
¼ teaspoon salt
Sugar

Cream shortening and 1 cup sugar; beat well. Add egg. Add sorghum or molasses. Sift together flour, baking soda, cinnamon, cloves, ginger and salt. Add to creamed mixture. Chill 1 hour. Roll into balls the size of hickory nuts. Roll in sugar. Place on greased cookie sheets. Bake 10 minutes.

Cookies

Shaw's Holiday Cookies
Good for all seasons

Preheat oven 350°

Yields 4 dozen

1 cup butter
1½ cups sugar
1 egg
1 tablespoon vanilla

3 cups flour
1 teaspoon baking powder
½ teaspoon salt
1 teaspoon cinnamon (optional)

Cream butter until fluffy. Add sugar, egg and vanilla. Beat. Sift together flour, baking powder, salt and cinnamon. Fold into butter mixture. Roll dough on lightly floured surface. Cut in desired shapes with cutters. Place on ungreased cookie sheet. Bake 10 minutes. Do not brown. Cool.

Butter Frosting

¼ cup butter
1 teaspoon vanilla
¼ teaspoon salt

1 1-pound box powdered sugar
⅓ to ½ cup cream
Food coloring (optional)

Cream first 5 ingredients together. Beat until smooth and of spreading consistency. Add food coloring. Spread over cookies.

Toffee Strips
Excellent finger food

Preheat oven 350°

Yields 2 dozen

24 graham cracker squares
1 cup butter

1 cup brown sugar, firmly packed
1 cup walnuts, chopped

Arrange graham crackers in lightly greased 10 x 15-inch jelly roll pan. Combine butter and sugar in medium saucepan. Bring to boil. Cook 2 minutes. Stir in nuts. Spread over graham crackers. Bake 10 minutes. Remove from pan while still warm. Cut each square in half.

Pumpkin Bars
Nutritious snack

Preheat oven 350°

Yields 55 bars

2 cups flour
2 teaspoons baking powder
½ teaspoon salt
2 teaspoons cinnamon
1 teaspoon baking soda
2 cups sugar

2 cups pumpkin, cooked
4 eggs
1 cup oil
1 cup raisins
1 cup walnuts, chopped (optional)

Stir together all ingredients. Pour into 9 x 13-inch oblong pan and 9-inch square pan. Bake 25 minutes. Ice with vanilla frosting, if desired. Cut into squares.

Vanilla Frosting

1½ cups powdered sugar
¼ teaspoon vanilla

3 tablespoons hot water

Combine all ingredients; stir until smooth. Spread over pumpkin bars.

Quickee No Bake Cookies
Kid pleaser

Yields 3 dozen

2 cups sugar
½ cup butter
3 tablespoons cocoa

½ cup evaporated milk
3 cups quick cooking oatmeal
1 teaspoon vanilla

Mix sugar, butter, cocoa and milk in saucepan. Bring to boil, stirring constantly. Boil 3 minutes. Remove from heat. Stir in oatmeal and vanilla. Drop from teaspoon onto waxed paper to harden.

Tip: Decrease butter to ⅓ cup. Add ⅓ cup peanut butter for variation.

Candy

Almond Toffee
Outstanding

Serves 16

2 cups butter
2 cups sugar
6 tablespoons water

2 cups almonds, chopped
6 1¾-ounce Hershey chocolate bars

In heavy large pan, heat butter, sugar and water, stirring, but not scraping, sides. Boil 5 minutes. Add 1 cup almonds. Boil to 295°. Pour on greased cookie sheet with sides. Cool 2 minutes. Place 3 chocolate bars on top. As they melt, spread chocolate with spatula. Sprinkle with ½ cup almonds. Cover with foil. Place another cookie sheet on top of foil and invert. Repeat chocolate covering process. Sprinkle with remaining almonds. Cut into squares.

Apricot Almond Balls
Excellent for Christmas

Yields 4 dozen

1¾ cups vanilla wafer crumbs
1 cup almonds, toasted and chopped
¾ cup powdered sugar, sifted

½ cup dried apricots, finely chopped
¼ cup light corn syrup
2 tablespoons apricot brandy

In large bowl, mix wafer crumbs, almonds, ½ cup powdered sugar and apricots. Stir in corn syrup and brandy until well blended. Knead with hands until well mixed. Shape into 1-inch balls. Roll in remaining ¼ cup powdered sugar. Store in tightly covered container.

Best-Ever Popcorn Balls
Children love to help with this

Yields 30

2 cups sugar
1 cup light corn syrup
1 tablespoon butter
2 tablespoons vinegar

½ teaspoon baking soda
3 to 4 batches popped corn, buttered
   and salted

In 3-quart saucepan, bring to boil sugar, syrup, butter and vinegar until mixture reaches 250° or forms soft ball in cold water. Add baking soda; mix. Pour over popcorn. Butter hands; form mixture into balls. Wrap in waxed paper.

Tip: Color syrup orange for **Halloween; red and green for Christmas.**

Buck Eyes
You will love these

Yields 75

½ cup butter
1 1-pound box powdered sugar
2 to 3 cups Rice Krispies

2 cups crunchy peanut butter
1 12-ounce package chocolate chips
¼ bar paraffin

Mix butter, sugar, Rice Krispies and peanut butter. Form into balls about the size of a quarter. Melt chocolate chips and paraffin over hot water. Stick toothpick into ball and dip in chocolate, leaving top open. Cool on waxed paper.

Candy

Microwave Fudge
For working mothers

Serves 16

1 1-pound box powdered sugar
½ cup cocoa
½ cup butter

¼ cup milk
1 teaspoon vanilla
½ cup nuts, chopped (optional)

Put powdered sugar and cocoa in bowl; mix with fork. Put butter on top and pour milk over mixture. Microwave 2 minutes. Mix with wooden spoon. Add vanilla and nuts. Mix until creamy. Pour into buttered 8 x 8-inch pan. Chill 20 minutes. Cut into squares.

No Cook Cheese Nut Fudge
A delight to make

Chill   Yields 30 squares

3 ounces cream cheese, softened
2½ cups powdered sugar

¼ teaspoon almond extract
½ cup blanched almonds, walnuts, pecans or Brazil nuts, chopped

In small bowl, with mixer at medium speed, beat cream cheese with sugar and almond extract until smooth. Stir in nuts. Press into buttered 9 x 5-inch loaf pan. Refrigerate. Cut into squares.

Tip: Substitute ½ cup coconut for nuts.

Caramel Candy
Chewy, old-fashioned candy

Yields 3 dozen

1 cup blanched almonds, toasted
   and halved
2 cups sugar
½ cup butter

2 cups light corn syrup
¼ teaspoon salt
2 cups evaporated milk
1 teaspoon vanilla

Put almonds in greased, shallow pan. Bring sugar, butter, syrup and salt to boil slowly in large saucepan, stirring frequently. Add milk slowly to keep boiling constant, stirring often. Cook to firm ball stage, 255°, stirring constantly about 1 hour. Add vanilla. Quickly pour over almonds. Cool. Cut in bite-size pieces and wrap in waxed paper. Store in cool place, not refrigerator.

Caramel Corn
Great snack

Preheat oven 250°

Serves 10

½ cup butter
2 cups brown sugar
½ cup corn syrup

¼ teaspoon cream of tartar
½ teaspoon baking soda
5 quarts popped popcorn, salted

Mix butter, brown sugar, corn syrup and cream of tartar. Bring to boil; boil 5 minutes. Add baking soda (mixture will foam and turn light). Pour over popcorn in large container. Cover and bake 1 hour. Stir every 15 minutes.

Tip: Leave in unheated oven overnight to completely dry out.

Candy

Peanut Brittle
Patience is most important ingredient

Serves 8

1 cup sugar
1 cup light corn syrup
¼ cup water

1 cup Spanish salted peanuts
1 teaspoon baking soda

Mix sugar, corn syrup and water thoroughly. Bring to full boil for exactly 6 minutes. Solution will start to discolor. Add peanuts and stir about 1 minute. Solution will start to slightly darken. Add baking soda and stir rapidly 1 to 3 minutes. Put on and off heat while stirring; solution will continue to darken. When color appears to be light brown or golden color, remove from heat while continuously stirring. Place solution on ungreased flat metal sheet. Spread to desired thickness. Cool 1 hour.

Peanut Butter Balls
Let your child make this one

Preheat oven 250°

Yields 30

1 cup sugar
1 teaspoon vanilla

1 cup peanut butter
1 egg

Combine all ingredients; mix well. Roll mixture into 1-inch balls. Place on greased cookie sheet. Bake 20 to 30 minutes or until browned.

Peanut Butter Fudge
A change from chocolate

Yields 80 squares

4 cups sugar
1 13-ounce can evaporated milk
½ cup butter
1 tablespoon white vinegar

1 tablespoon light corn syrup
12 ounces crunchy peanut butter
1 cup pecans, chopped
7 ounces marshmallow creme

Combine sugar, milk, butter, vinegar and corn syrup in large pan. Cook over low heat about 30 minutes to softball stage or 236°. Remove from heat; stir in peanut butter, nuts and marshmallow creme. Pour into buttered 9 x 13-inch pan. Cut into squares when cool.

Restaurants

* Alexander's
* Café L'Europe
* The Colony
* Columbia
* The Copperfield Inn
* Euphemia Haye
* Far Horizons
* The Flight Deck
* Four Winds
* Miguel's
* Oasis Restaurant
* Old South Oyster Bar
* Ristorante Casadio
* Saint Georges

Restaurants

ALEXANDER'S
A Former Sarasota Landmark
Chilled Cherry Soup

Chill

Serves 8

1 pound ripe or frozen Bing or red
   cherries
1 cup sour cream
1½ ounces Marsala or sweet
   red wine

1 pint vanilla ice cream
1 cup sugar
1 ounce Grenadine
Whipped cream

Place pitted cherries in blender on purée until they are liquid, 2 to 3 minutes. Add next 5 ingredients and mix slowly until creamy. Do not overmix. Pour into soup cups and chill. Serve with dab of whipped cream on top.

ALEXANDER'S

Blender Béarnaise

Yields 2 cups

⅓ cup tarragon vinegar
1 small onion, minced
1 tablespoon tarragon leaves

1 cup sweet butter
8 egg yolks, at room temperature
Dash salt and pepper

Combine vinegar, onion and tarragon leaves in saucepan and boil 5 minutes. In separate saucepan, bring butter to slow boil. Place egg yolks, salt and pepper in blender. Blend on slow speed 3 to 4 seconds and let stand. Strain vinegar mixture into boiling butter, allowing a few of the onions and leaves into mixture. Pour liquid slowly into blender; purée 3 to 4 minutes or until fluffy. Sauce can be refrigerated 1 week and warmed at room temperature. It should not be placed on direct heat.

Veal Chop Orloff

Preheat oven 400°

Serves 6

6 10- to 12-ounce veal chops
Flour

Salt and pepper to taste
6 tablespoons butter

Lightly flour each chop. Season with salt and pepper. Sauté chops in a hot skillet, until golden brown on each side. Finish cooking veal chops in oven for 10 minutes.

White Sauce

6 tablespoons roux
2 cups veal stock

1 cup heavy cream
Salt and white pepper to taste

Cook roux (equal amounts of fat and flour) over low heat. Add veal stock, cream and seasoning. Simmer for 10 minutes.

Sauce

½ pound mushrooms, chopped
10 medium shallots, chopped
2 tablespoons butter

3 cups white sauce
1 tablespoon sherry
Salt and white pepper to taste

Sauté mushrooms and shallots in a hot pan until cooked. Add white sauce and contine cooking for a few minutes. Add sherry and season to taste. Top each chop with sauce. Serve.

Vichyssoise

Chill   Serves 6

2 leeks, finely chopped   Salt and white pepper
½ celery stalk, chopped   1 whole clove
1 medium sweet onion, chopped   1 bay leaf
6 tablespoons butter   ½ pint heavy cream
1 pound potatoes, peeled and sliced   Leek, chopped
2 pints chicken stock

Sauté leeks, celery and onion in butter without browning. Add potatoes, chicken stock, salt, pepper, clove and bay leaf. Boil 40 to 60 minutes. Strain juice into large bowl. Purée vegetables and add back to juice. Refrigerate until cool. Before serving add cream and garnish with green part of leek.

Marinated Shrimp and Dill Salad

Serves 6

2 pounds large shrimp, cooked and   ¼ teaspoon Herbs de Provence
  cleaned   ¼ teaspoon sweet basil
2 cups blended oil   ¼ teaspoon oregano
1 cup wine vinegar   ¼ teaspoon garlic, chopped
¼ cup fresh dill, chopped   ¼ teaspoon salt
⅛ cup shallots, chopped   ¼ teaspoon freshly ground white
⅛ cup parsley, chopped   pepper
⅛ cup scallions, chopped

Cut shrimp in half lengthwise. Combine remaining ingredients. Pour over shrimp and marinate overnight in refrigerator. Chef Caldwell suggests serving this salad in half a cored apple or on a bed of shredded lettuce. Top with fresh dill.

Snapper Alicante

Preheat oven 350°

Serves 2

1 pound snapper fillets
1 onion, cut in round slices
¼ cup olive oil
½ teaspoon salt
Pinch of white pepper

½ cup brown gravy
½ cup white wine
12 almonds
2 green peppers, cut in rings

In a casserole (preferably clay), place snapper fillets on top of sliced onions. Combine olive oil, salt, white pepper, brown gravy, white wine, almonds and green pepper rings. Pour over fish. Bake uncovered for 25 minutes.

Spanish Bean Soup

Serves 4

½ pound garbanzos
1 tablespoon salt
2 quarts water
1 ham bone
1 beef bone
¼ pound salt pork

1 onion, finely chopped
2 potatoes, cut in quarters
½ teaspoon paprika
Pinch of saffron
1 chorizo (Spanish sausage)

Wash garbanzos. Soak overnight with a tablespoon of salt, in sufficient water to cover beans. When ready to cook, drain the salted water from the beans. Place in 4-quart soup kettle, add 2 quarts of water, ham and beef bone. Cook for 45 minutes over slow fire, skimming foam that forms at the top. Cut salt pork in thin strips and fry slowly in a skillet. Add chopped onion; sauté lightly. Add to the beans along with potatoes, paprika and saffron. Add salt to taste. When potatoes are done, remove from fire; add chorizo that has been cut in thin, round slices.

Shrimp Supreme

4 large shrimp, shelled and
   marinated with lemon juice
2 strips bacon
1 egg, beaten

¼ cup milk
Flour
Salt and pepper
4 slices of breaded eggplant

Cut bacon in half; wrap 1 slice around each shrimp. Skewer in place with toothpick. Dip shrimp in batter made of egg and milk. Roll in flour, salt and pepper. Fry in deep fat. To serve, garnish snapper with shrimp, and breaded and fried eggplant slices.

Veal à L'Mandarine

Serves 4

2 pounds veal, boned
Salt and pepper
Flour
2 tablespoons oil
3 tablespoons butter
2 tablespoons sugar
3 tablespoons vinegar

2 tablespoons lemon juice
1 cup chicken or veal stock
1 16-ounce can Mandarin oranges,
   drain and reserve juice
1 tablespoon cornstarch
2 tablespoons curacao
1 tablespoon orange marmalade

Salt and pepper cut-up veal pieces. Dredge in flour. Sauté in oil and melted butter until brown. Reduce heat, cover, and simmer 1 hour or until tender. Melt sugar in saucepan, stirring until golden. Add vinegar, lemon juice, stock and drained juice and simmer for a few minutes. Transfer veal to a serving pan when tender. Pour sauce into pan in which veal was cooked and blend with pan juices. Mix cornstarch with curacao and add to sauce mixture with orange marmalade. Simmer 5 minutes or until thick. Add salt and pepper to taste. Arrange slices of orange sections over veal and pour sauce over top.

far horizons
Beach● Resort

Gulf White Fish

Preheat oven 450°   Serves 6

2½ pounds white fish   6 basil leaves, finely chopped
2 ounces shallots, chopped   Salt
2 ounces butter   Pepper
8 ounces white mushrooms, finely   1 head Bibb lettuce
  chopped   1 cup dry white wine
Juice of ½ lemon   1 cup heavy cream

Combine shallots in butter, adding mushrooms, lemon juice, basil, salt and pepper. Cook this mixture over a high flame quickly. Stuff fish with this mixture. Blanch lettuce leaves by dropping them into boiling water for a few seconds only, and place them under the fish pieces and wrap them around the fish as well. On a buttered baking sheet, arrange the fish, pour the wine over the fish and add a few of the finely chopped shallots; cover the entire pan with aluminum foil. Bake for 6 minutes. After cooking, pour off the wine and juices into a small saucepan and reduce this sauce to ¾ of the amount over medium heat. Add the cream and reduce again; season to taste with salt and pepper. Pour the sauce mixture through a strainer over the fish. Serve as soon as possible.

THE FLIGHT DECK

Oyster Soup

Yields 1½ quarts

½ cup butter   2 dozen large oysters
1 cup celery, finely chopped   Oyster water plus water to make 6 cups
1 cup shallots, finely chopped   2 bay leaves
1 tablespoon flour   Salt and pepper to taste
1 teaspoon garlic, chopped

Melt butter in saucepan. Sauté celery and shallots until tender. Blend in flour and cook 5 minutes more, stirring, over low heat. Add remaining ingredients and simmer 20 minutes. Remove bay leaves.

far h**o**rizons
Beach• Resort

Fishermen's Sauerkraut

Preheat oven 350°   Serves 6

2¼ pounds sauerkraut   ½ cup water
2 ounces butter, softened   1½ pounds grouper or white fish
4 ounces shallots, thinly sliced   6 slices smoked salmon
1 cup dry white wine   1½ pounds salmon
1 pound red bliss potatoes   1 pound large shrimp
Salt and pepper   Juice of 1 lemon
Pinch thyme   ½ pound butter, softened
2 bay leaves   Parsley

Boil cabbage and strain. Melt butter in heavy skillet and add shallots. Cook until golden brown and add strained cabbage, white wine, potatoes, spices and water. Cover and bake 1 hour. Remove from oven and add to the cabbage, the slices of grouper, salmon and the shrimp. Place in oven and bake 8 minutes. Heat juice of 1 lemon and bring to boil; add ½ pound butter and bring back to boil. Add spices to taste and remove from heat. Place in double boiler to keep warm. Dress with elegance on a large platter, the cabbage, the two fish, the potatoes around them, the shrimp and the smoked salmon on top, a few sprinkles of parsley, then the whole covered with sauce. Bon appetit.

Old South Oyster Bar
Shrimp in Soy Butter

Preheat broiler   Serves 4

48 large shrimp   ½ cup soy sauce
½ cup butter, melted   1 lemon or 1 teaspoon lemon juice
½ cup water   concentrate
                                     Paprika

Peel shrimp leaving only the tail. Cut the shrimp down the back, deep enough that the shrimp lie flat. Devein. Do not cut the shrimp all the way through. Next, lay the shrimp in a 9 x 11 x 1-inch baking pan. Do not overlap shrimp. Add butter, water and soy sauce. Squeeze lemon over shrimp and sprinkle with paprika. Place pan of shrimp under broiler and cook about 5 minutes or until shrimp begin to curl. Serve shrimp in individual casserole dishes. Pour remaining sauce over shrimp and garnish with parsley.

Bouillabaisse

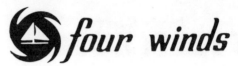 *four winds*

Serves 6 to 8

3 to 4 1-pound Florida lobsters or
  8 to 10-ounce tails
2 pounds red snapper or red fish,
  deboned and cut into filets
3 pounds blue fish, deboned and
  cut into filets
30 to 40 shrimp, peeled
1 to 2 crabs
4 ounces olive oil
1 pound onions, chopped
½ pound white leeks, chopped
1 garlic head, crushed (about
  10 cloves)

3 bay leaves
1 teaspoon thyme
2 teaspoons fennel seeds
½ teaspoon saffron
4 large tomatoes, sliced
¼ orange, peeled
3 teaspoons Pernod
Salt to taste
Freshly ground pepper to taste
2 dozen mussels, washed
Parsley
Dry French garlic bread (2 slices
  per person)

In a large pot, combine bones, heads, shrimp shells, crabs and 1 gallon water to make fumet. Bring to a boil and simmer for 20 minutes. Remove fish parts from bouillon. In a separate pot, heat oil and sauté onions and leeks until golden brown. Combine all ingredients except mussels, parsley and French bread. Boil 15 minutes. Do not stir, but occasionally shake the pot to avoid sticking without breaking the fish filets. Add the whole mussels. Cook 5 minutes more and serve at once. At the Four Winds, the Bouillabaisse is served in one large dish for each person: ½ lobster, fish filets, mussels, shrimp, 2 slices French bread and chopped parsley. Stir the broth in the pot and divide it over the above ingredients in each dish.

Chicken Saltimbocca

OASIS RESTAURANT

Serves 1

Chicken breast fillet (1 whole
  breast per person)
Rubbed sage
Proscuitto ham (1 slice per person)
Flour
2 eggs, beaten

1 tablespoon olive oil
1 tablespoon butter
⅛ cup lemon juice
⅛ cup white wine
Butter
Artichoke hearts, halved

Lightly season inside of chicken breast with rubbed sage and sandwich 1 slice of ham between 2 fillets. Dip chicken in flour, pat off excess flour, dip in egg. Heat oil and butter in teflon skillet. When oil is hot, place chicken in skillet. Brown on 1 side and then turn to other side. Turn down heat and cover so fillet will cook in the middle. Heat lemon juice and wine to reduce liquid by one-half. Add cold butter cut into cubes. Add artichoke hearts. Pour over fillet and serve immediately.

Cernia Piemontese
Grouper Piedmont

Preheat oven 350°

Serves 4

2 tablespoons white raisins
¼ cup white wine
¼ cup olive oil
1 small onion, finely chopped
1 clove garlic, minced
1 celery stalk, finely chopped
1 sprig sage, finely chopped or
  ⅛ teaspoon dry sage

1 sprig rosemary, finely chopped or
  ¼ teaspoon dry rosemary
2½ pounds grouper
5 tablespoons wine vinegar
1 lemon rind, grated
1 cup fish or chicken stock
4 teaspoons flour
Cold water

Soak raisins in wine. In a large pan, heat the oil. Add chopped vegetables and herbs, and sauté very gently until soft but not brown. Add fish, vinegar, lemon rind, stock and raisins with their liquid. Cover and simmer over low heat 10 minutes. Remove fish and bone it. Arrange on hot 14-inch oval serving dish and keep hot in oven. Mix flour with enough cold water to make a thin paste. Bring fish sauce to a boil; add flour and water paste. Stir until sauce is thick and smooth. Pour over grouper and serve immediately.

Ossobuco Milanese

6 2½-inch slices shin of veal
Flour
6 tablespoons butter
½ cup carrots, diced
½ cup onion, diced
½ cup celery, diced
4 sprigs parsley, chopped
1 clove garlic, finely chopped

1 anchovy fillet, chopped (optional)
4 bay leaves
6 whole cloves
Salt and pepper
½ cup red wine
2 tomatoes, peeled
4 cups veal or chicken stock

Roll the shin in flour. In a large pan, sauté shin in butter until brown. Add all vegetables, spices, salt and pepper. Pour the wine over and cook for 15 minutes. Finally add the tomatoes and stock and let cook 1½ hours. Serve over a bed of saffron rice.

Fresh Gulf Pompano Ostendaise

Serves 4

4 6-ounce fillets of pompano,
    boneless and skinless
8 shrimp
8 large oysters
8 large mushroom caps
Chives

4 shallots, chopped
1 bay leaf
Juice of 1 lemon
2 ounces butter
2 ounces white wine
4 cups water

Simmer the above ingredients for 12 minutes. Remove fish and garniture and place in ovenware baking dish.

Sauce

Butter
Flour

2 egg yolks, beaten
1 cup whipped cream

Thicken broth with butter and flour; add egg yolks and whipped cream. Pour over fish and broil until golden brown.

Artichoke Farci

Preheat broiler

Serves 4

1 pound shrimp, cleaned, deveined
    and cut into ½ inch pieces
4 ounces mushrooms, sliced
2 artichoke hearts, sliced
4 ounces garlic butter
1 ounce Pernod (optional)

Pinch salt and pepper
2 ounces flour
4 ounces cream
1 ounce parsley, chopped
4 artichoke bottoms
6 ounces Hollandaise

Sauté shrimp, mushrooms and hearts quickly in butter and Pernod with salt and pepper. Add flour, cook to paste. Add cream; simmer to creamy sauce. Add parsley. Heat bottoms in oven and stuff with mixture. Cover with Hollandaise and glaze under broiler.

Tip: May be served in smaller portions as an appetizer.

Apple Walnut Pie

Euphemia Haye Restaurant

Preheat oven 350°   Serves 6

Crust

4½ cups cake or pastry flour   1 teaspoon salt
½ cup shortening   ⅓ cup ice water
1 cup butter

Place flour, shortening, butter and salt in food processor. Work machine on and off until tiny beads are formed. Add water and process just until it forms a ball - stop immediately. DO NOT OVER PROCESS.

Filling

10 to 11 medium red delicious   1 teaspoon allspice
   apples, peeled, cored and sliced ¼ teaspoon ground cloves
1¼ cups sugar   ½ teaspoon ginger
1 tablespoon flour   1 cup walnuts
1 teaspoon cinnamon   1 10-inch pie crust

Combine all ingredients and place in pie crust. Top with streussel. Bake about 1 hour or until crust is brown and inside is bubbling.

Streussel Topping

½ cup butter, softened   1¾ cups cake flour
½ cup sugar   1 teaspoon vanilla

Mix until crumbly.

A Pinch of History
Notes

Mrs. Matthews wishes to cite the following sources consulted in preparation of her historical narrative: Henry Ringling North and Alden Hatch, **The Circus Kings, Our Ringling Family Story,** (Doubleday, New York: 1960), Gene Plowden, **Those Ringlings and their Circus,** (Caldwell, Idaho: 1968); Henry Ringling North to author; Sallie North Wadsworth to author; Florida Master Site Files for Caples-Ringling estates historic district and St. Armands division of John Ringling estates, and correspondence Division of Archives, History and Record Management, Fla. Depart. of State: Marian Murray and A.E. Austin, **Asolo Theater** (1952), John Daniels, Director of Education JMRMA to author February 16, 1983; Peter Tomory, **Catalogue of the Italian Paintings before 1800,** (John and Mable Museum of Art, Sarasota: 1976); Nathional Archives and Records Service, Washington, D.C.; Greta L. Banzhaf, "Thompsons Knew, Loved Area Long Ago," Sarasota **Herald Tribune,** Sunday, July 20, 1975; Owen Burns biographical data given in Karl Grismer, **The Story of Sarasota,** appendix; Lillian G. Burns to author; Gene Plowden, "John and Mable," Sarasota **Herald Tribune,** Sunday, January 9, 1983; Levoie Hipps, charter class clown college graduate, to author, February 1983; Sarasota County Deed Books; Robert Perkins, Selby Foundation, to author, February 18, 1983; Obituaries, Sarasota **Herald Tribune,** December 5, 1956; Irv Edelson, "Students Main Beneficiaries from Estate of late William B. Selby," Sarasota **Herald Tribune,** n.d. 1959; Curtis Haug, Managing Director, Van Wezel Performing Arts Hall to author, February 21, 1983; **Sarasota Life** vol. 1, no. 1 (March 1970); Kenneth Thompson, City Manager to author, February 22, 1983; Paul Stannard to author; Mrs. Robert L. Garrison to author, February 23, 1983; Adelaide K. Bullen, "The Oaks: A Moment Out of Time;" **The Florida Gardener,** Nov.-Dec., 1959; Janet Matthews, Philip Werndli, and James Miller, nomination of Osprey archaeological and historic site at The Oaks to the **National Register of Historic Places,** March 25, 1975, Florida Division of Archives, Department of State; Master Plan The Oaks Preservation Center, for Sarasota County Historical and Natural Science Center, Inc. (a.k.a. Gulf Coast Heritage Association, Inc.), December 1980; Allan Horton, "Ceremony Marks The Oaks Being Named Historic Site," February 29, 1976, p. 2-B; "A Proposal concerning Utilization of the Osprey Elementary School" presented to the Sarasota County School Board by The Sarasota County Historical and Natural Science Center, Inc. (a.k.a. Gulf Heritage Association, Inc.), March 16, 1976; Allan Horton, "The Oaks — Man's Dream of Tropical Solitude," Sarasota **Herald Tribune,** April 19, 1975; from the Lilian G. Burns collection: "Plat No. 1 St. Armands Division, The John Ringling Estate, August 23, 1925," and "Plat No. 2 Ringling Isles ... The John Ringling Developments, John J. Watson, December 1924," and "General Plan, John Ringling Isles John Ringling Developments," and Owen Burns/John Ringling correspondence August 1923-October 1924. Cerita Purmort, former President of the Junior League of Sarasota, Inc., was President of Gulf Coast Heritage Association, Inc. in 1980.

Index

Index

Index

Index

Index

Index

Index

Index

Index

Index _____

Index

Index _____

Contributors

We would like to thank the following members and friends who contributed their recipes for our book. Each recipe has been tested for accuracy and excellence. We do not claim that all of the recipes are original, only that they are our favorites. We regret that we were unable to include many recipes which were submitted, due to similarity or lack of space.

Mary Beth Abel
Pamela Allen-Jones
Weezie Anderson
Lisa D'Andrea
Mary Appleyard
Bill Arthur
Vicki Arthur
Ellen Ayers
Nancy Bailey
Margaret Banker
Ann Bartels
Verda Beachey
Jan Bell
Marla Bell
Michelle Beroli-Solatin
Sue Bissell
Kay Blix
Suzanne Bolan
Dorcas Bongaardt
Linda Bonnett
Linda Boring
Nancy Boyle
Virginia Bradshaw
Barbara Brame
Mary Jane Brantley
Shanna Breen
Pam Brewer
Betty Brooksbank
Alanson Brown
Barbara Brown
Sandra Buehler
Pat Byers
Jeanette Byrd
Lee Byron
Nancy Campbell
Brenda Cannon
Chee Carlton
Jane Carroll
Ann Cassadio
Betsy Chapman
Jeri Christensen
Vivian Clack
Barbara Colton
Sharon Corbridge
Charlotte Crosby
Nancy Curry

Martha Davis
Donna Dooley
Linda Dooley
Grace Duffey
Dode Dusler
Bonnie Early
Edith Eden
Betty Empkie
Susan Featherman
Mary Jim Ferguson
B. James Ferkes
Susie Field
Nancy Finlay
Tish Fitzgerald
Anita Fleming
Eileen Frayne
Carol French
Keith French
Dot Garber
Patricia Garner
Shirley Garvin
Claudia George
Patti Giorgetti
Beth Gourlay
Ellen Groover
Noni Hacker
Leslie Hahn
Mary Hall
Jan Harnden
Pamela Hart
Barbara Haskins
Martha Heagerty
Peggy Heagerty
Mrs. David Herchman
Ruth Hereford
Ruth Hess
Judy Hockett
Karen Hoefer
Jean Holzer
Wendy Hopkins
Martha Horton
Vicki Hosmer
Carol Houpe
Betty Howard
Mary Ann Hoyt
Jan Hudson

Cynthia Humphrey
Betty Huss
Evelyn Hutchison
Janice Hutchison
Amy Jeffrey
Anne Johnson
Margot Jonsson
Ann Judd
LaVergne Jung
Jan Jung
Susie Keller
Sherry Kerber
Lorraine Kermaghan
Lois Kiehl
Jane Kirschner
Lane Kimbrel
Mary King
Kathy Knapp
Louise Koss
Suzanne Krill
Jane Kusic
Kim LaCivita
Jerri LaCivita
Diane LaCroix
Irene Lindstrom
Patricia Linn
Alice Lolli
Cookie Long
Karen Long
Jane Longino
Marjorie Lonsdale
Nita Lortz
Sandra Lovner
Sherri Ludwig
Andrea Lyon
Jim Malachowski
Sally Malatesta
Cindy Malkin
Peg Marek
Ann Marshall
Barbara Martin
Susan Matuszak
Carolyn McClelland
Jane McDaniel
Joan McGill
Libby McGinness

Contributors

Spot McGrath
Theresa McKenny
Charlotte McPheeters
Doris Mitchell
Susan Mitchell
Nancy Monihon
William Monihon
Karen Montgomery
Pam Morris
Sally Morse
Bobbie Muenzmay
Lilli Anne Murphy
Julie Myers
Darlene Natherson
Barbara Nelson
Judy Nimz
Karen Oliva
Linda Olivieri
Diane Otis
JoAnn Padgett
Debbie Partridge
Wilma Perez
Kathy Peterson
Debbie Pietraniec
Gloria Pons
Susan Pore
Angela Postlethwaite
Floria Preston
Pat Primrose
Diana Profant
Cerita Purmort
Judy Quealy
Susan Radcliffe

Susan Reaves
Barbara Reese
Sue Renfrew
Helen Reppert
Shirley Ritchey
Schansa Roberts
Bitsy Robertson
Christine Robie
Linda Roe
Mineava Rolli
Catherine Rosevear
Hattie Rostan
Peggy Rutledge
Chris Scarbrough
Robert Scheidt
Carol Scherer
Kay Schlabach
Sandra Schwenk
Carole Sears
Carolyn Simmons
Terri Shaw
Betty Smith
Lib Smith
Stephanie Smith
Carol Spalding
Linda Spivey
Pam Steves
Sandi Stewart
Catherine Stickler
Marilyn Stone
Hope Streeter
Karen Stutz
Regin Swilley

Linda Swisher
Gerry Tausch
Deedie Taussig
Jennifer Thatcher
Tricia Tiano
Duchess Tomasello
Bonnie Topjun
Carolyn Travers
Susan Treibly
Sharon Tritschler
Helen Tucker
Doro Turner
Velda Turner
Blanche Tweedy
Ann Van Steenburgh
Tommy Vaughan-Birch
Judi Voight
Mary Walker
Jeannette Ward
Suzanne Webb
Jane Wieland
Myrna Welch
Ethel Wendland
Linda Weinrich
Pat Wheeler
Beaven Whitlock
Peggy Wilhelm
Nancy Lee Williams
Dee Ann Wilmot
Lori Witham
Carroll Drew Wood
Margaret Wrigley
Karen Zittel

FARE BY THE SEA
P.O. Box 25074
Sarasota, FL 34277

Please send me _____ copies of "**Fare By The Sea**" $10.95 each $_____

add postage and handling $ 1.50 each $_____

add gift wrap (if desired) $ 1.00 each $_____

FL residents add 5% sales tax $ .55 each $_____

Total $_____

Name _____
please print

Address _____

City _____ State _____ Zip _____

Please make checks payable to "**Fare By The Sea**".

- -

FARE BY THE SEA
P.O. Box 25074
Sarasota, FL 34277

Please send me _____ copies of "**Fare By The Sea**" $10.95 each $_____

add postage and handling $ 1.50 each $_____

add gift wrap (if desired) $ 1.00 each $_____

FL residents add 5% sales tax $ .55 each $_____

Total $_____

Name _____
please print

Address _____

City _____ State _____ Zip _____

Please make checks payable to "**Fare By The Sea**".

Please list any book stores or gift shops in your area that you would like to handle this book.

_____

_____

_____

_____

_____

_____

- -

Please list any book stores or gift shops in your area that you would like to handle this book.

_____

_____

_____

_____

_____

_____

FARE BY THE SEA
P.O. Box 25074
Sarasota, FL 34277

Please send me _____ copies of **"Fare By The Sea"** $10.95 each $_____

add postage and handling $ 1.50 each $_____

add gift wrap (if desired) $ 1.00 each $_____

FL residents add 5% sales tax $ .55 each $_____

Total $_____

Name _____
please print

Address _____

City _____ State _____ Zip _____

Please make checks payable to **"Fare By The Sea"**.

FARE BY THE SEA
P.O. Box 25074
Sarasota, FL 34277

Please send me _____ copies of **"Fare By The Sea"** $10.95 each $_____

add postage and handling $ 1.50 each $_____

add gift wrap (if desired) $ 1.00 each $_____

FL residents add 5% sales tax $ .55 each $_____

Total $_____

Name _____
please print

Address _____

City _____ State _____ Zip _____

Please make checks payable to **"Fare By The Sea"**.

Please list any book stores or gift shops in your area that you would like to handle this book.

_____

_____

_____

_____

_____

_____

_____

- -

Please list any book stores or gift shops in your area that you would like to handle this book.

_____

_____

_____

_____

_____

_____

_____

FARE BY THE SEA
P.O. Box 25074
Sarasota, FL 34277

Please send me _____ copies of **"Fare By The Sea"** $10.95 each $_____

add postage and handling $ 1.50 each $_____

add gift wrap (if desired) $ 1.00 each $_____

FL residents add 5% sales tax $ .55 each $_____

Total $_____

Name _____
please print

Address _____

City _____ State _____ Zip _____

Please make checks payable to **"Fare By The Sea"**.

FARE BY THE SEA
P.O. Box 25074
Sarasota, FL 34277

Please send me _____ copies of **"Fare By The Sea"** $10.95 each $_____

add postage and handling $ 1.50 each $_____

add gift wrap (if desired) $ 1.00 each $_____

FL residents add 5% sales tax $ .55 each $_____

Total $_____

Name _____
please print

Address _____

City _____ State _____ Zip _____

Please make checks payable to **"Fare By The Sea"**.

Please list any book stores or gift shops in your area that you would like to handle this book.

_____

_____

_____

_____

_____

_____

Please list any book stores or gift shops in your area that you would like to handle this book.

_____

_____

_____

_____

_____

_____